Senator Howard Cannon of Nevada

Wilbur S. Shepperson Series in Nevada History

T0288260

Senator Howard Cannon of Nevada

A Biography

MICHAEL VERNETTI

UNIVERSITY OF NEVADA PRESS   RENO & LAS VEGAS

Wilbur S. Shepperson Series in Nevada History

Series Editor: Michael Green

University of Nevada Press, Reno, Nevada 89557 USA

Copyright © 2008 by University of Nevada Press

All rights reserved

Cover photos: (front) Howard Cannon at Nellis Air Force
Base in the 1960s. Photo courtesy of U.S. Air Force;
(back) Senator Cannon and President Johnson. Photo
courtesy Nancy Cannon Downey Collection.

Cover design: Nicole Hayward Design

Manufactured in the United States of America

Library of Congress Cataloging-in-Publication Data

Vernetti, Michael, 1945–

Senator Howard Cannon of Nevada : a biography /
Michael Vernetti.

p. cm. — (Wilbur S. Shepperson series in Nevada history)

Includes bibliographical references and index.

ISBN 978-0-87417-761-9 (hardcover : alk. paper)

1. Cannon, Howard W. 2. Legislators—United States—
Biography. 3. United States. Congress. Senate—
Biography. 4. Nevada—Politics and government—20th
century. 5. Nevada—Biography. 6. Las Vegas (Nev.)—
Biography. 7. Mormons—Nevada—Biography. I. Title.

E840.8.C36V47 2008

328.7309—dc22

[B]   2008014523

The paper used in this book is certified by FSC, and meets the
requirements of American National Standard for Information
Sciences—Permanence of Paper for Printed Library Materials,
ANSI/NISO Z39.48-1992 (R2002). Binding materials were selected
for strength and durability.

ISBN 978-1-943859-02-3 (paperback : alk. paper)

ISBN 978-0-87417-747-3 (ebook)

This book has been reproduced as a digital print.

Dedicated to the workhorses of the world.

They beat the show horses every time.

Contents

Illustrations follow page 90

Acknowledgments

There would be no biography of Howard Cannon were it not for the tenacious desire of his daughter, Nancy Cannon Downey, to have one written. Nancy believed that history had slighted her father, and it particularly galled her that he left the public eye under the taint of impropriety. She knew him to be a shy man who naturally shunned the spotlight, so feared that an incomplete public record would be the legacy of his reticence. For years, she labored to bring the facts—just the facts—to light. One incomplete manuscript, bits and pieces of biographical material, and a trove of private memos, letters, and official documents were the result of her efforts. Those unfinished gestures were the genesis of this book.

Another key ingredient was Cannon's public papers, housed in the Lied Library of the University of Nevada–Las Vegas (UNLV). The Special Collections Department of the Lied Library is the most comfortable and attractive setting one could imagine for conducting research. The friendly and competent staff, along with manuscript librarian Su Kim Chung, was unfailingly helpful in filling my unending document requests. Although I spent far less time there, the University of Nevada–Reno (UNR) library and its manuscript librarian, Jacquelyn Sundstrand, were equally helpful.

The State of Nevada has a unique resource in its archivist, Guy Rocha. There was no research deadend I encountered that Guy wasn't able to help circumvent. In the course of my conversations with him he had managed to correct the records of the U.S. Senate historian concerning the closest U.S. Senate election in history: the 1964 Cannon-Laxalt race, decided by eighty-four votes after a recount (the original margin was forty-eight votes). Thanks to Guy and to veteran Carson City AP correspondent Brendan Riley for introducing me. Like all good newsmen, Brendan has excellent sources.

Howard Cannon was ninety when he died, which means he does not have many contemporaries. Those who remain, the Old Guard of Nevada public life, were indispensable in piecing together his life. Las Vegas attorney Ralph Denton, his wife, Sara, Harry Claiborne, Chet Smith, Mike O'Callaghan, Herb Jones, Florence Murphy, J. Kell Houssels Jr., Jeanne (Houssels) Stewart,

George Foley, John Squire Drendel, Prince Hawkins, Bill and Barbara Thornton, and Gene Gastanaga are an honor roll of Nevadans who remember an era long past. I cannot thank them enough for sharing their memories and insights. If Ralph Denton were billing me at his normal rate, I could not pay the bill in this lifetime.

Cannon's sister, Evelyn Jay, belongs in the category of old-timers with an excellent memory, although her field of reference is St. George, Utah, not Las Vegas. Not only was Evelyn able to provide details of her brother's life, but she also gave tours of St. George that brought life to Cannon's early days in Utah.

A special thanks to those who read portions of the manuscript and provided their comments and edits. Randolph Hils is a dedicated steward of the history of the 440th Troop Carrier Group, that unsung bunch of pilots— Cannon among them—who labored in the background of World War II. He made sure that what I wrote about this group, which, like Cannon, has been wrongly remembered by history, was factually correct. Thanks, too, to Christine Goyer, daughter of Frank Krebs, for introducing me to Mr. Hils and for her helpful insights.

John Dowd, Aubrey Sarvis, Will Ris, and Chip Barclay also read long portions for accuracy, and I am in debt to them. William McPherson provided valuable editing of the early part of the book, which owes much of its structure to his wise suggestions. Likewise, Eric Engles helped immeasurably to shape up the latter chapters. Also, friends and relatives read sections of the book to make sure it was accessible to people not directly connected to Cannon: Michele Boyer, Candy and Andrea Vernetti, Celeste Miller, and Gayle Walker. Ellen Eggers, a Sacramento attorney defending the rights of death row inmates, never failed to find errors in the sections she read. Thanks to all of you.

Senator Howard Cannon of Nevada

Introduction

An Honorable Man

"My father was an honorable man." The words hung in the still mortuary air. She repeated them, determined, insistent, demanding. "My father was an honorable man!"

Her father was Howard Walter Cannon, U.S. senator from Nevada for twenty-four years, who had died five days before, on March 6, 2002, at the age of ninety. Twenty years earlier, charges of corruption filling the air, he had lost his bid for a fifth term. Nancy was his only daughter. Although others spoke at her father's funeral that Monday morning in the chapel of the Palm Mortuary in Las Vegas, none spoke so memorably as Nancy.

The mortuary itself was large, modern, efficient—a structure distinguished only by the incongruities of its setting. Little more than two miles directly south, the outlandish, gaudy, mesmerizing world of the Las Vegas Strip beckons. In a single glance, a mourner leaving the chapel that day could take in both the mountains rising serenely, timelessly, above the valley and the neon Strip where the billboards shout, "Defeat Reality."

As a retired major general in the Air Force Reserve, Cannon was accorded full military honors. The Honor Guard came from nearby Nellis Air Force Base. There was a twenty-one-gun salute. A military funeral is an impressive event, and many of the four hundred or more people overflowing the chapel that day were impressive, too. The Republican governor of Nevada, Kenny C. Guinn, was there, as well as the most popular governor Nevada ever had, Mike O'Callaghan, who received many assists in his political career from Cannon. O'Callaghan became executive editor of the *Las Vegas Sun* after leaving office, and his boss, *Sun* publisher Brian Greenspun, was there, too. Cannon and Brian's father, Hank, who founded the newspaper, were friends from their early days in Las Vegas.

U.S. Senator and former lieutenant governor of Nevada Harry Reid and former governor and U.S. Senator Richard Bryan gave eulogies, as did Sara Denton, who had managed Cannon's Las Vegas office for many years and was very close to the senator. She could tell him things others hesitated to say. Virtually the entire Nevada political establishment paid their respects, as well as many former members of his senatorial staff in Washington.

A little more than a month after the funeral in Las Vegas, Cannon's body was flown to Washington for burial in Arlington National Cemetery. A pre-internment ceremony in a chapel near the cemetery's entrance was small, intended mostly for family members and Washington-area friends. After the service, a brass band and a contingent of Air Force Honor Guard riflemen accompanied the caisson, pulled by six horses, through the solemn, grassy expanse of Arlington. Finally, in a section of the cemetery lying in the shadow of the terrorist-damaged southwest wall of the Pentagon, Cannon was laid to rest to the echo of another twenty-one-gun salute. Construction cranes completing the task of restoring the Pentagon's exterior after the September 11 attack formed an eerie backdrop to the ceremony. Cannon was a dedicated defender of his country's military forces throughout his career, and his burial so near the shocking reminder of a new American enemy seemed to underscore his concern over perpetual peril.

Cannon had been a genuine World War II hero, although he rarely talked about his wartime exploits. He flew the slow-moving, unarmed c-47s that ferried men and matériel to the most dangerous battlegrounds in Europe. As a young man, Howard had been a carefree cowboy roping cows in small-town rodeos in the West. He played the clarinet and saxophone, and when he was in college earned money by leading his own dance band. He learned to fly. He was handsome, he loved fun, he liked the girls, the girls liked him, and he was successful at almost everything he tried. When he moved from rural St. George, Utah, where he had been born, to bustling, seductive Las Vegas after the war, he found himself in a city of gamblers, hustlers, mobsters, movie stars, even Mormons like himself.

Among such a roisterous and colorful group, neither the staid, churchgoing Mormons in general nor the thirty-three-year-old Cannon in particular drew much notice. The dashing hero and ladies' man was now married and settling down. His wife and a few close friends constituted his social life. It was almost as if he were returning to the inward-looking mores of his Mormon upbringing. It was hard to see the saxophone-playing, rodeo-loving, daredevil Romeo in this serious new, buttoned-down, and very respectable Cannon.

I first came to grips with Howard Cannon as a reporter assigned to cover the 1970 elections for the *Las Vegas Review-Journal,* familiarly known as the *R-J.* On that assignment, I encountered many memorable Nevada politicians—gubernatorial candidate Mike O'Callaghan and U.S. Representative Walter Baring for two—but Cannon was different. He seemed uncomfortable with the press. He did not speak in easily quotable bites. To me, he was an unrepentant hawk on Vietnam when it was becoming increasingly apparent that the still-raging war had been a big mistake. I wanted to label him an unprincipled opportunist who changed positions on major issues out of political expediency, but he undermined that line of attack simply by refusing to acknowledge it. He responded coolly and without emotion to my aggressive questioning. He was unflappable, almost Zen-like. I had been expecting passion and rhetoric, but he was detached and logical. In the end, I was left with the reporter's hackneyed "on the one hand, on the other hand" approach to the story. "In Nevada," I wrote, "where conservatives are elected while liberals snap at their heels, one of the state's most successful careers has been forged by a man who alternately delights and confounds both philosophical poles." In retrospect, that was his genius.

My profile was anything but laudatory, and I had heard that the Cannon camp didn't care much for it, so it came as a great surprise when, little more than a year later, a call came asking if I would be interested in joining the senator's Washington staff. At the time, I was working for the Associated

Press in Reno and liking it, but after some inner debate I accepted the job. Two or three weeks later I was in Washington, knowing almost as little about my new boss as I did about the workings of the U.S. Senate. I was given a vague assignment at that time under the title of special assistant. The charter was to somehow enhance Cannon's stature in the Nevada media, but I found it confusing and, ultimately, unsatisfying, so I left after a little more than a year. When I returned to Cannon's staff in 1977 with the title of press secretary, my duties were straightforward—be the middleman between the media-shy senator and a press corps that was growing as his stature and importance in the U.S. Senate grew. I stayed through his fourth and final term.

In the Senate, it was often an open question which way Cannon would vote on key issues. Often not even his staff knew. During the dramatic vote on the Panama Canal treaties, we huddled over scratchy radio receivers on our desks listening to the Senate floor debate. The emotional issue of "giving away the Panama Canal" had elicited more negative voter reaction than any other matter Cannon encountered during his Senate career. All of us, including his wartime commanding officer and longtime Senate aide Frank Krebs, listened anxiously to the roll call. When he voted in favor of the treaties, bucking an avalanche of criticism from antitreaty forces in Nevada, we cheered him for his courage—but none of us would have wagered on his vote in advance.

There is something admirable about a politician who keeps his own counsel and makes his own decisions. Although Cannon possessed a fine mind and great self-confidence, he was the least arrogant of men. To his mind, vigorously refuting his critics gave their charges more credibility than they deserved. His oratory was uninspired—no one would call him charismatic—and he was not adept at the glib riposte. He was a man of great courage, but some deep inner reticence seemed to prevent him from explaining or defining himself to the voters. His political opponents, most notably Paul Laxalt and Jim Santini, were only too happy to undertake the task for him. They presented an image of an unscrupulous, even corrupt politician. That image—baseless in reality—stuck and eventually cost him his beloved Senate seat.

Early on, Cannon made a bargain with the voters of Nevada: You may not warm up to me, but if you vote for me I'll work harder for you than you can imagine and I'll produce results like you've never seen. Cannon fulfilled his end of the bargain. As a freshman senator, his record was outstanding. That record and his hard work enabled him to prevail—by the narrowest of margins—against Laxalt's ferocious attack in 1964. His accomplishments sheltered him from serious political opposition until 1980, when allegations of a corrupt deal with the Teamsters Union put him on the defensive. Cannon again failed to respond strongly, quickly, and decisively enough. The facts later proved him right, but the facts were not enough against the calculated attack on his integrity during his last campaign.

Howard Cannon's rise and fall is a very American story: how a young man from the small town of St. George, Utah, became one of the most powerful men in the Senate before his innate shyness mixed with stubborn pride—an Achilles-like flaw—helped bring him down. It is also a universal story. Only the details are different. When Cannon came back from the war in late September 1945, he had already decided to make Las Vegas his home. He was hardly alone in recognizing that Las Vegas had enormous potential for growth. The population almost tripled in a decade, growing from 8,422 in 1940 to 24,624 in 1950. The new residents were a colorful lot. Nevada had legalized gambling in 1931, and casinos were beginning to flourish. There was money to be made in gambling, a lot of money, and men like Bugsy Siegel and Benny Binion, who would have been considered outlaws in any other state, found a place within or near the law in Nevada. Nevada's divorce laws, the most liberal in the nation at the time, drew stars of stage and screen, heiresses and chorus girls, the rich, the famous, and the notorious. They did not stay long. It took only six weeks to establish residency and then the divorce became final, but something had to fill the empty hours. Ordinary people—that is, those without a major bankroll—dropped their nickels, dimes, and sometimes quarters in the slots at the closest gas station. But the men and women who put Las Vegas on the map did not come all the way from New York or Los Angeles to mess around amid the gas pumps with sacks of quarters in their hands. The divorce may or may not have been devastating, but after a week or two of decorous seclusion the soon-to-be-single-again wanted action.

In the desert, the place for action was the casino. It was not long before Walter Winchell, the New York tabloids, and the Hollywood gossip columnists were telling all, or at least all they safely could. Photographs of famous faces at the roulette table or playing blackjack while quaffing champagne appeared in newspapers across the country. Las Vegas began to epitomize glamour and glitz, with an emphasis on the glitz. It also had a reputation for being just a bit risqué. Brothels, after all, were legal in many Nevada jurisdictions, and Las Vegas had its own red-light district, the notorious "Block 16," that dated back to the founding of the city in 1905. The last brothel in Clark County was closed in 1954. It is now one of only two counties in the state where prostitution is prohibited by state law. In other counties it's a matter of local option. Nevada has never had a major problem in reconciling the raffish and the respectable.

In the excitement of the postwar boom, nobody thought much about the workers who built Boulder Dam in the 1930s and stayed on to build Las Vegas in the 1940s and 1950s, or the defense workers who came to the Basic Magnesium Plant in nearby Henderson, liked the climate, and remained to do the work of the city. The high rollers were making the city famous, but those who put down roots made the city work and made it grow. Among them were the lawyers who migrated to Las Vegas to lead all those people through the divorce process, or to keep the men in the gaming business out of the kinds of trouble that are often associated with it. Among those lawyers was a small-town Mormon boy—right there at the center of the city that sin built.

CHAPTER 1

Blood Matters

Descendants of the original *Mayflower* colonists take great pride in their lineage. The same is true of those who trace their roots back to the Huguenot founders of South Carolina, or to the early planters in Virginia, to George Washington's officers, to one or more of the signers of the Declaration of Independence—the list goes on. In Utah and other parts of the West settled by the first Mormon pioneers, descendants of church founder Joseph Smith and of his successor Brigham Young and their close associates make up the Mormon aristocracy. Like most aristocracies, it is more a matter of blood and breeding than of wealth.

Howard Cannon was a Mormon aristocrat. His great-grandfather George, known in the family as "the Immigrant," was prospering as a woodworker in the British port of Liverpool and raising a family with his wife, Ann Quayle, when he encountered the missionary John Taylor, one of the young church's most important leaders. Taylor spoke compellingly of a new Zion that the Church of Jesus Christ of Latter-day Saints was establishing in America. In 1839, when Taylor had embarked on the second Mormon mission to the British Isles, the church was barely nine years old and known only to a relative few, but by the time Taylor and his group returned home in 1841, they had made four thousand new converts, George and his wife among them.

On September 18, 1842, the Cannons, along with Ann's family and other converts, set sail on the long and perilous voyage to New Orleans. Ann was carrying another child. She became seasick at the beginning of the journey, her condition worsened, and she died twenty days later, leaving a young husband and four children. It is said that her four-year-old son, David Henry, the senator's grandfather, had to be physically restrained from following his mother's coffin into the sea. For the Cannons, it was a terrible voyage, and the journey was not over.

From New Orleans, they continued up the Mississippi River to St. Louis, where they spent the winter of 1842. The following April they traveled overland to the Mormon colony in Nauvoo, Illinois, Taylor's "new Zion" and the seat of the prophet Joseph Smith, whose series of visions from the time he was a boy of fourteen formed the basis of the church.

Nauvoo was then the second-most-populous city in Illinois and prospering under the Mormons. The state granted Joseph Smith the right to form an independent militia, which he then commanded. He was also mayor of Nauvoo, justice of the peace, and university chancellor, in addition to being prophet and president of the church. The doctrines of the new church did not set well with their neighbors of other more established faiths. Smith preached—and practiced—the union of spiritual, economic, and political matters under the priesthood, as well as a new scripture that had been revealed to him called the Book of Mormon. Other unorthodox doctrines, including the practice of polygamy, contributed to the heightening of political and economic tensions within Nauvoo and the neighboring communities. Non-Mormons and a few Mormon defectors rebelled against Smith's rule. He declared martial law in Nauvoo, and as a result he and his brother Hyrum were arrested for treason and jailed in Carthage, the county seat. There, a mob attacked and shot them on June 27, 1844. John Taylor, one of the church's twelve governing apostles and the missionary who had converted the Cannons, barely escaped with his life.

The Immigrant, the woodworker of Liverpool, was chosen to build the coffins and mold the death masks for Joseph Smith and his brother

Hyrum. Not long afterward, and shortly after taking a new wife, he himself died of sunstroke. The following spring his wife, Mary, gave birth to a daughter, Elizabeth.

Smith's death caused a rift among the Mormon settlers, but most—including the surviving Cannons—decided to throw in their lot with Smith's successor, Brigham Young. More violent incidents the following year convinced Young that the Saints, as church members called themselves, should leave Nauvoo and look for new headquarters in the West. After much planning, the exodus began in February 1846. Mary, the infant Elizabeth, and the Immigrant's four older children joined the pilgrimage. By late spring, 16,000 Saints with their animals and wagons were making the arduous trek across the Great Prairie. It did not end until July 1847, when Young beheld the valley of the Great Salt Lake in Utah, deemed it the site for the new city, and marked the spot for the temple. It stands on that same spot today.

For a time, the Cannons were settled in Salt Lake City and the family grew in importance within the church. Howard's great-uncle, George Quayle Cannon, served as Brigham Young's private secretary and, after Young's death in 1877, as chief executor of his estate. The Immigrant's family was among the first group of settlers directed by Young to colonize the sparsely populated desert region of southern Utah, some four hundred miles away. They left Salt Lake City in 1861 on a thirty-seven-day trek through wilderness and hostile Indian territory to the New Dixie, so-called because Young and other church leaders were convinced the area could grow cotton, an important consideration should the traditional supply from the South be cut off by the Civil War. By November more than two hundred wagons were drawn up on the site of St. George.

In April 1862, the Immigrant's son Angus was elected mayor. Howard Cannon's grandfather, David, who had so mourned the loss of his mother on the voyage from Liverpool, became the third president of the St. George Temple. George Quayle Cannon was the only child who remained behind. In 1862, at the age of thirty-five, he went to Washington as a delegate from the Territory of Utah to the U.S. House of Representatives, and his son, Frank J. Cannon, was elected as one of Utah's first U.S. senators in 1897.

David had spent years helping build the temple while managing his own farm and fathering a large family with two wives, Wilhelmina and Josephine, ten children from the former and eleven from the latter. At the

1877 dedication ceremony for the temple, which is still in use, David met the woman who would become his third wife and Howard's grandmother, Rhoda Ann Knell. Of the eleven children David fathered with Rhoda, the sixth was Howard's father, Walter, born on July 5, 1888. Like his brothers and sisters, Walter was reared as much by his father's earlier wives, affectionately called Aunt Willie and Aunt Jo, as by his own mother, and he turned to whoever was closest to hand for comfort. For companionship, he had his thirty-one brothers and sisters and even more numerous cousins. It is easy to see why the town grew rapidly.

Until Walter's generation, all the Cannons practiced polygamy, and, after federal law abolished it in 1882, all suffered for it. Angus was married six times and served six months in jail in 1890 rather than abandon any of his wives. His brother George fathered thirty-four children with five wives and served 175 days in prison in 1888, using the time to write a book on the life of Joseph Smith.

In 1909, less than a month away from his twenty-first birthday, Walter married Leah Sullivan, a local girl of the same age. Their son Howard, the future senator, was born three years later, on January 26, 1912. Walter and Leah's life together was less daunting than their forebears'. There were no more directives from Salt Lake City to conquer unexplored new lands for the church, and much of the wilderness of St. George had been transformed by the hard work of their parents' generation. Instead, they faced the day-to-day challenges and joys of rearing and sustaining a family in a rural farming community formed by the deeply held values of the Mormon Church. In 1914 Walter began his two-year commitment as a missionary in the city of Liverpool that he had last seen in 1842, when he was four years old. The family home was rented out, and Leah and two-year-old Howard moved in with her parents while she earned $2.50 a week working as a clerk in A. R. Whitehead and Sons' department store.

When Walter returned from his mission abroad, Leah suggested he complete his studies at Dixie College, the local junior college that was housed in the same building as the high school, which Howard later attended. Walter graduated from Dixie and began teaching there. In 1921 he became postmaster of St. George, a patronage position that he held until 1932 when Franklin Roosevelt's election cost Republican Walter his job. In those years he began investing in local real estate ventures. He owned a farm south of town that was worked by tenants, and later he built a motel that his children invested in to the tune of $2,000 each. It was a good investment. The children sold the motel in 1953 for $60,000. Walter joined the board of directors of the Bank of St. George, and in time he assumed his role as patriarch with the industriousness and stolidity that had made the Cannons respected and admired since the early days of St. George.

For Howard, the firstborn, life in Walter and Leah's home was safe, predictable, rigorous but not harsh, and filled with love. The home that he and his two younger sisters, Evelyn and Ramona (a third sister, Ellen, lived only three weeks), shared and where each of them had been born was a small white adobe structure facing north on a deep lot just northeast of the temple Howard's grandfather had helped build. In keeping with the Mormon tradition of laying out cities in relation to the Tabernacle, the Cannons' address was 167 East 300 South. That meant it was one block east and three blocks south of the Tabernacle block. They bought it for $200. It had electricity but, as in most parts of rural America, no running water. The toilet, Howard's sister Evelyn recalled, was a "three-holer" in the backyard. The Cannons did not have an indoor bathroom until 1936, when Walter built a new home of red brick on the same lot as the old adobe structure.

There was order and regularity to life in St. George. Saturday was bath day, with everyone getting cleaned up for Sunday church services. Water was heated on the cookstove, and baths were taken in an aluminum tub in the kitchen. On Sunday children were given religious instruction in the morning, followed by worship services. Monday was wash day. The laundry was done in a big tub of water sitting on hot coals in the backyard. Two more tubs were used for rinsing. Bluing was the bleach of the day.

Early in the morning, Howard milked the cows before walking the short distance to Woodward School, which he attended through eighth grade and is still in use today. He, and later his sisters, came home for lunch. After school Howard tended to the second milking and groomed and trained his horses, which were kept in a large corral that surrounded the barn. His mother loved music, and insisted that her son practice the clarinet daily. Howard described her as "a stern but loving woman with an Irish temper that one didn't want to challenge."

In 1936, when Howard was twenty-four and studying law at the University of Arizona, resourceful Leah rented a basement room to teachers in the new house that Walter had just built. A spirit of uncomplaining hard work extended throughout the Cannon household: They looked for opportunities and seized them as they found them. Howard's favorite hymn exhorted, "Put your shoulder to the wheel, push along, do your duty with a heart full of song." Among many lessons Howard learned from his father were a willingness to work hard and a respect for real estate as an investment. After he had finished law school and returned to St. George, Howard bought a small house for investment purposes on Main Street right across from Dixie College. Later he invested profitably in numerous properties in Las Vegas and in the Washington, D.C., area.

Howard enjoyed a loving and respectful relationship with his father, signified by a son's appreciation for a hardworking parent. That this example stuck with him was indicated by a wartime letter to his sister inquiring about their father's health, with questions about how hard he was working and expressions of hope that he could stop working the farm before too long. The concern was well founded, as Walter lived to be "only" sixty-nine, a relatively young age compared with the ninety years of Howard's life.

For his part, Walter emphasized the importance of higher education to Howard, as if to impress upon him that the hard work of a farmer wasn't the only option available to him. Howard learned that lesson early and well, recalling nearly seventy years later in an interview with his daughter, Nancy, "Through his example, I knew I wanted to do something else in life other than farm, which meant hard work, mending fences, and knowing the future would always be more of the same. I was willing to do everything I could to follow higher education away from the farm in St. George."

Howard's intelligence and maturity soon registered with the neighbors and family acquaintances, and in the summer before he turned six, the first-grade teacher, Miss McAllister, urged Walter and Leah to send him to school a year early. She said she knew the boy was ready for class despite his young age.

By family accounts, Howard competed successfully with his older classmates. Woodward was not a one-room schoolhouse, as Howard's classes were taught by separate teachers from the first through eighth grades. One childhood trait, his affection for horses, would remain with Howard throughout his life, whether riding in small-town rodeos, cantering through

Washington's Rock Creek Park as a new senator, or riding his golden palomino, Edgewood Sunrise, in full western regalia at the annual Helldorado Days parades in Las Vegas.

"It was kind of a rough-and-tough town back then," he recalled of St. George years later. "There were cowboys; I was a cowboy myself during those early days. I used to ride horses to school." His favorite was Old Queenie, a bay mare who lived in the barn behind the house in town and helped him on his paper route delivering the *Deseret News* around St. George. Howard recalled a specific hallmark of Queenie's service. "Queenie knew the delivery route so well she would stop in front of every gate or house where I needed to throw a paper," he remembered. "When I was sick or couldn't take my route, I had a friend ride her and told him to throw one wherever she stopped, which worked out fine."

The pattern of work, school, and activities that was fostered in Howard at an early age continued in high school. Dixie High was located within a stone's throw of Woodward, continuing the close-knit nature of Howard's upbringing. In addition to playing guard on the football team and fostering a dedication to pole vaulting on the track team, Howard polished the musical skills instilled by the dogged determination of his mother during those daily clarinet lessons. He had added the saxophone to his repertoire somewhere along the way and joined the Dixie High band as a saxophone player.

Although Howard would initially settle on education as a way to take him away from farm life in St. George, his growing prowess as a musician provided another route. In the summers during high school, Howard and two friends from Dixie High—Vella Ruth and LeGene Morris—landed jobs at the North Rim Lodge of the Grand Canyon. "Howard and Gene were employed as bellhops, and I was a waitress," recalled Vella Ruth. "But we all knew that the real reason for our employment was to entertain the guests. We would work at our regular jobs during the day, then put on a program in the evening for about an hour. Then we would have a dance in the recreation hall," she added.

The transition from high school to junior college was as easy geographically for Howard as that from elementary to high school, since Dixie Junior College was in the same building as Dixie High. He decided to continue an emphasis on music when he entered Dixie JC. His first two years of college were centered on studying music, debate, and German. According to the 1930 Dixie yearbook, he was also "the only man brave enough to take dramatic art." He became a member of the college's advanced band, playing at basketball games and devotional services. One of the purposes of the advanced band was to prepare students for dance orchestra work, and Howard was quick to take advantage of the opportunity. He became a member of the college's prestigious dance orchestra headed by Earl J. Bleak and later sat in on other dance bands around St. George. He was developing the skills that would provide him both experience and income in his later college and law school days.

Musical studies at Dixie also engendered Howard's first attempt to use music for wider career goals. He competed in a music contest sponsored by Brigham Young University and was awarded a music scholarship to the well-known school that was considered the epitome of Mormon higher education. The career-minded Howard was at war with the Utah cowboy part of his makeup, however, and he turned down the Brigham Young University scholarship because he thought he might want to play polo at the University of Arizona. If polo was more intriguing to the college sophomore than studying music at BYU, still another opportunity appealed to him at the time: a scholarship to West Point. Howard was eligible to apply to the military academy because he shared top academic ranking at Dixie with classmate Henry Nicholes, whose father was president of the institution and a friend of Howard's father. Howard first passed the physical part of the West Point entrance requirements, which Henry failed, and then sat for the formal entrance examination.

For perhaps the first time in his life, he met an obstacle he could not overcome and failed to pass the mathematics portion of the exam. This puzzled him because, as he recalled, "I was pretty good in math, too." He was later informed that an unusually high number of applicants that year also failed the math exam, so West Point allowed all of them to be renominated the following year. For the restless Howard, however, whose mind was mulling everything from music to polo to the military, a year was too far away. "By that time I was ready to go away to school and just skipped it and didn't take the exam again," he said.

Still another interest was roiling the college sophomore's mind, one that would supersede music as an important part of his life: aviation. "I had a yen for flying, for becoming a pilot," he remembered. "I was probably five or six years old when I first saw an airplane. It landed on Black Hill in St. George. I was about fourteen the first time I got a chance to ride on one. It probably would have been a two-passenger plane. I enjoyed it."

While passing on some options and seeing others evaporate, Howard eventually focused his career thoughts on two staples of his upbringing: education and music. Specifically, he began to think in terms of becoming a music educator and enrolled in Arizona State Teachers College (ASTC) in Flagstaff, Arizona, which is now Northern Arizona University, majoring in education. Although this was a reasonable compromise between his ambition and his development to that point, he made the decision sound almost accidental in recalling it years later. "I went with two fellows from Santa Clara [outside St. George] down through Flagstaff, where they were going to play basketball," he said. "When the three of us got there and visited around with the people in the athletic program, they offered all three of us scholarships and work, so we stopped off there and I went to school at Flagstaff rather than going on down to Tucson [the University of Arizona and its polo team]."

Howard recalled that he "did very well in school," receiving his education degree and graduating from ASTC. An article in a local newspaper gave more details, including Howard's receipt of a gold key for being named the college's honor student in music. He had also been president of the Delta Phi Alpha music fraternity in his junior year and president of Sigma Eta Alpha, a local honor society, in his senior year.

The article also mentioned his stewardship of the Lumberjack Collegians, "a dance orchestra which has won a very good reputation in Arizona for its ability to entertain." It noted that Howard planned to remain in Arizona for the summer, booking his band in resorts such as the dance hall at the South Rim of the Grand Canyon (harking back to his summers at the North Rim), Lake Marie's Summer Resort near Flagstaff, and the Big Indian Pow-Wow in Flagstaff. Although acknowledging that he "could have been a school-teacher" at this time in his career, that choice was not enticing enough to the college graduate, who was making a name for himself as a musician and mulling over other possibilities. "For some reason I wasn't interested in teaching right then," he recalled, so he turned to his father for counsel. Then a teacher at Dixie College, Walter enlisted a friend, Dixie president Joseph K. Nicholes, to discuss the idea of a law career with Howard.

Those two, along with mother Leah, prevailed upon Howard to apply for law school, and he was accepted at the University of Arizona. The ever-practical Walter impressed his son with the argument that even if he did not practice law, it was a good background for business.

Repeating the pattern of Dixie and Flagstaff, Howard combined stewardship of the University of Arizona Concert Band—an impressive group with up to seventy members—with private bookings of musicians he knew. He soon became known throughout the Tucson area and back home in St. George, where his dance band played a weekly fifteen-minute radio program over station KVOA that was carried on Monday nights. Walter, Leah, and Howard's sisters gathered around the large curved radio on the dining room table to hear him play. These were the early days of the Depression, and the Cannon family's spirit of opportunistic hard work manifested itself in Howard's entrepreneurship—he certainly kept his shoulder to the wheel, even as the national economy faltered.

Howard's managerial skills were challenged in his dealings with the American Mail Line, which he had contacted while at Flagstaff to book a band on one of its cruise ships sailing between Seattle and the Far East. Rebuffed in 1933, Howard met success the following year and created a great deal of press interest in a planned booking. The boys had a major disappointment, however, when they arrived in Seattle—a longshoremen's strike. A photo in the *Seattle Post-Intelligencer* pictured three of the American Mail Line's ships resting at anchor in a cove, "where they are being held in idleness pending the reopening of the port."

Howard scrambled to find employment for his group, landing a booking at Seattle's Edmond Meany Hotel, near the University of Washington. A hotel announcement stated that the University of Arizona Pep Orchestra, under the direction of Howard Cannon, "will furnish music for dancing during dinner, from seven until nine o'clock in the Marine Dining Room."

As his third year of law school drew to a close, Howard finally capitalized on the enterprise he exhibited by securing the American Mail Line tour of the Orient. His group was booked for the summer of 1936 to play aboard the SS *President Jefferson,* sailing from Seattle to Yokohama, Japan. According to the ship's program, Howard played the saxophone, clarinet, and drums. James Williams, his friend from Flagstaff days who had been recruited to participate in the aborted tour in 1933, played the piano, while three new recruits, Lawrence Campbell on oboe, George Davis on guitar, and Corwin Larson on violin, rounded out the group. Dinner music included Akimento's "On the Volga," Donizetti's "Sextette from Lucia," and Wagner's "Song to the Evening Star."

That memorable cruise played havoc with Howard's law school schedule, as it made him late for the beginning of classes that fall—an additional semester of study that would wind up law school for him. His excellent grades up to that point held him in good stead, though, and he recalled that he "was able to get in okay and make up the work." He completed his studies in December 1936, but stayed in Tucson to study for the Arizona bar exam and complete some orchestral commitments. He received his LL.B., bachelor of laws, in June 1937.

Music and law school did not occupy all of Howard's time while attending the University of Arizona. During summer breaks he roped cattle and rode horses for fun and entered rodeos for competition. At some point he capitalized on his nascent interest in flying. The catalyst was his law school roommate, Johnny Milner, whom Howard described as "nuts about flying."

The two "chummed around together," Howard told *Air Line Pilot* magazine in a long interview in 1971, and took flying lessons in Tucson. "We flew a number of different planes, like the Piper Cub and the Curtiss Pusher that had the little gondola on it. You sat right out in front with just a stick and throttle in front of you; the engine and prop were behind you. Flying that was an experience and a lot of fun. . . . I found myself with an earnest desire to fly, not with the thought of making it a profession, however, but as a hobby."

Something else had entered Howard's life in those busy days as he was nearing the end of law school. Home in St. George for a while in the summer of 1936 before his final year, Howard wandered into the Big Hand Cafe, a beer-and-sandwich grill operated by a local man, Andy Pace, whose family was well known in the area. Visiting at the time was Andy's cousin from Alamo, Nevada, Dorothy Pace. The imagination must reconstruct the effect meeting Howard—the handsome local celebrity who was on the radio, led dance bands in Arizona, and flew airplanes to boot—had on Dorothy. Likewise, one can imagine how the beautiful Dorothy struck Howard, who had been fully involved with the pretty, sophisticated coeds at the University of Arizona. Dorothy was, simply, a stunning young woman, with beautiful skin and eyes, a cute, petite figure, and flowing dark hair. Shy like her future husband, not given to elaborate descriptions of her personal experiences, she allowed only that she was instantly impressed by the twenty-four-year-old law student. "I had a date that night with someone else," Dorothy remembered years later with a laugh. "He took me home and Howard picked me up later." She was more concerned with the impression she made at the café after ingesting a sandwich that was full of onions. Dorothy's wholesome beauty undoubtedly overcame any effects of the onions. Indeed, it would have taken someone of her movie-star looks to turn Howard's head, as he had developed a widespread reputation as a ladies' man. "Howard always had girlfriends," his sister Evelyn recalled with a smile, looking at clippings from his college scrapbook and unremembered photos inscribed to her brother from numerous comely young women. One of the main subjects of the scrapbook Cannon began in 1933 was his dating career. An entry in the scrapbook notes that his first date at the University of Arizona was with Dorothy Greer, a sorority girl from Houston, Texas, who was featured in a campus newspaper photo under the caption, "Most Beautiful Arizona Co-ed." Another memento is a simple dance card for the Aggie Hoe Down on October 21, 1933, inscribed "with Barbara Bush." Card entries show Howard had Ms. Bush's hand for five of the evening's twelve dances, sharing her with the likes of "Ed," "Slotzy," "Frizzy," and "Jack." Underneath another glamorous campus newspaper photo of Ercelle Amanda Caldwell of Phoenix, Howard wrote, "'My Pal' Ercelle."

The budding romance between Howard and Dorothy did not flower immediately, as Howard left for the cruise-ship engagement shortly afterward and Dorothy left St. George within a year for Los Angeles, where she graduated from the Sawyer School of Business and went to work for her uncle's company, Physicians' Business Counselors. But a spark had been ignited, as indicated by a letter Howard sent his new acquaintance a few weeks later. Addressed to "Friend Dorothy," Howard's letter on the stationery of the SS *President Jefferson* was postmarked from Yokohama. "I suppose you will be very surprised to hear from me after so long a time," he opened. "That is if you even remember who I am." After providing a few details about Japan and the cruise-ship engagement, Howard noted that he planned to be in Los Angeles in August, "and I would like to see you if that is possible." Howard and Dorothy corresponded and occasionally saw each other throughout the ensuing years. Howard would visit his old grade-school friend and cousin Horace MacArthur, who lived in Los Angeles with his wife, Ethel, and see Dorothy at the same time.

Although romantic, the relationship had a star-crossed element to it as well. Both Howard and Dorothy suffered the loss of sweethearts before exchanging vows in 1945. Dorothy's fiancé, Ray B. Nelson, was killed in an oil-well explosion on the outskirts of St. George on March 6, 1935, an incident described as "the worst disaster Dixie has ever known." Howard's girlfriend Carma Fawcett was killed in a car wreck outside St. George on April 14, 1940, a setback Evelyn described as "devastating" to her brother. Howard arrived too late to pick up Carma following her shift at a local restaurant, and she accepted a fateful ride with another boy who owned a convertible automobile. Howard's sense of regret and loss was understand-ably overwhelming, as Carma was not just another of his dates. "He was really in love with her," Evelyn said. After the accident, "he looked like death warmed over."

Although Cannon traveled far away from St. George throughout his life, his upbringing there stamped him in many ways. He would not adhere strictly to the tenets of Mormonism, but he remained conservative socially and kept alcohol consumption under control. He never lost his focus on family concerns and always reflected the cautious financial outlook of those reared during the Depression. His forebears' interest in political concerns was also ingrained in him, and that, combined with an unrelenting drive, accounted for his most telling accomplishments.

CHAPTER 2

War Clouds

Wars interrupt lives—or take them. All healthy young men are swept up in great international conflicts, some interrupting careers, some leaving school, some enlisting or being drafted in the absence of alternatives. The lucky ones return to their former lives, changed but able to carry on. Such was the fate of Howard Cannon.

Following receipt of his law degree in 1937, Cannon quickly passed the Arizona and Utah bar exams. He then returned to St. George and began solving the perplexing question of how to live the rest of his life. He had been pulled in several directions, from taking a music scholarship to Brigham Young University to enlisting in an Army Air Force (AAF) flying school to attending West Point.

In addition, his experience in leading and managing dance bands and orchestras had broadened his views of the world and exposed him to a more glamorous life than available in St. George. But family ties were strong, and the pull of the familiar exerted more influence on him at twenty-five than the lure of the exotic. Thus, he hung his shingle in a suite of offices on the second floor of the Pickett Building on St. George Boulevard, within sight of the Woodward School and Dixie College. Small advertisements in the local paper, the *Washington County News,* showed two aspects of his career: Howard W. Cannon, Attorney at Law, and Cannon Realty Company, specializing in "abstracts, rentals, fire & auto insurance." The telephone number for both was 49.

He became active in the Mormon Church, assuming a position as South Ward Sunday-school superintendent, and bought the house on Main Street for investment purposes. By these actions, Cannon seemed capable of settling into a small-town businessman's life that would have been similar to his father's. Not content with a predictable future, however, the young lawyer entered almost immediately into local politics. The sitting county attorney was Orval Hafen, scion of a St. George family of equal prestige with the Cannons. Hafen was a graduate of the University of California law school and had first been elected to the two-year county attorney post in 1932. He was also first cousin to Preston Hafen, with whom Cannon attended college in Flagstaff and who married Cannon's summertime entertainment companion, Vella Ruth Morris. Notwithstanding this formidable opponent and despite the fact he had been out of law school for barely a year, the twenty-six-year-old Cannon filed for the office as a Democrat against Republican Hafen in 1938.

Cannon was not a memoirist, and no other record exists to account for his party affiliation, which is somewhat unusual, considering that his father was a Republican. He may have simply been infected by the popularity of Democratic president Franklin Delano Roosevelt, who had already been elected twice by the time Cannon filed for his first office. He came close to unseating Hafen, losing by 218 votes out of 3,110 cast, and wasted no time taking his next political step. In January 1939, he accepted a position as reference attorney for the twenty-third session of the Utah legislature in Salt Lake City.

The reference attorney was essentially a clerical job, ensuring accuracy as bills were "enrolled"—or put in final form—after passage. But the larger significance was exposure to the legislative process and the men and women who were involved in it. Cannon had cultivated a friendship with one of the most influential Democratic officeholders in southern Utah, State Senator Glenn E. Snow, who was also the current president of Dixie College. Shortly after the legislative session was concluded in March 1939, a letter from Senator Snow appeared in the *Washington County News* under the head-line, "Howard Cannon's Work Praised by Sen. Snow." Snow wrote: "He is commended for his efficient and effective service, working into the problems that were presented in a most creditable way."

Cannon also became active in the St. George Lions Club, latching onto a local Lions-sponsored rodeo called the Dixie Round-Up. The rodeo was scheduled for September 5–7, 1940, just months before the November election. As chairman of the event, Cannon received continuous coverage in the weeks leading up to the rodeo. With that, his friendship with Senator Snow, and a more established law practice under his belt, he presented a more confident image in the rematch with Hafen. Cannon's election ad in the *News,* running on October 31, 1940, was larger and more prominently placed than Hafen's. Boasting "four years active practice of law" along with the stint in the 1939 Utah legislature, the ad described Cannon as "a young man attempting to establish himself in Washington County where youth, training and leadership is needed." Hafen's ad, by contrast, acknowledged that the incumbent had been ill for some time during the summer, but assured voters that for several weeks "he had been doing all the work required of the county attorney." Cannon prevailed by 284 votes, roughly equal to the 348-vote margin by which President Roosevelt carried Washington County over Wendell Wilkie.

Cannon also followed up on a bent for military service during this period, enlisting in the Utah National Guard as a member of a combat engineers unit, the 115th. This was a humble introduction to the World War II flying career that would bring Cannon to some of the most momentous combat theaters of the war. Combat engineers are the workhorses of the military, building bridges and other structures that enable ground forces to advance across enemy terrain. Notwithstanding his lack of preparation for such work, Cannon quickly attained the rank of first lieutenant in the Utah Guard. When guard units across the country were called into active duty in early 1941, twenty-nine-year-old Cannon found himself company commander of the 115th. Thus, his hard-won victory over Orval Hafen in the county attorney's race proved for naught, as he was not able to fulfill the duties of that office.

Cannon was assigned to a combat engineer's school at Fort Belvoir, Virginia, in February, then was transferred to the Fortieth Division of the combat engineers in San Luis Obispo, California. A newspaper story in November 1941 featured the exploits of the Fortieth Division during a field demonstration in Los Angeles. Captain Howard Cannon was cited for leading his group of engineers in constructing a 308-foot floating footbridge across Echo Park Lake in less than nine minutes. Cannon was with the Fortieth Division in San Luis Obispo when the attack on Pearl Harbor came. "I was playing a little Sunday morning bridge with three of the guys in the outfit when we heard FDR on the radio," he recalled. "That meant for me to get my unit loaded up and find out where we were going next. We went down to Los Angeles, and from there up to Seattle." He was subsequently transferred to the 133rd Combat Engineers and assigned to Fort Lewis, Washington, training new recruits and itching for action. In an April 6, 1942, letter to his parents, he complained of the slow pace at Fort Lewis compared to what had been happening in California. "They don't seem to know there's a war on," he wrote, noting that no new recruits had arrived in camp.

It was at Fort Lewis, however, where his preparation as a pilot met opportunity. Cannon had followed up on his flying adventures with Johnny Milner to obtain a private pilot's license, so was elated when a call went out from the Army Air Force for anyone with flying experience. "I didn't hesitate taking advantage of this opportunity," he recalled in a later interview. "I was transferred in grade [as captain] and went to light aircraft and glider school in New Mexico [Kirtland Air Force Base, near Albuquerque]. There, we received light aircraft and basic free-flight glider training. We would fly the small planes to altitude, cut the switch and bring them in. This exercise went on day and night." Although definitely a step up from building pontoon bridges, Cannon was still a long way from being a combat pilot. A friend he met at Kirtland in 1942, Bernard G. Parks, recounted the many long steps taken by the pair to get ready for a larger role: further training in Plainview, Texas; Twentynine Palms, California; and Fort Sumner, New Mexico.

After a stint at Bowman Field in Louisville, Kentucky, Cannon and Parks moved to the Air Force School of Applied Tactics near Orlando, Florida, flying C-47s with the 439th Troop Carrier Group (TCG). Cannon upgraded himself from glider pilot to service pilot by the time he and Parks were reunited at another base in Alliance, Nebraska. "I was amazed at what Howard had done in the short time he had been there," Parks recalled. "You've got to remember, we were glider pilots. We had not gone to regular flying school which had the glamour and so forth that some of them had. So we sort of struggled through. But it was no problem for Howard. By the time I got there he was acting operations officer for the whole group. Howard was the only one I knew of who advanced from the glider pilot rating through the service pilot."

Having successfully transformed himself from a combat engineer to a full pilot, and having won the admiration of those who served with him, the former bandleader and small-town lawyer from Utah was about to take another fateful step in a remarkable military career. In keeping with his track record, however, it was not through conventional means.

The Troop Carrier Command, with which Cannon was affiliated by joining the Air Force School of Applied Tactics, had a "shaky beginning," according to one of its most illustrious graduates, Col. Francis X. Krebs. This is the same Krebs who eventually served as Cannon's best man and one of his closest and longest-lasting friends, but found himself in 1943 commanding the 440th Troop Carrier Group.

Troop carrier as a concept—flying massive amounts of men and matériel into a combat zone and parachuting them into action—came into being only after Hitler showed the effectiveness of such tactics by capturing the British island of Crete in 1941. Hitler transported 32,000 German troops to Crete and captured it within ten days, Krebs recounted in a postwar history of his group, and the United States organized its own Troop Carrier Command about a year later. Thus it was that Krebs was commanding the 440th TCG in Florida when it was transferred to Nebraska, where the 439th was also stationed—along with its rising star, Captain Howard Cannon. Fate then played a baffling card, much as it had done to create the possibility of Howard and Dorothy Cannon becoming man and wife after the war. The commander of the 439th, Ralph Zimmerman, flew to California to visit his family one weekend. Returning to the base, he decided to buzz his home, flew too low, and was killed in the resulting crash. As a result, Krebs recalled, "They took my deputy, Charlie Young, and gave him the 439th. In exchange I was given Howard Cannon, who had been in the 439th."

They formed a colorful and effective duo that stayed together throughout the war and for decades thereafter. Krebs was a tall, skinny Catholic from Chicago, and Cannon a shorter, huskier Mormon from Utah. Krebs was the commanding officer, pilot to Cannon's copilot, and a brusque, no-nonsense officer with an infectious, cackling laugh that spawned imitators wherever he went. Although hardworking and responsible, Cannon had a playful side that cropped up even in the grim wartime environment. He wrote his parents of the sites he and Krebs encountered on their way to the European war zone much as a tourist would. Reading Cannon's letters, one could get the idea that training for battle involved as much beach time as serious preparation. He rattled off glowing accounts of his many layovers and postings, always noting the condition of local beaches and documenting the deepening of his tan. Notwithstanding their differences, Cannon and Krebs meshed in that unexplainable chemistry that sometimes occurs between two seemingly mismatched humans.

Cannon and Krebs spent the next six months, from September 1943 until February 1944, in England, getting the 440th into shape for its historic role in the liberation of Europe. The outstanding fact about this preparation was the novelty of it—Krebs, Cannon, and others involved in the development of troop-carrier tactics were operating on a clean slate. The 440th was created only in June 1943, four months before Cannon and Krebs were teamed up in Nebraska. The overall command structure had been solidified only the previous October, and the role of airlifted troops was in a state of flux amid planning for the invasion of Europe.

Although military leaders included plans for a considerable airborne contingent as part of the cross-Channel invasion as early as 1942, initial plans proved to be too ambitious. There simply were not enough aircraft and trained crews to meet an original deadline of four transport groups ready to go to England by the first of August 1942 and another ready by September. Also, plans for the invasion of Europe changed, with Allied leaders deciding in 1942 that the invasion of North Africa would have to precede an attack on Europe. Thus, the initial troop-carrier wing that had been rushed into being was assigned to assist in the North African invasion, which was code-named Operation Torch. As these strategies evolved, a similar transformation was taking place in the availability of aircraft for troop-carrier operations.

The plane chosen for this task was the famous Douglas DC-3, which had revolutionized commercial passenger air travel with its reliable long-distance flying capabilities. At the beginning of 1942, however, U.S. airlines had a combined total of fewer than three hundred DC-3s, of which the Army Air Force appropriated ninety-two by May.

The Army Air Force version of the DC-3 became known, after a few revisions, as the C-47. The plane could carry a combat payload of three tons, or eighteen fully equipped paratroopers. It could carry a jeep or a trailer, or a 75mm pack howitzer, and could take off fully loaded on a dirt strip of less than three thousand feet. It could tow one or even two of the U.S.-built Waco CG-4A gliders, which were towed behind the C-47s to carry additional men and matériel. If equipped with extra fuel tanks, the C-47 had a range of 1,500 miles at a cruising speed of 150 mph. It could also slow to 110 mph to give paratroopers a steady platform from which to jump. The military managed to train nearly four thousand troop-carrier crews on C-47s between 1942 and 1945, and made available eleven hundred crews in Europe by June 1944. Training was made difficult by the peculiar requirements of troop-carrier operations, which included pilots capable of glider towing, flight engineers knowledgeable in attaching glider tow ropes and operating additional pickup equipment, and crew members adept at dropping cargo containers into small clearings. One thing the crews didn't have to worry about, however, was proficiency in aerial gunnery, as the C-47s carried no armament—a mixed blessing, most crew members would agree.

For their part, Cannon and Krebs oversaw formation of a group of fifty-two C-47s and crews by February 1944, when they took off on a long, slow trip to England and an unknown mission. They took a southern route via Puerto Rico, British Guiana, Brazil, Ascension Island in the South Atlantic, Liberia and Marrakech, Africa, and eventually to their first destination, Bottesford, England. Later they moved to Exeter, from which their role in the Normandy invasion was launched.

A heavy schedule of training awaited the 440th in Bottesford and later in Exeter: flying formations "in weather they wouldn't even let single ships fly in the states," night flying, and paratroop and glider work. Preparations for the invasion were well under way.

Cannon and Krebs provided their own accounts of their historic night of flying on D-day, each revealing glimpses into the operation, and other eyes told the story from a different vantage. It began with the buildup, which, Cannon recorded, "began to get hot about 1 June." He continued: "On 2 June we loaded. 3 June the entire base was restricted. On 4 June the weather was bad. . . . 5 June photographers and war correspondents were with us all day getting stories and taking pictures. At 1700 (5 p.m.) we briefed the crews.

At 23:15 (11:15 p.m.) the paratroopers were loaded. . . . [A]t 23:50 we were on our way leading the Group."

Cannon and Krebs flew the lead airplane of forty-five in the 440th's assault on Normandy, the plane bearing the unusual name *Stoy Hora* across its nose. The derivation—even the meaning—of that name is lost to history. Commanding officer of the paratroopers, who were from the Third Battalion, 506th Parachute Infantry Regiment, was Lt. Col. Robert Wolverton. He had sixteen paratroopers under his command, and a BBC war correspondent named Ward Smith took the place that would have been an eighteenth trooper. The flight crew numbered six, with Lts. Edward J. Sullivan and George Arnold as navigators, Sgt. Bill Quick as radio operator, and Sgt. Frederick Nagy as crew chief, in addition to the pilots.

To guide them on their circuitous route to the drop zone near Ste-Mère-église, Cannon and Krebs relied on picket ships in the English Channel with familiar names like *Flatbush, Gallup, Hoboken, Paducah,* and *Spokane.* "After the formation was formed, I headed for *Flatbush,* a point where the friendly land of England would be left behind," recounted Krebs. "As we hit *Flatbush,* we dropped to 1,000 feet and kept descending until we were 500 feet above the water—hitting a steady 140 mph airspeed in order to conform to the rigidly established time schedule."

Cannon picks up the narrative: "Crossed the ship markers Gallup and Hoboken. . . . Anti-aircraft fired at us as we passed the Channel Islands, but we were too low and out of range for them. Three minutes to the French coast we climbed to 1,500 feet. As we crossed the coast there was tracer and anti-aircraft fire on our right. Ran into an overcast so climbed and topped out at 1,700 feet. As we approached the target, we let down through the stuff and broke out at 700 feet over green fields of France." Cannon noted that enemy fire intensified as the plane neared its target, and there were many bomb fires burning on the ground below. He noted a big explosion below and to the right of his craft and concluded that one of his group's planes had been hit and exploded when it crashed. "Many positions firing tracers," Cannon continued. "Many of them had me flinching. Over target—green light—there go the troops. Time 0140 (1:40 a.m.) 6 June 1944."

Krebs noted that "the men stepped out very fast. In one minute the planes were empty. . . . Our mission accomplished, we headed for the coast of the [Cotentin] Peninsula." Krebs saw that several planes were now being hit by flak, and Cannon noticed that one gun about 40 degrees and on their right "about had our position." A few searchlights came on as the Germans tried to pinpoint their plane, and one of the guns "caught our tail and our rear elements."

Cannon and Krebs climbed to 3,000 feet to retrace the route back to Exeter and turned on their navigational and recognition lights as they approached the English shore, which Cannon recalled dryly "really looked good." They landed at Exeter at 0305, with forty-two of their forty-five planes back. Of all loads carried, only four paratroopers came back without having jumped, Cannon recalled. "One was shot in the head, but will live," he explained. "Three were knocked on the floor by flak and couldn't get up with their heavy loads on."

Cannon and Krebs had no way of knowing it, but the Germans were lying in ambush for Lt. Col. Wolverton and his crew. They had soaked a farm-house with oil, and when the paratroopers began to jump torched the build-ing, providing plenty of light to shoot the helpless soldiers as they drifted to earth. Casualties were heavy, and both Wolverton and his executive officer were killed before they touched the ground.

In vivid contrast to the methodical account of the mission provided by the two pilots, the BBC's Smith recounted a far different experience in his story. The sporadic flak that the pilots recorded almost nonchalantly struck Smith differently: "All around the plane, rocketing less than 100 feet from the ground, a Brock's benefit of flak rainbowed us for something like eight minutes on end by my watch, though I could have sworn it was at least half an hour," he wrote.

Smith touched on another subject absent from the accounts of Cannon and Krebs—the extreme vulnerability of the C-47s. "I knew we were a sit-ting pigeon," he wrote as the flak intensified at one point, flak he saw vividly through the still-open door in the side of the plane. "We didn't have a gun or any armor-plate. Our only safeguard was our racing engines and the cool-headedness and skill of the pilot, Colonel Krebs, as he twisted and dived."

A chronic problem of supplying fuel for Gen. Eisenhower's fast-moving ground troops pulled Cannon and Krebs into their second momentous bat-tle. One solution was to open another port closer to the ultimate target of the invasion—Germany. That problem seemed to be solved with the fall of Antwerp, Belgium, on September 4. Antwerp was the second-largest port in

Europe, adjacent to an area occupied by British field marshal Montgomery and less than 100 air miles from Patton's Third Army.

British troops failed to seal off the port from the remaining German troops, however, and the Germans reinforced their defense of the vital estuary that controlled entrance to the port facilities of Antwerp from the North Sea. With Antwerp temporarily delayed as a resupply solution, Montgomery concocted an alternative plan: to secure a narrow road 85 miles into German-held territory over the numerous canals and rivers of the Dutch coastal plain, to Arnhem. From there, Montgomery proposed establishing a beachhead over the Rhine River, from which the Allies could launch an assault on the German interior.

The key ingredient in Montgomery's plan was a massive airdrop of American, British, and Polish paratroopers during three days of daylight missions. He called this airborne portion of his plan Market, to be followed by the ground assault called Garden. Books have been written about the machinations behind this mission, and the internal fighting among Montgomery, Eisenhower, and other leaders to win its approval. For all its apparent flaws, however, the plan was approved by Eisenhower, with ominous consequences for Krebs, Cannon, and thousands of other soldiers.

Orders for the Holland invasion came on September 11, requiring the 440th to relocate to Fulbeck, England. Bad weather held them there until the seventeenth, when the operation that Cannon described as "almost my Waterloo" began. The 440th provided forty-two C-47s to the huge force of five thousand aircraft enlisted to carry out Montgomery's Market operation. Just as at Normandy, Cannon and Krebs led the formation, whose destination was Groesbeek, south and east of Nijmegen. The mission required them to make a 68-mile run each way over enemy-held territory, in a sky full of planes. Unlike the Normandy invasion, they did not have the cover of night.

Conditions for the mission were not just daylight, but "a bright afternoon, a clear and sunny day," as recalled in a postwar account written by Ward Sullivan, group navigator in the Krebs-Cannon crew. The *Stoy Hora* crew had flown together unchanged until that mission, when they were assigned a different plane, named *Miss Yank* and adorned with the familiar depiction of a scantily clad woman. Along with the new plane came a new crew chief, Task Sgt. Frederick Broga, replacing Nagy. "Perfect flying weather for over

2,000 troop-carrying planes and gliders, their fighter escort and, of course, the German Luftwaffe," Sullivan added.

Krebs, not given to overstatement, described the flight in as "difficult," with considerable ground fire and the disconcerting sight of planes in adjacent groups catching on fire around him. He watched as his fellow pilots would try for a belly landing, "only to explode on impact." Cannon's account noted the commanding officer of the paratroopers aboard, Lt. Col. L. G. Mendez of the Third Battalion, 508th Parachute Infantry Regiment, had given them a "pinpoint location" to drop him. "We put him right on it," Cannon noted.

Cannon recalled seeing one ship burning on the ground and another catching fire on his left and hearing a report from their crew chief of another burning as they turned from the drop zone. "We climbed to 3,000 feet, and the formation assembled on us pretty well intact," Cannon recalled. "We headed home. Passed Breda on our left, but near Standarbisten there was a terrific explosion." Cannon thought initially they had been hit by antiaircraft fire, and, indeed, many accounts of that day report that he and his crew were "shot down over Holland." What actually happened was more frightening than a flak burst, however: A lone C-47 from the 441st TCG, disoriented or perhaps hit itself by enemy fire, crashed into their plane from underneath the left engine.

Krebs's account is graphic, although it leaves out the panic that must have been felt by the crew, struck unexpectedly from below just as they were starting to relax from their harrowing mission. "The left prop came off and walked through the fuselage," Krebs said. "All the windshield glass blew out and there was hydraulic juice all over the place. The incoming air was like a hurricane. We had crew members falling all over each other trying to pick up their chest packs [parachutes]."

As Cannon recalled, the plane lost its controls as the propeller from the stray C-47 cut through the fuselage, sending them nose down into a spiral. "I groped for my parachute but slipped on the fluid and fell on my face. When I regained my balance, I had a hard time getting out of my flak suit, but I finally hooked on the 'chute pack and managed to reach the cabin door with the aid of Colonel Krebs. The balance of the crew had already bailed out." Cannon reckoned he was only at about 800 feet when his parachute opened after he dived, almost blinded by the hydraulic fluid, from the stricken C-47.

Krebs cracked a bone in his left foot in the fall. "As we drifted into the wind, German patrols below began shooting at us," Cannon recalled. "To put it mildly, it was uncomfortable." Cannon landed in a potato field near Krebs and Sgt. Broga. They got rid of their 'chutes and ran and limped for cover in a nearby ditch as Germans on bicycles headed toward them. "We lay flat on our backs in the watery ditch, tall brush and grass pulled over us," Cannon recalled. "Our .45s were cocked while we listened to the searching Germans yelling and jamming bayonets into piles of straw. After an interminable time, they left."

What began shortly thereafter constituted a bonding with the valiant Dutch citizenry that rivaled the kinship that the war had created between Cannon and Krebs. The bonding began unbeknownst to the frightened aviators as they drifted to earth following the midair collision. A Dutch farmer, Piet Withagen, had spotted them and began burying their parachutes and other equipment as soon as they landed. He then came over to the ditch in which the nervous soldiers were hiding. Unable to communicate because of the language barrier, the parties managed through hand signals and pointing to dials on their watches to agree to a later rendezvous after dark, at 9 PM. As Cannon recalled, "For the next five hours we sweated it out."

Krebs, who spoke German, decided to use that language when the lone farmer returned at the appointed hour, but it had the opposite effect than he intended. "I frightened him by talking to him in German," Krebs said, and the farmer asked, "You are Americans, yah?" Krebs reassured him, and the farmer led them to what they thought would be a meeting with other downed aircrew members. But, as Cannon recalled, they were given a start when two uniformed men stepped out of the shadows as they reached the top of a nearby hill. Wary, tired, nerves on edge after the long wait in the ditch, the Americans drew their guns on the two strangers. But the strangers smiled back, managing to explain they were members of the Dutch Underground who also happened to be village policemen. Their role was to escort Cannon, Krebs, and Broga to the nearby town of Oudenbosch, where they would hide until they could be safely escorted to underground headquarters in Breda. Arriving there, the group found its destination was a large department store, Vroom and Dreesman, which had been closed to civilians but was used by the Germans to obtain items for their own use. "We were quartered on the top floor in the upholstery department," Cannon related. "There was plenty of furniture and coverings and we were able to make up comfortable beds every night. . . . The Dutch provided excellent food—they even brought us ham and fresh eggs for breakfast—and gave us candy and American cigarettes. They set up a stove with plenty of food and even brought in a ping-pong table and many English books and magazines for us to read."

In two weeks of hiding in the department store, Cannon had perhaps his first opportunity to reflect on the courage and ingenuity of the Dutch. On September 23, less than a week after parachuting from his burning plane, he wrote a letter to his parents on the department store's letterhead, which he would send after his return to Allied lines. Along with optimism that the advancing Americans would soon improve his precarious condition, Cannon marveled at the treatment he and his fellow soldiers had received. "It is hard to believe [the Dutch] have such a wonderful Underground system," he wrote. "We have eaten even better than in the Army, tho [*sic*] I'm sure they are undergoing great hardships to take care of us so well. . . . The people here have been so kind we could never repay them—they really treat us like kings."

It would have been comforting to his parents to know of Cannon's relative safety at that point, because on October 7 they received the stark military telegram sent to thousands of other parents during the war: "The Secretary of War desires me to express his deepest regret that your son, Major Howard W. Cannon, has been reported missing in action since 17th Sept. over Holland."

The group of department-store refugees eventually climbed to thirteen, and the Underground determined it was too dangerous to keep so many in one place. They paired up the captives, and Krebs and Cannon moved across town to the home of a Dutch army officer. After weeks of anxious waiting, Cannon and Krebs decided they were endangering their hosts by remaining in their home any longer. They decided to head south through the lines, toward where they reckoned the Allied forces were located, and seek freedom. The Underground provided fresh disguises and papers for Krebs and Cannon, and their final outfits became the stuff of World War II lore. "The colonel was dressed as a poor farmer, while I was his even-poorer assistant," Cannon said. "Our papers were as official appearing as identification could be." Krebs carried a long hoe over his shoulder with some sandwiches wrapped in a rag tied to the end. Cannon carried a bundle of twigs. Their goal was some fifteen miles away, where they figured the Allied columns were, but those fifteen miles were packed with Nazi troops, Cannon said. They began their "walk to no-man's-land" at a prearranged time toward a bridge in Breda where two young Dutch brothers, Frans and Charles Marijnissen, were munching apples. "This was our recognition signal," Cannon said. "I took an apple out of my pocket and bit into it."

The tension mounted as they continued walking through the close-knit, rural communities, where everyone knew everyone else and years of living under German occupation had increased wariness toward strangers. They ascertained that many villagers were commenting on their strange appearance and the fact that they were not recognizable. At one time, Krebs's heart raced as he picked up a conversation in German between a young couple, with the girl commenting, "I've never seen those farmers around this area before."

Finally, after what Cannon described as "the most nerve-wracking afternoon we had ever spent," they reached their assigned destination: the foundation of a silo beside a farmhouse. A cover had been built over it and a woodpile stacked on the cover, so by pulling aside a few sticks of wood the men could get into a small room under the woodpile. There was a small amount of food left by the Underground, and Cannon and Krebs "were sure that we could stay safely hidden until the right moment to make a break for it." But waiting until that right moment proved as harrowing as their "walk to no-man's-land." They had been in the shelter only a short time when a battery of German 88s (artillery) rolled up and started firing. "They were so close that we could hear the Nazi officer give his orders to fire each time the battery let go a salvo," Cannon recalled. "Shells were whizzing around us for the better part of three days—going both ways."

The artillery onslaught ended abruptly in the middle of the third night, as the German battery hurriedly pulled out. Cannon and Krebs emerged cautiously from their hiding place the next morning to hear a sound that thrilled them: Allied soldiers marching across the fields. The unmistakable tip-off was the reams of profanity coming from the soldiers. "They would say, 'There goes one of the s.o.b.s over there. Get him' and so forth," Cannon said. "When we heard that, we knew they had to be Americans."

In a movie version of this scene, Cannon and Krebs would encounter one of the American GIs and the GI would ask something like, "Who won the 1944 World Series?" Cannon and Krebs would name the winning team, and they would be welcomed into the ranks of their comrades. Real life was crueler, as Cannon related. "As they worked their way up near where we were located, I went out to talk to the one fellow on the end of the platoon line. I identified myself and said I was an American airman that had been shot down and there were others over there with me, both US and non-US," Cannon said. "He looked at me and said, 'Don't f—— with me buddy, I've got work to do.'"

The gruff American apparently relented, however, and soon returned with his sergeant and an officer to where Cannon, Krebs, and the other escapees were waiting. The bedraggled escapees were placed under guard and marched back to the command post of the advancing regiment. On the way, they passed through the little town where the young girl had speculated on their appearance just a few days earlier. "She recognized us again," Cannon said, and "immediately began pointing at us." He did not speculate on what thoughts were racing through the townspeople's minds.

Finally able to convince the Americans of their bona fides, Cannon, Krebs, and the others were sent to Antwerp by jeep, where they took a welcome bath and enjoyed their first good night's sleep in a long time. "In fact, three buzz bombs came over and hit Antwerp that night, but did not wake us up," Cannon said. "We didn't hear a sound. We were really exhausted."

They were pronounced in good physical and mental condition after forty-two days of hiding from the Germans—a testament to the good care of the Dutch people as much as to their own conditioning—and continued flying combat operations from that date in early November 1944 until VE Day on May 8, 1945. During their absence, Krebs had been promoted to full colonel, and, soon after, Cannon was promoted to lieutenant colonel.

The story of Cannon and Krebs, dressed as farmers walking silently through German troops to join their compatriots, resonated strongly through the U.S. Armed Forces. They were reminded of the heroic proportion of their ordeal years later, during Cannon's first term in the U.S. Senate.

Col. Roy Weinzettel was a former intelligence officer in the 440th Troop Carrier Group who was knowledgeable of the entire episode. He presented Senator Cannon with a large oil painting depicting two shabbily dressed men walking side by side over a country bridge. The destruction of war is evident in the background, but a positive symbol is prominent in the foreground—a large red apple with a bite missing: the recognition symbol that enabled Cannon and Krebs to contact their escort to freedom.

Cannon hung the painting over the fireplace mantel in his private office in the Russell Senate Office Building, where it remained until he left the Senate in 1982. As Krebs joined his staff in ensuing years, there were many meetings of the two men underneath that painting. Visitors to the office could observe the two conferring on problems of the day and reflect on the trial by fire that had brought them to their postwar careers. Soldiers then, commanding officer and chief adjutant, they continued to work as a team with their roles reversed. No one ever got the impression that Cannon outranked Krebs in civilian life, or that Krebs deferred to his former subordinate. They were simply a team, forged by events that superseded mundane concerns.

Cannon and Krebs and the rest of the 440th were not finished playing their part in the liberation of Europe. They participated in the relief of Bastogne in southern Belgium during the Battle of the Bulge, flying C-47s loaded with supplies, "despite the most terrific concentration of German anti-aircraft fire yet encountered on the continent."

Then came the long-awaited Allied crossing of the Rhine into the German heartland. The 440th, with Cannon and Krebs reversing pilot and copilot roles because Krebs had broken his left arm and leg in a glider crash that July, towed ninety heavily loaded gliders to their target without a single loss. The group then undertook a mission that would occupy it until VE Day: hauling planeloads of gasoline and ammunition to Gen. Patton's tank columns plunging into Germany. As one of Cannon's combat citations noted, the resupply mission "often brought the unarmed C-47s directly under enemy ground fire while unloading at forward airstrips on the front lines."

To the victors go the spoils. That is the law of war, and it proved true in Cannon's case, as accolades soon came streaming in for his wartime contributions. In a July 12, 1945, story in the *Salt Lake City Tribune,* later re-created by the *Washington County News* in Cannon's hometown of St. George, one of his most gratifying moments was captured: receiving the French government's highest honor, the Croix de Guerre with silver star, from a general in the French Air Force. The photo of that moment in Chartres is a memorable one. Cannon, his chest bursting with pride and his heart undoubtedly full of gratitude that he had survived great peril, stands rigidly at attention as the revered French decoration is pinned to him. He was thirty-three years old at that moment, already having experienced more than most people do in a lifetime, yet poised on the brink of still more memorable accomplishments.

His own government was not stinting in its praise, awarding Cannon a Purple Heart and a second Oak Leaf Cluster to the Air Medal he had been previously awarded. Several months later, Cannon and Krebs participated in one of the most stirring tributes ever staged, a parade of thirteen thousand paratroopers down New York's Fifth Avenue with forty C-47s flying over-head. "It was the greatest military parade the nation's metropolis had seen since Sept. 11, 1919," reported one newspaper of the January 12, 1946, event. The period between VE Day and his return to the states was a time for reflec-tion by Cannon. His letters home reveal some of the things that were on his mind.

One issue had to do with his civilian career. A result of his aviator's role in the war was acquaintance with a number of pilots from American commercial airlines. He recounted an offer from one of them, a United Air Lines pilot, in a letter to sister Evelyn. "Lt. Col. Jack Bridgman . . . is trying to get me to fill out an application to fly for the lines, but I'm too old for that," wrote Cannon, reflecting the concern that thousands of wartime young men shared about "falling behind" their Stateside peers because of years of service abroad. He also doubted he had the patience to withstand the airlines' bureaucracy after all that he had been through. "I wouldn't be able to take sitting on the 'right seat' [as copilot] for a couple of years. By the time I would be checked out as captain so I could make some money, I would be too old to fly." This was updated conjecture on a postwar career, reflecting his changing ambitions. A year earlier he had postulated a humbler future in a letter to Evelyn that also expressed concern about their father's health. "Sure wish father would take it easy," he wrote. "Too bad he can't sell the farms and retire, though I might be glad to have them after the war is over, so I can make a living."

Cannon also had time to concentrate on his relationship with Dorothy Pace that had been kept alive after their meeting in St. George in the summer of 1936 through numerous letters and occasional visits with her in Los Ange-les or her family's home in Alamo. Dorothy's younger sister, Sydney, recalled that during the war, "Howard would fly in to Los Angeles, and he swept her off her feet." In mid-August 1945 he wrote her that he expected to return to the United States by mid-September, and hoped to be in St. George a week later. "How about coming to St. George when I get there?" he asked, and Dorothy complied. Soon after that meeting their letters began containing plans to be married, and the wedding was set for December 21 in Las Vegas.

That fall, Cannon and Krebs, his commanding officer and close friend—and about to be his best man—were preparing Laurinburg-Maxton Army Air Base in North Carolina for closure after returning from the European theater. To get to Las Vegas in time for the wedding and Krebs back to North Carolina for Christmas with his family, they commandeered a C-47 transport, the same plane the two had flown on many missions over Europe. Two days before the wedding, Cannon and Krebs flew west, lumbering along at a top speed of 150 MPH. The weather was terrible. They arrived in Las Vegas the morning of the wedding and secured the marriage license, and that afternoon Howard Cannon and Dorothy Pace were married. So began Cannon's fifty-seven-year relationship both with his wife and with Las Vegas. A contemporary of Cannon's wrote that Las Vegas then, with a population of twenty thousand, was "still a small town with more dirt roads than sidewalks, replete with swinging-door saloons, blanketed Indians, bearded prospectors, and burros." At the time, many would have thought his wife was definitely the better bet.

The small but elegant ceremony took place in the family home of Cannon's prewar friend Clifford A. Jones. In October, Jones had been given a temporary appointment as judge for the Eighth District, so in addition to hosting the wedding he was able to perform it as well. Jones was the same age as Cannon and a dashing, well-liked figure in town as well as a controversial one. Tall, handsome, outgoing, he dressed like a cowboy from his shirt to his boots. He had lived in Las Vegas since 1938 and had already served as a state assemblyman and as a Clark County delegate to the 1940 Democratic National Convention. After his judicial appointment he was elected lieutenant governor. The two men had gotten to know each other when they competed in calf-roping contests at small-town rodeos before the war. Their friendship was an important factor in Cannon's decision to settle in Las Vegas, and to Cannon, Jones embodied the excitement and promise of the burgeoning city.

Indeed, there must have been an element of the Old Guard considering the New on that wedding day in the Jones house at 121 South Thirteenth Street. Cannon could certainly match Jones's western roots, having grown up milking cows and herding cattle on his family's ranch. The calf-roping contests where he competed with Jones were an echo of the real-life cowboy environment in which he grew up.

Although he wasn't as tall as the lanky six-foot Jones, Cannon, at five feet eight inches, had a commanding presence buttressed by his beribboned Army Air Force uniform. An athlete throughout his youth, Cannon also had an air of self-confidence gained from many years as a college and professional bandleader of wide repute. He did not pale in Jones's company.

The couple spent a quick honeymoon at one of the town's newest resorts, the Last Frontier, located even farther from downtown than the daring El Rancho Vegas, which had earlier broken precedent by setting up outside the city limits, at the edge of the desert. When the Last Frontier opened in 1942, it was the ultimate in Vegas splendor, going the El Rancho Vegas one better in every way. Enormous stuffed animals gave the trophy room its name, electrified wagon wheels lit the showroom and bar, and the banquet room seated six hundred. Each guest room featured a cow horn on the bed.

After the honeymoon, Howard returned to North Carolina to complete his military duties, and Dorothy headed back to work in Los Angeles. Howard's father, Walter, an experienced real estate investor in St. George, found them a small two-bedroom house on Bell Drive, just blocks from the Las Vegas business center. Cannon needed to establish his Nevada residence by March 1946 in order to take the state bar exam in September. While studying for the bar, Howard fixed up the house. When it was livable, Dorothy joined him, and soon after passing the bar he began earning a living as a lawyer in Las Vegas, the city he had first visited in 1929 as a seventeen-year-old high school senior competing in a track meet. Even though he won a medal in the pole vault with a jump he recalled as eleven feet two inches—a medal he kept his entire life—"the thing that excited all of us most," he said in 1958, "was that we got a chance to visit Las Vegas."

As he wound up his active-duty responsibilities in the military and began making his postwar plans, Cannon dealt with the Army Air Force's desire to keep him among the enlisted ranks. He was offered a commission in the AAF, with the promise of greater responsibility with the expected creation of a new service branch, the U.S. Air Force. Already having made the calculation that Las Vegas was the preferred locale for launching his civilian life, Cannon wanted to take the Nevada bar exam before accepting the military's offer. He didn't have that option, however, as the Air Force insisted he decide on its offer immediately. So he compromised, deciding to stay in the Air Force Reserve but refusing the full-time officer's commission.

Cannon had truly completed a "grand tour" of much of the world during his military service. If privileged Americans gained knowledge of geography and appreciation of culture from their experiences, Cannon received a remarkable history lesson from his. He had not only participated in some of the most crucial phases of World War II—the Normandy and Market-Garden invasions, the relief of Bastogne, crossing the Rhine—but also supplemented these experiences with his private excursions. Rome, Paris, Berlin, Africa, England, the Caribbean, and many points in between came under his gaze.

He had completed a memorable personal ascent, from humble National Guard officer building portable bridges across a lake in Los Angeles to decorated AAF lieutenant colonel flying troops and equipment to the most crucial battlefield sites in history. Whereas in 1937 Cannon had stood on the edge of a new career and shortly thereafter began expanding the boundaries of possibility with a run at local politics, in 1945 he stood on the brink of a much larger universe. He had seen the world in distress, made a name for himself in the most difficult situations man can face, and thought seriously about his role in the future of his country. His life from that point forward showed a single-minded dedication to making that role a meaningful one.

CHAPTER 3

Citizen Cannon/Senator Cannon

That Howard Cannon was an ambitious young man was clear from his three and a half years in St. George following law school, from mid-1937 to 1940. His maturing sense of himself was reflected not only in what he did but also in what he stopped doing. Almost overnight he shed his identity as a musician and bandleader, even though his musical adventures during high school and college had brought him attention, experience, and money. It is as if he decided, upon returning to St. George, that leading the Lumberjack Collegians or a cruise-ship quintet was not the image he wanted to cultivate any longer.

If an intensified sense of purpose informed his immediate prewar years, it was nothing compared to his actions following the war. He had no patience for a conventional airline career, as his letter to Evelyn made clear, because he would have to waste too much time as a copilot before he could make any money. Time was wasting for the thirty-three-year-old war hero who had blazed such a trail in St. George and the Air Force, and time was money.

There was money to be made in postwar Las Vegas, as two of Cannon's contemporaries recall. Herbert Jones, brother of the more famous Cliff Jones who performed Cannon's wedding ceremony, followed a legal career beginning in Las Vegas in 1947 that led him to head a prestigious firm, Jones Vargas, fifty-five years later. Still practicing in 2002 at age eighty-eight, Jones surmised the carrot his brother dangled to attract Cannon to Las Vegas as the two competed in small-town rodeos before the war. "If you're asking me, they would have talked [at the rodeos]. And Cliff would have said, 'Gee, Howard, why don't you come on down and practice law in Las Vegas because the money is good.' That would have been what was attractive to him."

The late Harry Claiborne was a colorful attorney whose high-profile, high-income defense of various criminal defendants over the years earned him fame, an appointment as a federal judge courtesy of Cannon's Senate influence, and conviction on income tax–evasion charges. Like Cannon, Claiborne was a new resident of Las Vegas in 1946, and he recalled some particulars of the Las Vegas legal profession at the time. "It wasn't uncommon for attorneys to handle four to six divorces a day at a one hundred–dollar minimum fee," Claiborne said.

Cannon was not averse to making money, and his career both as a private citizen and as an elected official was a testament to the industrious, practical Mormon upbringing he received. He provided well for his family and left a sizable estate upon his death in 2002. But there was always more than the desire to make money driving Cannon, a need to channel his seemingly boundless energy. Given the history of Cannon relatives attaining public office in Utah and Cannon's own exposure to elective politics in St. George, it was not surprising he took that path after arriving in Las Vegas.

His first order of business, however, was earning a living. Cliff Jones took him under his wing in his first days in Las Vegas in March 1946, escorting him to the courthouse to "make connections." He soon was able to write Dorothy that he had opportunities with several law offices. "Think I'll do some work with an ex-judge" was his brief description of how he joined forces with his first employer, sixty-five-year-old former Nevada district court judge L. O. Hawkins, who had established a growing practice in association with J. R. Lewis. Lewis and Hawkins opened their firm in late 1942, following Hawkins's decision not to seek another term as judge of the sixth judicial district in Winnemucca. He had served on the bench for seventeen years.

Their firm was dedicated to "general and trial practice," and Hawkins was soon representing some of the city's high-profile murder defendants. Once aboard the Lewis and Hawkins team, Cannon soon found himself plying the same criminal-defense waters as Hawkins, albeit on a much lower level. The crime blotter of the *R-J* records him as early as December 21, 1946, defending a suspect in a jewelry holdup. Other cases covered in subsequent months ranged from the mundane (a man accused of building a home addition without a permit) to the mildly sensational (suing a suspect in a hit-and-run killing for $25,000 on behalf of the victim).

Claiborne remembered Cannon as "a damn good lawyer" some fifty-six years after the two worked the criminal scene together, but added a qualifier as one who became the preeminent Nevada criminal-defense lawyer of his time. "Howard didn't have the charisma or jury appeal to be a good trial lawyer, but he was damn knowledgeable and he was damn smart," Claiborne said. "And he could try a good case. He wasn't spectacular as a trial lawyer."

The young Lewis and Hawkins attorney achieved his first fame in 1950, representing a woman, Ruth Kring, who was injured in a frightening accident at the Las Vegas air force base (soon to be renamed Nellis Air Force Base) on the morning of March 15. The forty-nine-year-old Ms. Kring was a civilian employee of the base snack bar, which was housed in a single-story cinder-wall base-operations center. Around nine in the morning an F-51 training jet that had experienced engine trouble while attempting to land plowed nose-first into the side of the operations building, injuring seventeen persons. Ms. Kring and another civilian resident of Las Vegas, Monte Sager, were among the most seriously injured.

In the inevitable lawsuit that followed, Cannon represented Ms. Kring, and Roger D. Foley, one of five lawyer sons of Nevada federal district court judge Roger T. Foley, represented Sager in a $225,000 action against the U.S. government. Judge Foley recused himself from hearing the case because of his obvious conflict, so it was turned over to a colleague in San Francisco, where Cannon and Foley made their arguments in May 1952. On June 5, San Francisco judge John Murphy awarded Ms. Kring $100,000 and Sager $40,000. The award to Ms. Kring, Cannon's client, was the largest personal-damage judgment ever rendered in Nevada at that time.

Another case revealed Cannon's ability to maintain confidences. The client in this instance was a man known for fanatical concern about concealing details of his private life, Howard Hughes.

Biographical accounts state that by 1957 Hughes was concerned that business enemies might attempt to institutionalize him because of his numerous eccentricities. He had learned that one way to avoid such a fate was through marriage, since his wife would have to agree to any institutionalization. The problem was in convincing any of his multitudinous girlfriends to attempt marriage with someone who had shown himself singularly unfit for the institution. The choice of actress Jean Peters for the role of wife-savior seems to have been made as much because she was receptive to the specific requirements of being Mrs. Howard Hughes—that she wouldn't agree to put him in an insane asylum—as because of undying love felt by either party. Whatever the reason, Hughes won her consent and set about arranging a marriage that no one would know about.

How Hughes or his legal advisers hit upon Cannon as the man to help with this task is not known. Indeed, Cannon to his death never even acknowledged he played a role in the marriage, much less gave any details. It is known that Cannon received an inquiry in January 1957 from a Los Angeles lawyer named James J. Arditto, asking whether a wedding in which neither party used their legal name would be considered binding in Nevada. Indeed it would, Cannon replied, and the game was on.

Reporters over the years—none receiving any assistance from Cannon—surmised the following scenario for the bizarre wedding: Cannon prevailed on an acquaintance in Las Vegas who had previously worked in Tonopah, an isolated former mining boomtown some two hundred miles north of Las Vegas. The task assigned this gentleman was to smooth the way for a clandestine wedding in Tonopah with the Nye County clerk, Eudora Murphy.

Cannon's friend ascertained that Murphy would accommodate someone seeking a marriage license if they arrived after normal business hours. On the evening of January 12, Murphy received a phone call at her house asking if she could issue a license. She met a beautiful twenty-nine-year-old woman using the name Marian Evans, who was seeking a license to marry a gentleman from Houston named J. Johnson. Murphy issued the license, and later that evening the marriage was conducted by the Nye County justice of the peace.

The unwitting Nye County officials might never have learned that the famous couple wed that day was Hughes and Peters if news of the wedding was not leaked to the Hollywood papers sometime later—without any details as to time and place. Also unmentioned was the role played by Cannon, even though he had flown to Tonopah by private plane to ensure the event came off without a hitch.

This and other colorful marital engagements added flavor to Cannon's early life in Las Vegas, but were far from his primary preoccupation. His cheeky opposition to the sitting county attorney in St. George in 1938 was not an aberration, as Cannon attempted an almost identical step in Las Vegas in April 1947, filing as a candidate for city attorney, this time with even less experience in the city's legal and civic affairs—about five months of service with Lewis and Hawkins.

The city charter, however, required two years' residency and two years as a taxpayer to be a candidate in city elections, and even by some creative rearrangement of his résumé, Cannon couldn't meet the standard. In announcing his candidacy, he stated he had been "a constant visitor" to Las Vegas over the past twenty years, and when faced with the legal challenge embellished the record even more. He had, according to a newspaper story, "been a resident [of Las Vegas] since 1941 except for the time he spent in service."

Considering he had been elected county attorney in St. George in November 1940 and began active service in the National Guard by February 1941, that doesn't leave much time for residency in Las Vegas. These facts notwithstanding, Cannon was belligerent about the charter restriction, claiming it discriminated against veterans even as he withdrew his name from the 1947 ballot. Showing a finely honed instinct for seeing the legal trees instead of the forest, Cannon reasoned this way: Since the charter requires candidates to be property taxpayers for two years and since veterans received an exemption from property taxes, "No veteran could ever be eligible for office in this city."

Thus, his anger over being barred from the election was couched in terms of discrimination against veterans, not about where he had actually lived for the two years preceding the filing deadline. Although upsetting to the hardcharging young attorney, this setback proved only a minor obstacle, as he filed again for the city attorney post in April 1949.

The 1949 election, pitting Cannon against incumbent George Gilson and two other local lawyers, William G. Ruymann and George E. Marshall, was expected to be "hot and close." Indeed, Cannon's victory margin of fewer than one thousand votes over Marshall, who would later run unsuccessfully for the U.S. Senate against the formidable Pat McCarran, was the second closest of the election. It is unknown to what extent Cannon expected the city attorney's post to occupy his attention, or whether he foresaw the tumultuous events that would soon overwhelm city hall. The part-time position paid only three hundred dollars a month and allowed Cannon to retain his private practice with Lewis and Hawkins. But given his track record of moving quickly up the ladder and his postwar reluctance to spend even a few years as a commercial copilot before moving into the pilot's seat, it is unlikely he foresaw spending nine years as city attorney. But that was what was in store for him, and it proved to be a providential turn of events. His time as city attorney gave him a high profile among the public and Las Vegas business and political leaders and isolated him from a turbulent period of political upheaval that harmed other challengers for high public office.

In several respects Cannon moved to city hall at a propitious moment, as the city was under the direction of a strong mayor, E. W. Cragin, who was adopting policies to end a recent history of comic-opera ineptness. Cragin had been returned to office in 1943, following his defeat in 1935 largely over the issue of public ownership of power and water supplies in Las Vegas. Even though he built a reputation for aggressively improving the city's infrastructure, Cragin was close to the ultraconservative—and solidly antigrowth—Samuel Lawson and other trustees of Southern Nevada Power and Telephone.

A public-power reform movement in 1934 found Cragin on the wrong side of a political storm that resulted in a referendum dramatically in favor of replacing Southern Nevada Power with a city-owned facility. Before the city could implement the citizens' wishes, however, the public-power advocate who ousted Cragin, Leonard Arnett, bowing to extreme legal pressure applied by Lawson confederate (and local bank owner) Ed Clark, took a sudden leave of absence and later resigned. The public-power movement died.

Arnett's departure put his ally John Russell in line to be the next mayor (after an interim reign by one of the city commissioners), and he was elected in May 1939. Russell, however, was unable to bring calm and purposefulness to city government, and engaged in a series of violent disagreements with the city commission over the next year, a period called "the worst political crisis in Las Vegas history." Russell was eventually removed in a trial conducted by the commissioners, and businessman Howell Garrison was appointed to finish his term. For good measure, the four commissioners all either resigned or were defeated in a house-cleaning frenzy.

That was the situation Cragin inherited in 1943, and he moved quickly to clean up the mess in city hall. He endorsed a city-charter amendment establishing a city manager, which laid the groundwork for a better-organized city government. Things were looking up, but there was still a lot of work to be done to move Las Vegas into the modern postwar era. Among many unsolved problems for Cannon and other officials at city hall, the most severe reflected the conservative stewardship of the city's telephone, water, and power supplies by the Las Vegas Land and Water Company and Southern Nevada Power and Telephone. The LVL&W Company, as the water company was known, was a subsidiary of the railroad company that had given Las Vegas life in 1905 by establishing it as a division point on the route from Los Angeles to Salt Lake City. Although the power and telephone companies had been split into two entities in 1929, they remained under control of the private investors who had been in charge before the split, particularly Lawson, the telephone company's general manager. The LVL&W Company was under control of another rock-ribbed conservative, Walter Bracken.

By 1947, the power company's ability to supply electricity had been outstripped by the city's growth, and a moratorium on electric space heaters in new commercial buildings was enacted by the state Public Service Commission (PSC). This amounted to a ban on heating of any kind for new buildings since Las Vegas had no supplies of natural gas. When the PSC extended that moratorium to residential properties in December 1951, the public uproar dragged the mayor and city commission into the fray. Cragin had been defeated in 1951 by C. D. Baker, a no-nonsense former engineer who had also been seasoned in electoral politics through two terms in the Nevada state senate, in 1947 and 1949.

Baker's platform in the 1951 mayoral race concentrated on the intertwined issues of water, power, and phone services, which he derided, and the failings of the state PSC in rectifying them. He had joined the battle over the water issue while in the state legislature, helping win passage of legislation creating the Las Vegas Valley Water District, eventual successor to the anachronistic LVL&W Company. Thus, the agenda for the new mayor and city attorney was clear, and they addressed it in their first months together as a team.

Fighting for better electrical service, for water distribution in his desert community, and for better and more frequent air transportation provided Cannon a convenient way to forge a political career. Cannon and Baker found themselves in pitched battles against entrenched political and regulatory forces located in the state capital, Carson City, hundreds of miles away and operating under a socioeconomic mind-set far different from the free-wheeling gambling spirit of Las Vegas. Mining, and the riches that flowed from the Virginia City and Goldfield strikes, had created a powerful ruling class centered in Reno.

Although fading by the time Cannon and Baker teamed up in city hall in the 1950s, Reno's power in the state was still formidable. Nevada's two U.S. senators, Pat McCarran and George (Molly) Malone, and its lone U.S. congressman, Walter Baring, all had their main Nevada offices within a few doors of the courthouse and city hall in Reno in 1950. Moreover, there had never been a governor from southern Nevada, and until Harvey Dickerson was elected attorney general in 1954, Clark County had never had an elected official in state office except for lieutenant governor, a part-time position.

So, as Cannon grilled PSC members about inadequate power supplies in Las Vegas or deficiencies in telephone service under the telephone company controlled by Lawson, he was aligning himself with popular causes. He took the same public-spirited stance against another monopoly that bedeviled Las Vegas in its early days, that of Western Air Lines. The airline had provided Las Vegas its first scheduled air service as early as 1926, when it won a government charter to deliver mail between Los Angeles and Salt Lake City and soon after added two parachute-wearing passengers to the forward compartment of a Douglas M-2 biplane. As Las Vegas began growing rapidly following World War II, however, Western was reluctant to add flights or make other service improvements, particularly on the key route between Las Vegas and Los Angeles.

Already popular because of widespread news coverage of his fights against the utilities, Cannon received more acclaim for leading a community effort to force Western Air Lines to improve service or, later, to win permission from the federal Civil Aeronautics Board (CAB) to allow additional carriers to compete against Western. Each of these battles was chronicled by the city's two daily newspapers, the entrenched *Las Vegas Review-Journal* and the upstart *Las Vegas Sun,* Hank Greenspun's pugnacious competitor that was born as a strike-breaking alternative to the *r-j* in 1950. In a typically lauda-tory commentary in his front-page "Where I Stand" column on September 5, 1952, the vigilant and increasingly influential Greenspun called Cannon "as level-headed and hardworking a fellow as you will ever meet."

Another concern of Cannon's toward the end of 1952 was one that affected many young men of the postwar years—starting a family. Both Cannon and his wife, Dorothy, came from close-knit, multigenerational Mormon families, and both desired to continue that tradition in their mar-ried life. Sometime after settling in Las Vegas, however, they discovered they were unable to have children of their own, so they turned to adoption. In September 1952, the Cannons were notified that a newborn baby girl was available for adoption in Reno, and they began the process that brought them their daughter, Nancy. A son, Alan, would be found two years later in Las Vegas, and the two children fit smoothly into the Cannon family, trav-eling with their parents to the Washington, D.C., area in 1958, remaining there through their high school years, and returning to Las Vegas to start their careers.

As 1952 ended, Cannon could be excused for feeling pleased about his postwar relocation to Las Vegas. He had won two terms as city attorney, built a substantial private practice, participated successfully in efforts to improve the critical infrastructural needs of Las Vegas, and won favorable media attention. His announcement in March 1953 that he would seek reelection to his third term as city attorney was treated as an important matter of state. The *Sun* related that a petition signed by 240 Nevadans had convinced Can-non to make the reelection bid, and he consented to the will of the populace. The *r-j* sniffed out the artifice behind the petition claim, however, noting, "It was understood that Jack Conlon, local insurance man, was instrumental in starting petition activity for Cannon."

This was the first public indication that Cannon was relying on Conlon for political advice and support, the beginning of one of the most successful collaborations in Nevada political history. Conlon was a charismatic figure who bridged the McCarran era of the '40s and the resurgence of Nevada Democratic fortunes in the middle-1950s. A Runyonesque former boxing champ on the famous University of Nevada–Reno teams of the '30s, Con-lon was a tough-talking, hard-drinking Irishman with a sentimental side revealed to relatives and close friends. When Cannon was elected chairman of the Clark County Democratic Central Committee in 1950, one of his first actions was to appoint Conlon as secretary of the committee.

Their association had begun shortly after Cannon began his legal career in Las Vegas following the war, as indicated by a letter in his private papers. Dated July 7, 1949, the letter is from Conlon to a friend in New York who was seeking a lawyer in Las Vegas. "We have a varied assortment of lawyers in this town," Conlon noted wryly. "A few are competent, one of which is our newly elected City Attorney, Howard Cannon, who I can recommend and assure will get the job done with alacrity and dispatch even though it might be a contested case."

That Cannon kept this letter in a file throughout his life attests to the warmth of his relationship with Conlon and Conlon's early recognition of Cannon as a person of merit. Like Cannon's partnership with Frank Krebs, which spanned World War II and his career in the U.S. Senate, the friendship with Conlon was one of the seminal relationships in Cannon's life. Conlon became Cannon's political mentor and close friend, from his early political career through his election to the Senate, where Conlon served as Cannon's administrative assistant (head of office) until his death by heart attack in 1968.

Regardless of the *R-J*'s revelation that the 1953 petition drive was a gimmick, Cannon's strength chased off challengers, and he ran unopposed, as he had in 1951.

With all the favorable political and civic developments that went Cannon's way as city attorney, there was one that presented him a challenge unlike the others. And, unlike the others, it was one that cost him in terms of public reputation and political support. For decades, Las Vegas had been living a double life concerning the growing African American population of Las Vegas—presenting an image of tolerance to the outside world while repressing its own nonwhite citizens. Institutionalized bigotry started slowly, evolving from color blindness in the 1920s—when the African American population numbered only around 50—to segregation of business establishments and, ultimately, to ghettoization of the African American populace.

As that populace grew in numbers, and as national recognition of civil rights as a pressing social issue increased, tensions grew in Las Vegas. Migration of African Americans to Las Vegas to work in the Basic Magnesium, Inc. (BMI), plant in Henderson in 1941 was the starting point of overt racial tension, as these workers found a completely segregated workplace, segregated housing at Carver Park—a housing development built for BMI workers—and denial of admittance to the casinos and other entertainment venues that were making Las Vegas famous.

While subtle discrimination was countenanced with an African American population of 178 in 1940, overt segregation did not go unnoticed when the population of the Westside area in Las Vegas reached 3,000 by 1943. The Westside had become a de facto ghetto through housing covenants outlawing African Americans in other areas. There was not nearly enough housing stock in the Westside to accommodate the influx of workers, however, so it eventually became a "tent and shack city." Furthermore, since none of the roads leading into or out of the area had been paved, the traffic going to and from the BMI plant "created a dust bowl with huge clouds of dust rising up into the sky." To complete an agenda of urban misery in a desert setting, "Sanitary conditions were terrible and public facilities non-existent."

As more educated African Americans moved to the Westside, they gradually became more organized and began petitioning the city to make improvements, particularly to pave the streets. The standard reply of the city commission beginning in 1945 and repeated often during the coming years was that the assessed valuation was too low in the Westside to permit issuance of a bond to pay for improvements. In other words, the ghetto that whites forced African Americans to live in was so run-down that the city could not afford to improve it. It was logic that guaranteed perpetuation of the deplorable conditions of the Westside.

It was inevitable that these festering conditions would find expression in the political process, and that finally happened in 1953. The catalyst was George Rudiak, a Las Vegas attorney who had been elected to the state assembly in 1952. Rudiak was among the small group of whites in Las Vegas who were outspoken advocates of civil rights, and had campaigned among the African American population on a promise to introduce civil rights legislation if elected. On February 20, 1953, he kept his promise, introducing a bill that provided that all Nevada citizens were entitled to "full and equal accommodations, facilities and privileges of inns, restaurants, motels, eating houses, ice cream and soft drink parlors, barber shops, bath houses, skating rinks, theaters, public conveyances and all other places of amusement, recreation and the like."

The assembly gave the bill short shrift, voting 30-14 on March 16 to indefinitely postpone it, but its supporters had already calculated their next move—to the Las Vegas City Commission chambers. Las Vegas members of the NAACP, notably Woodrow Wilson and Lubertha Warden, both veterans of the BMI and Westside segregation battles, said they would seek a local ordinance similar to the one considered by the legislature. They made good on that promise on August 5, 1953, appearing before the commission to officially present a proposed ordinance. It was referred to Cannon for an opinion as to its legality, as Commissioner Rex Jarrett stated he felt such matters were covered by the U.S. Constitution and should not be addressed by state or local laws.

The *R-J* called the NAACP presentation an "impassioned plea" and quoted Warden's description of conditions in Las Vegas as "discouraging and humiliating." She said that persons "with more pigmentation in their skin—no matter how intelligent or well-dressed—cannot enter most of the licensed establishments in the city or must accept inferior Jim Crow service."

Greenspun chimed in strongly behind the NAACP delegation in his "Where I Stand" column the next morning, contradicting an opinion he said he heard at the meeting that the issue was a "hot potato." "It seems that some of our citizens have forgotten that there is such a document as the Constitution, so the . . . NAACP has asked that the city supplement the Constitution with an ordinance declaring that any hungry person who has just returned from facing death in Korea fighting for this country should not be denied a sandwich in a restaurant. . . . It's just as simple as that," Greenspun concluded.

But not to Cannon and his employers on the city commission. They answered to constituents, including owners and employees of the thriving resort industry who felt tourists would not come to the city if they had to pull slot-machine handles and eat next to African Americans. So Cannon began a three-month investigation of the legal issues involved in a city taking steps to end discrimination that the State of Nevada and the U.S. Congress had balked at doing. In a memo to Mayor Baker dated November 30, 1953, Cannon cited an earlier case that "makes it appear that the enactment of a Civil Rights ordinance without specific Charter authority would not be within the power of the City of Las Vegas."

Cannon's opinion was all the city commission needed to refrain from acting on the issue, something it had clearly wanted a legal justification to do. But the opinion was far from a clear-cut statement that the city was without power to act if it wanted to. Cannon cited a recent U.S. Supreme Court decision holding that the police power of a municipality is as broad as that of the state. That decision was a departure from general practice, Cannon said, and "leaves the matter confused." He ventured that in subsequent decisions the Supreme Court could interpret municipal police powers more openly, leaving municipalities with the option of testing the waters with a civil rights ordinance. He then presented the commission with a choice: "If the Board of Commissioners of the City of Las Vegas desire to adopt such an ordinance and legal action should be brought for enforcement thereof to test the validity, this office will attempt to secure an early determination by the Courts," Cannon wrote. The ball was in the commission's court.

The local NAACP representatives gave their response to Cannon's opinion through the organization's San Francisco–based attorney, Franklin H. Williams. At a special meeting to debate the issue on January 8, 1954, Williams strongly contradicted Cannon's finding that the issue was "confused," arguing forcefully that there were no prohibitions in Nevada law on local entities enacting antidiscrimination laws. He cited twenty-two cities and sixty-one local commissions nationwide that had done so. Williams also increased the emotional temperature of the meeting by comparing Las Vegas to the state of Mississippi, thus giving public voice to the oft-repeated whisper among African Americans that Las Vegas was "the Mississippi of the West."

No action was taken that night, but Williams had clearly rankled the commission. Its official reply, revealed on January 14 in a letter from Mayor Baker to the NAACP, acknowledged Williams's comment by stating that "so long as the NAACP has branded the entire state of Nevada as the 'Mississippi of the west,' a law instituted on the scale of a state act seems mandatory to remove any stigma on the state as a whole and not to any area in particular." This must have caused Williams to scratch his head, as he had pointedly referred to Las Vegas alone as resembling Mississippi, taking pains to note that the rest of the state was, in his opinion, discrimination-free. That finding defied reality, but Williams was clearly focusing his attention on Las Vegas.

Baker's letter ended the civil rights matter for the commission, but not for Cannon, whose perceived weakness in the face of a plea for basic justice was never forgotten by Wilson, Warden, or other African American leaders. Wilson, who came to Las Vegas in 1941 to work at BMI, became a successful businessman in the Westside and president of the Las Vegas NAACP. When elected to the state assembly in 1966, he was the first African American legislator in the state's history and a Republican as well. Years later, he recalled his opposition to the NAACP's Voters League endorsing Cannon for the U.S. Senate in 1958, recollecting Cannon's role in the antidiscrimination fight. "[Cannon] came back with information advising the commission that it was unconstitutional. So I never could give him my support," Wilson said, not mentioning whether his party affiliation influenced his decision.

A fair assessment of Cannon's action on the civil rights ordinance would have noted the tenor of the times in which he was acting and the expectations of the people who turned to him for an opinion. As Ralph Denton, Las Vegas attorney, avowed liberal, and two-time unsuccessful Democratic candidate for Congress, put it, Cannon was merely "reflecting the attitudes of his superiors," and they would "probably have run his ass out if he opined any other way." Cannon was, after all, an elected representative of the city, and his private practice derived considerable income from representing its interests.

The engagement of northern Republicans by Las Vegas Democrats Cannon and Baker was indicative of a general sense of optimism among Nevada Democrats as the 1950s neared a close. National polls suggested the electorate was moving in a Democratic direction after six years of an Eisenhower administration that, although generally popular, was showing some cracks in its foundation. The president himself was hardly the powerful, energetic World War II conquering hero who had moved from victory over Hitler to the presidency in 1952. He had suffered heart attacks and a stroke and was perhaps better known to the general populace for playing golf than leading the country.

In addition, Sputnik was launched in 1957, causing Americans to fear that their national security was threatened for the first time since the relative calm following the conclusion of World War II. Ongoing civil rights clashes in southern cities, a recession in 1958, even Vice President Nixon's being jeered and stoned by riotous students during a visit to Peru in 1958 added to a spreading sense of unease. The time was ripe for political changes, and Nevada Democrats felt they were ready to capitalize. Their goals were obvious—the governorship and U.S. Senate seats held by Republicans who did not inspire fear or respect.

Cannon was among those who thought the time had come for political advancement. He had surprised many in late 1955 by announcing that he was considering running for an open U.S. Senate seat created by Senator Alan Bible's shocking decision not to seek reelection in 1956. Bible had served less than two years of the unexpired Senate term of powerful Democratic senator Pat McCarran, who died suddenly in 1954. Bible's abdication drew several prominent Democrats into the Senate race, including Attorney General Harvey Dickerson, whose father had once been interim governor; State Senator B. Mahlon Brown, a popular legislator from Las Vegas; and Reno's Julien (Jay) Sourwine, who had been working in Washington on McCarran's Internal Security Committee. Cannon's boss, Mayor Baker, was also prominently mentioned, but Cannon and Baker soon withdrew from contention, leaving Dickerson, Brown, and Sourwine to fight it out for the Democratic nomination.

Bible blindsided his fellow Democrats by changing his mind in May 1956 and deciding to seek reelection after all. He would dominate the race from the moment he entered, easily dispatching Dickerson, Brown, and Sourwine in the primary and defeating Republican Clifton Young, who had given up a safe House seat, in the general. Dickerson's son, Denver, believed that Bible was merely feigning an intention not to seek reelection as a gambit to draw the popular Young into a Senate race and open up a House seat for Democrats to capture. Given Bible's reputation for caution, Young's popularity, and Bible's painful loss to upstart Thomas Mechling in the 1952 Democratic primary that should have permanently cured him of taking an opponent for granted, that seems quite a stretch.

Whatever Bible's motivation, Cannon capitalized on the situation by first maneuvering himself among potential successors to Bible and later moving to fill the power vacuum created by Young's decision to seek the Senate. On May 1, 1956, Cannon announced his candidacy for the House of Representatives, conducting an uphill but energetic campaign against four other candidates for the Democratic nomination. Among them was Walter Baring, a former holder of Nevada's congressional seat who had been ousted by Young in the Eisenhower Republican sweep of 1952. Baring eventually beat Cannon by a little more than 1,000 votes (13,281 to 12,156) and easily recaptured his House seat in November's general election. The narrow loss, and Cannon's dogged determination in seeking the nomination, served notice that he should be taken seriously as a statewide candidate. The year 1956 "revealed Cannon's unreal drive to succeed in politics," said former *R-J* political editor and, later, longtime Cannon aide Chet Sobsey. "He had a very, very deep personal commitment." Others who knew Cannon at the time said the 1956 race was inevitable, given his ambitious conduct of the city attorney's post. "He knew where he was going," recalled Cannon's longtime secretary, Eileen Carson. "He told me to keep records of anybody who talked to him. We had cards on everybody. . . . All the businessmen in town would walk by his office [on city business], and Howard would ask, 'Who's that?'" Carson, a Las Vegas native who was hired by Cannon at the Hawkins law firm and followed him to city hall as his executive secretary, knew the answer. "That's Norm ——," she recalled, using one visitor as an example. "Hi, Norm!" Cannon would say as the gentleman passed by. "He was a smart politician," Carson continued. "He would make personal notes on everyone, their wife's name, names of their children." Carson didn't feel that Cannon was unduly shaken by losing the 1956 congressional primary. "Oh, he hated to lose," she said, "but he didn't waste any time crying about it. We kept doing the things we had done before, keeping track of contacts, meeting new people. He was a go-getter."

But what to go after? Cannon's clear preference in 1958 was to seek the governorship held by Republican Charles Russell, whom Cannon and Baker had nettled through their attacks on the state PSC. Russell was not considered particularly strong, and would be bucking a Nevada tradition of governors serving only two terms if he sought a third term in 1958. In the Senate was Republican George "Molly" Malone, who had served since 1946. The consensus among Democrats was that he would face his day of reckoning in 1958 because he had capitalized on internal disputes within the Democratic Party to win both in 1946 and in 1952.

Although his appetite for statewide office was clearly whetted by his close call in 1956, Cannon did not march resolutely to his fate as a challenger to Malone. Rather, he, like many of his fellow Democratic aspirants, tested the waters, sent up trial balloons, and eyed the competition. The process of winnowing the field of potential candidates unwound throughout 1957–1958, concluding only in the final days of filing for '58 office in mid-July.

One of the protagonists in this drama was Grant Sawyer, the boyish-looking Elko County district attorney, recent appointee to the University of Nevada Board of Regents, and former Democratic Party state chairman. Although Sawyer had made clear his desire to seek statewide office, he, too, was unsure which prize to seek, governor or attorney general. Sawyer moved first in the showdown with Cannon, as he announced on Wednesday, July 10, that he would file for governor and did so the next day.

This was seen by some as a preemptive strike to force Cannon into the attorney general's race, and, indeed, a headline following Sawyer's move proclaimed "Sawyer Spikes Cannon Bid." The paper also reported that "furious efforts were made to deter Sawyer from filing for governor in deference to Cannon," and there may have been some truth to that. Cannon was not leading those efforts, however, as he was not present in Secretary of State John Koontz's Carson City office in the final hours before all candidates had to file by 5 PM on July 12. Conlon, Cannon's close friend and political adviser, accompanied by prominent Las Vegas labor leader Al Bramlet, was representing Cannon in Carson City, carrying a signed declaration of candidacy in Cannon's name, with no office indicated. Cannon was in Chicago and conferring with Conlon by phone.

Cannon obviously wanted to keep his options open. Sending Bramlet, who headed the powerful Culinary Workers Union in Las Vegas, was a sign of power that would mean something to Sawyer, an independent sort who had no strong base of support in southern Nevada. But Cannon's practicality also figured in the last-minute deliberations. Although encouraged by a group of Las Vegas supporters that they would help him raise enough money to wage a strong campaign if he ran for the Senate, Cannon told the leader of the support group, Las Vegas builder and close friend Frank Scott, to make sure they had at least $50,000 in commitments before filing him for the Senate race.

Exactly what ensued in the final days and hours (even minutes) before Cannon eventually declared his intentions has been the subject of much speculation—and many conflicting stories—over the years. By most accounts, Cannon's decision to sidestep the crowded gubernatorial race and aim for the Senate is seen as proof of Conlon's uncanny political judgment. Conlon certainly let this version of events become part of the Cannon-Conlon political lore, even embellishing his role in some accounts. Conlon's sister Laurene (Lari) Bissell said years later that Conlon told her he filed Cannon for Senate without conferring with him and had to withstand Cannon's wrath when he told him what he had done. "Howard and Dorothy were very upset," Lari recalled. "They didn't want to leave Las Vegas," perhaps overlooking the fact that being governor meant living in Carson City. Although the idea of

Conlon pushing Cannon into a race he did not want to make seems unlikely, it was no secret that Cannon was thinking more about running for governor. "Cannon was programmed for governor," Sobsey said. "The Senate was never a major part of his calculations."

No matter how it came about, the 1958 Democratic lineup proved enormously beneficial to the party in Nevada: Cannon would run for Senate against Dr. Fred Anderson, a Reno physician, and, he hoped, face Malone in the general election; Sawyer was to oppose Dickerson, George Franklin, and another lesser-known candidate for the right to oppose Governor Russell in his bid for a third term; and the Democratic attorney general slot would go to Las Vegas attorney Roger D. Foley, who had joined Cannon in the lawsuit over the plane crash at Nellis several years earlier. It was a strong slate, notwithstanding the haphazard method of its construction.

Given his focus on the governorship, Cannon perhaps did not pay as much attention to Dr. Anderson's moves in the Senate race as he should have. If he were keeping a file, the accumulated data would have been unsettling: Anderson was a well-respected Oxford and Harvard Medical School–educated physician and surgeon, with a solid core of supporters in Reno. He also could claim the small-town Nevada ranching and mining roots that typified successful Nevada politicians from the Pittmans to McCarran to Bible and, most disconcertingly, to Baring, who had defeated Cannon just two years previously. To Cannon, he may have seemed the ultimate opponent—a Walter Baring with brains. Although respected as a campaigner and vote-getter, Baring was considered by many to be less than brilliant.

Specific responsibilities are difficult to reconstruct fifty years after the fact, but the differences between Cannon's lonely quest for the congressional nomination in 1956 and his '58 campaigns in the primary and general elections are stark: Where the 1956 effort had a slapdash, seat-of-the-pants air about it, Cannon's 1958 run for the Senate had all the characteristics of a modern, professional effort. Conlon was a respected, resourceful campaign manager who directed a coordinated advertising and public relations program and engineered Cannon endorsements from both organized labor and prominent business groups. Underlying everything else, there was sufficient money to keep the whole effort on course.

One source was the Frank Scott–led group of southern Nevada Cannon supporters, who certainly had the wherewithal to reach the $50,000 goal

Cannon set for them. Along with Scott, who was establishing himself as a major contractor in Las Vegas through the Roberts Roof and Floor Covering Company, there were fifteen people on a "Business Men for Cannon Committee," including labor leaders Bramlet of the Culinary Workers Union and Ralph Legion, president of the Southern Nevada Central Labor Council, whose contributions would take the form of support from the union members they spoke for; Albert Neumeyer, president of First Western Savings and Loan; Archie Grant, a member of the University of Nevada Board of Regents and a prominent auto dealer in Las Vegas; M. J. Christensen, owner of one of Las Vegas's original jewelry stores; Wendell Bunker, a city commissioner who had written a letter on Cannon's behalf in his congressional race and who had ties to the large Mormon base in Clark County; and G. C. "Buck" Blaine, a former rodeo buddy of Cannon's who attended his 1945 wedding in Las Vegas and was a partner in the Golden Nugget hotel-casino in downtown Las Vegas. Named chairman of the group was Ernie Cragin, mayor at the time of Cannon's first election as city attorney and owner of a prominent movie theater in downtown Las Vegas (the El Portal). Cragin was also a prominent member of the Roman Catholic community in southern Nevada, so he served as a comforting symbol for those who might have been put off by Cannon's Mormonism. Of this group, Cannon's private record of contributors—neatly typed on three-by-five cards—indicate only that Cragin gave $100 and Neumeyer $1,000, while other campaign reports indicate a $100 contribution from Wendell Bunker and $250 from Scott's company.

There were also less public supporters, including a member of the Las Vegas gambling fraternity who became a close friend and political ally of Cannon's, Ben Goffstein. Goffstein, who was from Omaha, Nebraska, first surfaced in Las Vegas in 1946. He was operating a legal bookmaking operation in partnership with the notorious Gus Greenbaum on the top floor of the Las Vegas Club, one of the earliest Fremont Street gambling joints. Goffstein, untarred by his longtime relationship with Greenbaum, combined a lucrative career as an executive at the Flamingo and Riviera hotels on the Strip and owner-founder of the Four Queens in downtown Las Vegas, with an active role in civic affairs. He founded the Las Vegas Hotel Resort Association, which, among other things, helped establish the School (later College) of Hotel Management at UNLV, one of the university's signature educational endeavors. As a vice president of the Riviera in 1958, Goffstein had the means to provide financial support to Cannon, as well as connections to other sources of campaign cash among the gambling fraternity. Cannon's three-by-five cards record no contribution from Goffstein, however, but a sizable one from Greenbaum: $1,000 in the primary and $1,500 in the general.

Although many of Cannon's 1958 contributors would remain supporters for years, Greenbaum's contribution was his last: He and his wife, Bess, were found murdered in their Phoenix, Arizona, home on December 3, 1958, stabbed to death by an unknown assailant. The brutal murders—police reports said Bess Greenbaum's head was nearly severed by a carving knife—gave credence to Greenbaum's reputation as one of gangland kingpin Meyer Lansky's chief lieutenants. This past notwithstanding, Greenbaum won respect in Las Vegas for his stewardship of the Flamingo Hotel after "Bugsy" Siegel's demise, and for later success in making the Riviera Hotel profitable.

Even more interesting than the totals on Cannon's cards is the contrast between them and what Cannon filed as official campaign contributions and expenditures with the secretary of the Senate under the then controlling federal Corrupt Practices Act. According to these reports, his contributions totaled $2,785 and expenditures $1,591, obviously far less than he actually took in and spent. Was Cannon, therefore, illegally concealing the true details of his campaign finances? Not at all, as the Corrupt Practices Act was riddled with loopholes that Cannon and other candidates freely took advantage of. The biggest one exempted committees working for candidates in only one state from reporting their contributions. Thus, the Business Men for Cannon group did not have to report how much money it raised or spent. "The bulk of Congressional campaign expenditures are channeled through such committees and thus never reported nationally," noted the *Congressional Quarterly Almanac* in 1965.

Even with an organized campaign effort at his disposal following the hectic filing-day maneuvering, Cannon had no time to waste. The first big challenge on his horizon was the state AFL-CIO convention in Las Vegas on August 1–3, where Nevada's labor forces were expected to endorse candidates for the primary election. It was crucial for Cannon's chances against Anderson that he receive labor's endorsement, a responsibility that would fall mainly to Conlon and his ally in the labor ranks, the Culinary Union's Bramlet. Bramlet, who had signaled his support of Cannon by accompanying Conlon to Carson City for the filing duties, was then a rising force in

Nevada labor. Like Cannon a 1946 émigré to Las Vegas, Bramlet had begun building up the Culinary Union, which represented the rank-and-file Strip workers—maids, porters, kitchen help, and so on—into a potent force.

Although he would eventually become a caricature of a cigar-smoking, limousine-traveling labor boss, Bramlet in the '50s was winning recognition not only as an advocate of the common working man but also as a broker between them and the Las Vegas hotel-casinos that more and more dominated the state's economic structure. He would receive credit for preserving labor peace in the casino industry while at the same time uplifting the wages and benefits of his members. That his life would end as ignominiously as dozens of nameless hoodlums—shot and dumped in the Nevada desert years hence—did not detract from his growing clout in 1958. "Significant in the 1958 labor conference is the increasing influence of Al Bramlet, top hand of the Culinary and Bartenders Union statewide, who controls more than a third of the entire delegation," wrote Sobsey as the AFL-CIO convention opened. "Bramlet's avowed support for Democratic Senate aspirant Howard Cannon should help give the Las Vegas city attorney a bloc of primary votes to solidify his position in southern Nevada, where his support makes the task of his opponent, Dr. Fred Anderson of Reno, a little rough."

Throughout his political career, Cannon chose the right staff person or campaign aide to handle the right problem. Nowhere was that more apparent than in his choice of Conlon as labor go-between. As Cannon's secretary Eileen Carson recalled, "[Conlon] handled the unions completely." Carson liked Conlon, as virtually all those who knew him did, but she was not naive about his strengths and weaknesses, as her remembrances indicate. "He was an alcoholic and he played dirty. He knew how to deliver the vote. . . . Jack sat right down with the heads of the unions. There was a whole different game of politics then. You approached the heads of unions. You knew them. You knew what they wanted. They told you what they wanted, and you delivered."

Taken together, Anderson and Cannon gave labor a lot to like as possible candidates against the conservative Molly Malone. Recognizing this, the convention voted not to endorse anyone in the upcoming primary election, a decision that was initially taken as a major victory for Anderson—until the other shoe dropped. Less than two weeks later, the Southern Nevada Central Labor Council, representing twelve thousand workers, gave its endorsement to Cannon. Making the announcement was council president Ralph Legion, a member of the Business Men for Cannon committee.

When the September 2 primary ended, Cannon needed every bit of his hard-won Clark County support to prevail over Anderson. Trailing throughout the evening because Washoe County had more advanced vote-counting equipment than Clark, Cannon finally edged Anderson by a mere 1,468 votes statewide. Cannon won 76.6 percent of the Clark County vote compared to Anderson's two-to-one edge in Washoe County and victory in fourteen of the other fifteen counties. In a face-to-face showdown with a strong, highly respected candidate with solid Reno and small-county connections, a Clark County politician had won the right to compete for one of the state's prestige positions. Moreover, Cannon had shown that Clark County could prevail over the northern- and small-county-led coalition that had dominated Nevada politics since the state's inception. The upcoming general election contest with another politician representing that coalition—and a sitting U.S. senator with twelve years' seniority to boot—promised to draw those battle lines more sharply.

It is a mighty task to unseat an incumbent member of the U.S. Senate absent any monumental event such as a scandal or economic upheaval. Members of an exclusive group, U.S. senators receive reams of media coverage, are considered contenders for presidential office, and can exercise innumerable levers to affect the economics, politics, and everyday lives of the people they represent.

In targeting George "Molly" Malone, the Cannon-Conlon team had chosen a man with all these advantages and more. Malone was an exemplar of the mining and ranching tradition that had dominated Nevada politics and an affable man-on-the-street campaigner who would remind the miners and ranchers in Nevada's cow counties of his days as an engineer and the names of his five horses (Aly Khan, Miss Pay Dirt, Gimick, Chispa, and Duke). A former Nevada state engineer, Malone had entered politics a generation before Cannon, losing to Key Pittman in the 1934 Senate race. He played a role in the early planning for Hoover Dam and kept his political hopes alive until opportunity struck in the 1946 contest against the controversial Berkeley Bunker, as many Democrats sat on their hands rather than vote for the upstart Clark County gas station owner who had defeated former governor Carville in the primary.

That he was an archconservative of the McCarran school, a Joseph McCarthy supporter who opposed the Senate's famous censure vote against the red-baiting senator from Wisconsin, and a tireless supporter of tariffs or other measures to protect Nevada's mining interests only endeared him more to his bedrock constituents. Malone's go-it-alone votes against even the modestly progressive policies of the Eisenhower administration—the mild 1957 civil rights bill, statehood for Alaska and Hawaii, foreign aid—may have alienated him in his own party but only added to his legend in Nevada.

Except in Clark County. Cannon had some advantages in battling Malone on his home turf, turf he had carefully cultivated through nine years as a conscientious city attorney coming down time and again on the side of everyday citizens as they dealt with poor utility, telephone, and airline services. One was the desire of Clark County business and political leaders to have one of their own in D.C. instead of another northern Nevada mining-ranching advocate. Another was the sense that the political agenda that inspired them went beyond opposition to reciprocal trade laws and support of farm programs. Cannon had targeted the growing awareness of an alternative agenda that included taxes, inflation, and education as key elements in both his '56 congressional campaign and his primary win over Dr. Anderson.

These strengths notwithstanding, Cannon and Conlon knew they needed plenty of ammunition to unseat a two-term incumbent with sharp political skills. Like the contest against the mild-mannered Anderson, Cannon carried the fight against Malone, attempting to convince voters they needed to change the status quo. He came out swinging, and continued an aggressive attack-style campaign through the election on November 4. Although Cannon would put out scores of statements, a Point-Ten Social Program, and numerous advertisements in both print and broadcast media, his initial theme was one that all voters could understand—Malone's attendance record in the U.S. Senate.

From the first days of the campaign, Cannon was charging that Malone had missed 41 percent of the Senate votes in 1957. Cannon later ran an advertisement consisting solely of a letter from the secretary to the Senate's majority leader, the not-yet-notorious Bobby Baker, delineating Malone's absences on Senate votes from 1953 to 1958.

A more telling use of a simple thematic element in the Cannon campaign was the series of "Molly's Follies" ads. These capitalized on one of Malone's well-documented traits—his taking extreme and, in some cases, bizarre positions on many issues. This tendency through the years, combined with a penchant for making long, tedious speeches on the Senate floor, contributed to Malone's image among his detractors as a clownish Senate figure. Partially as a result of this image, Malone consistently made lists of "worst members of the Senate" compiled by national news organizations. "Malone was rated one of the 10 worst Senators by *Time* magazine, seventh worst by the *Denver Post,* and is held in low regard by most of the writers and publications across the United States," Cannon charged in campaign speeches. Cannon increased the impact of the formal campaign charges by cleverly exploiting Malone's perceived quirkiness through the "Molly's Follies" ads, which were themselves one of the by-products of the freewheeling Conlon style of campaigning.

Although Cannon operated a standard campaign headquarters in downtown Las Vegas, many of the creative ideas came from a less traditional location—the Lido Bar on First Street that Conlon owned. There, Conlon gathered with people such as *Sun* newspaper columnist and artist Bill Willard to brainstorm campaign ideas. In Sobsey's view, Conlon "ran the campaign out of a bar he had on 1st Street," a fact Sobsey could verify because he visited the Lido frequently himself. "I think there may have been a campaign headquarters somewhere, but the bar was where the campaign was really run from," Sobsey stated. He described a group of from twenty to thirty people congregating at the Lido, with Conlon or his partner, Bill Elwell, tending bar, with music playing and some in the group dancing.

Willard's contribution was the stylistic representation of the "Molly's Follies" ads. They were constructed along the lines of a theater playbill, with the headline "Molly's Follies" depicted as stage lights. The text of the ads would be one of Malone's reported gaffes, run-ins with opponents, or long-winded orations, such as an October 19 ad that quoted a syndicated writer's account of a Malone speech on tariffs that made the Senate chamber "a sea of empty red leather chairs." In the forefront of the ad was an easel-mounted announcement of the current attraction, such as: TODAY (Headline) "Drone from Reno."

The tension between Cannon's unrelenting attack on Malone and the inherent strength of an incumbent U.S. senator was reflected in Sobsey's Sunday-before-election "Boiling Pot" column in which he gave odds on the statewide contests. Cannon and Malone were a toss-up—or "pick 'em" in gambler's parlance—at 11-10 each, Sobsey wrote.

In the end, it wasn't nearly that close. Cannon and Conlon's seemingly improvised decision to take on Malone proved to be an inspiration, and Cannon won handily, 48,732 to 35,760, capturing ten of Nevada's seventeen counties. In Reno, where he had been solidly beaten by Baring in '56 and Anderson earlier in '58, Cannon lost by fewer than 1,000 votes.

As national prognosticators had foretold, it was a Democratic year, with Cannon's party picking up an unprecedented twelve seats in the U.S. Senate. Cannon would join the heralded "Class of '58," a group of fellow Democratic senators that included such long-lasting party stalwarts as Robert Byrd and Jennings Randolph of West Virginia, Phillip Hart of Michigan, Frank E. (Ted) Moss of Cannon's home state of Utah, Eugene McCarthy of Minnesota, and Harrison (Pete) Williams of New Jersey. In a phrase, Cannon, the low-key but indefatigable attorney from small-town Utah, had caught the zeitgeist.

CHAPTER 4

Education of a Senator

National newspapers were taken by the powerful showing of the twelve Democrats elected along with Cannon. The *New York Times, Washington Post,* and *Washington Star,* among other publications, carried pictures and profiles of the newly elected senators spread across most of a page. Along with three new Republican senators, the Class of '58 represented one of the most sweeping injections of new blood into the Senate in its history—a nearly 17 percent turnover from the previous Congress. An additional two new faces were the Democratic senators from Alaska, Ernest Gruening and E. L. Bartlett, who were elected on November 25 in the new state's first senatorial election.

A subtext of the stories was the "liberalization" of the Senate that their success portended. Americans had become accustomed over the years to a Senate dominated by conservative southern Democrats who opposed civil rights and successfully defended southern-inspired institutions such as the oil-depletion allowance, which significantly reduced the tax burden of oil companies in Texas and Louisiana, among other regions. Opposing these southern barons was a coterie of well-meaning but outflanked liberals such as Democrats Hubert Humphrey of Minnesota, Paul Douglas of Illinois, Clinton Anderson of New Mexico, Henry "Scoop" Jackson of Washington, Lester Hunt of Wyoming, and Herbert Lehman of New York, along with Republicans Jacob Javits of New York and Clifford Case of New Jersey. With all the bright new faces of the Class of '58 added to this liberal core, the electorate wondered, would the conservative tenor of the Senate be changed? "The Democratic tide in state elections was viewed variously in newspaper editorials yesterday as a trend toward liberalism, a rebuke to the Republican leadership and notice that the nation was in a mood for change," stated the *New York Times* in a postelection analysis buttressed by snippets from newspapers across the country.

Speaking as one excited member of the class, Cannon certainly gave credence to the anticipation that a new day had dawned for America. Cannon had espoused a liberal platform including fairer income-tax policies and federal aid to education, had received solid labor support in his campaign, and had defeated an archconservative in Molly Malone. Sobsey, who had covered Cannon's campaign and would soon join his staff in Washington, agreed that Cannon was at least somewhat enthralled by the new political spirit. "He didn't mind being called a liberal—that was what was popular then," Sobsey recalled with a dose of cynicism that was ever present in his personality.

Even with his liberal-seeming record, however, Cannon was not as doctrinaire as Humphrey and others. Throughout his political career, Cannon evidenced disgust with the fringes of political opinion, although the far Right most often was the brunt of his spoken outbursts. A self-assured person without doubts about who he was and what he could accomplish, Cannon was uncomfortable with labels of any kind. By reducing himself to a label, whether liberal or conservative, Cannon felt he would lose the right to make an independent judgment on issues. He spent most of his political career denying that he was captive to any political category.

In his postelection media interviews, Cannon made one thing perfectly clear—Nevadans weren't getting just a Democratic version of Malone. "Senator-elect Howard W. Cannon (D-Nev.) met the press yesterday and left the impression that the best clue to his views would be to check the votes of the conservative he defeated . . . and reverse them," wrote the *Post*. As for the touchy issue of overhauling the Senate's storied "Rule 22," which permitted unlimited debate and had been the most effective weapon of Senate con-servatives in forestalling votes on civil rights legislation, Cannon indicated support for some change. He did not favor dropping the margin for cutting off debate from two-thirds to a simple majority, but he might support chang-ing it to two-thirds present and voting. He told the *Post* reporter that he "generally" supported civil rights legislation, but hedged his position when asked about the Eisenhower administration and Arkansas government's handling of the Little Rock school-integration conflict that had dominated the nation's news in late 1957 and 1958. This was a chance for Cannon to unequivocally demonstrate that he was breaking away from the mold of southern Democrats—and the reputation of Las Vegas as being the "Mis-sissippi of the West"—but he wouldn't do it. Instead of lashing out at the reluctance of Eisenhower to implement the Supreme Court's 1954 decision that the maintenance of segregated schools was unconstitutional, and the outright defiance by Arkansas governor Orval Faubus of federal interven-tion, Cannon said only that he disapproved of the way both men handled the situation. In a follow-up comment that could only have brought anguish to African Americans hoping for definitive action by the federal government to end years of civil rights abuses, Cannon stated that it "might be better for all" if school desegregation moved at a slower pace. If he was a liberal, he was a liberal with an asterisk.

Cannon's family was facing new challenges as it prepared to move to the D.C. area. Dorothy Cannon had established a warm and hospitable home in the family's two Las Vegas residences, most notably the house on West Charleston Boulevard to which they had moved a few years after taking up residence on Bell Drive. It was a "lovely home, typical of warm, casual South-western living," noted an *R-J* story following the election, and it had been the focus of the Cannons' family and social life. "Not given to excess party life, the Cannons prefer to entertain at home with friends, or to spend a quiet evening before the fireplace with their children," the story said.

The Cannons began their trek to Washington in the first week of January 1959 in order to make the January 7 opening of the Eighty-sixth Congress. Only Howard and Dorothy, along with friend Patsy Snow, made the cross-country automobile trip. The Cannons' first home was a sublet apartment in Arlington, Virginia, across the Potomac River from D.C. By August, the Cannons had settled in a new home in the Rock Creek Hills section of

Kensington, Maryland. Nancy, who was seven at the time, recalls the wooded setting, with bike trails and numerous trees. The house was fronted in natural stone, reminding her of their home on West Charleston. The deciding factor in selecting the home, Nancy said, was the excellent public school system in Montgomery County, then and now considered one of the finest in the country.

In putting together a staff for his Washington office, Cannon demonstrated that he greatly valued loyalty. Many of the original Cannon hires had ties to his '58 campaign or other aspects of his political career. Jack Conlon was the most obvious choice as the person to head the staff, and the announcement of his appointment as Cannon's administrative assistant came as no surprise. Beyond Conlon's acknowledged political strengths, he claimed a personal relationship with Cannon that no other aide would match.

On the surface, they were a political odd couple. Cannon was a circumspect Mormon, polished and gracious in his dealings as city attorney and candidate. Conlon was direct and gruff, and didn't hide his affection for alcohol. In the blunt assessment of Bob Revert, longtime state assemblyman from Nye County and a friend of Conlon's from college, the unusual association of Conlon and Cannon could be summed up briefly—"a Mormon and an alcoholic." Sobsey, who knew Conlon from covering the Nevada political scene and would serve under him on Cannon's staff for ten years, attested to his toughness during the '58 campaign. "When Cannon asked someone to do something, they took care of it in the appropriate time. When Jack told them to do something, growling out of the side of his mouth, they jumped," he said. Sobsey recalled that Conlon was fond of referring to people by nicknames, not always complimentary ones. Lee Walker, a recent University of Nevada graduate who became a key member of Cannon's '58 campaign organization and went on with him to D.C. as a legislative assistant, had a receding hairline. Conlon referred to him as "that bald-headed son-of-a-bitch," Sobsey said. Bill Woodburn, a prominent Reno attorney and Democratic National Committeeman from Nevada, was "Willie the Whale" to Conlon. Sobsey earned the sobriquet "Heywood" after New York newspaper columnist and American Newspaper Guild founder Heywood Broun.

But Conlon had a sentimental side as well, one that women were more likely to appreciate than men. His sister Laurene, whom Jack christened Lari, said he treated her and her three sisters like they were "queens of the world."

No matter where he was on Saint Patrick's Day, he would call home and sing the Irish ballad "Just a Little Bit of Heaven (That's How Ireland Got Its Name)." "He had the old Irish blarney about him," Lari said.

Conlon and Cannon were "joined at the hip," Lari commented, "a great combination. Howard was a staunch Mormon, and Jack loved his martinis. Jack taught him how to drink." They were similar in size, Lari noted, around five feet eight, and wore the same size suit. Like Cannon, Conlon possessed a rugged handsomeness, with a square-shaped head and close-cropped hair parted high on the left side. His eyes were dark in contrast to the startling blue of Cannon's, and his gaze was stern and appraising. Reflecting the self-assuredness of a man who boxed professionally (as "Billy Edwards"), Conlon was not someone to be trifled with. Their physical similarity was perhaps one of the reasons for the Cannon-Conlon friendship, as Conlon was one person to whom Cannon did not have to crane his neck to look in the eye. But there was more, and associates couldn't help but notice it even if they did not fully understand it. "They called each other 'Joe' and 'Little Joe' from the *Joe Miller Joke Book* [a popular publication of the time]," Lari recalled. Aides who knew only the serious, sometimes gruff Senator Cannon of later years would have marveled at such an exchange between their boss and another employee. Cannon's reference to Conlon as "Joe" even extended to memos and letters in his Senate office, which carried notations in Cannon's hand to "Joe" to handle delicate issues of a political nature.

Conlon was the only one of the Cannon staffers—including the senator himself—who had Washington experience from his days as an aide to Senator Edward P. Carville in 1945–1946. He and his wife, Lee, established quarters in a now-abandoned thoroughfare near the Senate office building called Schott's Alley, which was also close to a famous D.C. watering hole, the Quorum Club in the Carroll Arms Hotel. Thus, the contours of Conlon's life were neatly drawn: walking distance to both his job and his favorite hangout, where he could indulge in gossip and other political talk at the heart of the U.S. government. Reflecting the bravado of the community that provided him his sustenance, the car Conlon drove back to D.C. had a special license plate reading "Nevada 22." "He always joked that he was the only guy in Nevada to make a pair of deuces stand up," Sobsey recalled.

Sobsey was the next appointment announced by Cannon, ending a six-year stint at the *R-J* to become "executive secretary" in the D.C. office. The title was a euphemism for press secretary, perhaps reflecting sensitivity to public concern over elected officials employing professional media representatives. But in staff hierarchy, Sobsey was just below Conlon, indicating his importance to the Cannon political apparatus. Sobsey had graduated from the University of California–Berkeley with a degree in journalism and launched his career with the United Press in California, later serving as UP's bureau manager for Nevada. Joining the R-J as political editor in 1953, he penned the important "The Boiling Pot" political column from that point on, becoming city editor and later news editor of the newspaper before joining Cannon's staff.

Although he arrived in D.C. the first week of January 1959, Cannon had already been introduced to one of the key issues the Eighty-sixth Congress would deal with—revision of Rule 22, the cloture provision. This was a political chestnut that Senate liberals used to wage war with powerful Senate majority leader Lyndon Johnson (D-TX) and the southern arch-conservatives who cherished the right of unlimited debate as a way to stave off the evils of civil rights legislation. The liberals sought to lessen the requirement for a two-thirds majority of all senators to invoke cloture and cut off debate to a more lenient standard. Optimists hoped for a simple majority, while the more realistic among them sought to change the requirement to two-thirds of those senators present and voting.

Majority leader Johnson had opposed any loosening of Rule 22 in 1957, and there was no reason to think he had changed his position as the Eighty-sixth Congress convened. Cannon had been approached by the Senate's liberal coalition immediately after his election, and had agreed to cosponsor a measure offered by New Mexico's Senator Anderson that seemed reasonable to him. It declared that each Congress had the right to adopt its own rules instead of being bound by previous ones. Although Anderson's resolution did not mention Rule 22 by name, it had not been altered since its adoption in 1949 and was clearly his intended target.

Johnson, who ruled Senate Democrats with an iron fist, strongly opposed the Anderson resolution. He utilized his mastery of parliamentary procedure and legendary persuasive powers to convince Cannon and several other Democrats to support a motion to table—and thus kill—the Anderson resolution after Senate consideration. The tabling motion succeeded by a vote of 60-36, with Cannon and seven other freshmen senators siding with Johnson.

Showing more spine, ten freshmen, including Cannon's neighbor from Utah, Frank Moss, opposed the tabling motion. Was it a coincidence that only six days later Cannon learned that he had been given a coveted position on the Armed Services Committee, only the second time in Senate history that a freshman had received such an honor?

Johnson's influence on the new senators did not go unnoticed, as syndicated columnist Drew Pearson reveled in the Johnsonian show of power in his January 15 column, which was carried in the *R-J.* "Insiders who watched the hot and crucial vote to permit the Senate to adopt new rules at each session—to prevent filibusters—rubbed their eyes in amazement as some of the new senators answered the roll call," Pearson wrote. "Some of them completely reversed pledges made only 24 hours before. Their reversal was due almost entirely to the effective, fast-talking salesmanship of the man who dominates Capitol Hill—Lyndon Johnson of Texas."

Cannon may have done only what other successful politicians do routinely—make a deal to gain something he cherished—but to the ardent civil rights community he had sold out. That group focused on Cannon's vote to table the Anderson motion and on two succeeding votes—against a Douglas amendment to end filibusters with a simple majority vote and against an amendment by Senator Thurston Morton (R-KY) to shut off debate with a three-fifths vote of senators present and voting. On February 12, Cannon received a letter from David Hoggard, chairman of the Las Vegas branch NAACP's Legislative Committee, upbraiding him for his votes on the Anderson, Morton, and Douglas proposals. "It is disturbing to us to find such a record being written so early by so promising a young rising Democrat," Hoggard wrote.

Just as Cannon was digesting the information from Hoggard about the unhappiness of some African Americans over his cloture votes, he was presented with an opportunity to redeem himself. Robert Archie, an African American student at Las Vegas High School, was seeking to cap an outstanding career as a high school debater and all-around good citizen by applying to college in Washington. His ultimate dream was to become Nevada's first African American lawyer. Cannon received a letter in mid-February from James B. McMillan, president of the Las Vegas NAACP, informing him of Archie's dreams and asking for help in obtaining employment and a scholarship to Georgetown University for the Las Vegan.

Cannon leaped at the opportunity, responding to McMillan within a week that he would offer Archie a job as a Capitol elevator operator under his patronage. The elevator jobs, which were highly sought by students throughout the country as a means of paying for college or law school while participating in the daily life of the U.S. Senate, paid $3,523.37, Cannon informed McMillan. The new senator's personal interest in the matter was indicated by that figure, $3,523.37, written in Cannon's hand in the margin of McMillan's letter. The implication was that Cannon immediately contacted the Democratic Patronage Committee to inquire about positions available, and wrote down the salary figure as it was relayed to him.

Not only did Cannon assure the patronage position, but he also contacted the admissions director at Georgetown to find out what Archie needed to do to attain admission there. He had the director send a college catalog to Archie and informed McMillan that he should have Archie send his high school transcripts directly to Georgetown. Leaving no stone unturned, Cannon also informed McMillan that Archie had to take the admissions test administered by the Educational Testing Service, and then directed that body to send information about the test to Archie's high school. "My appreciation for what you have done cannot be expressed in words," Archie wrote. "I shall try to the best of my abilities to live up to your expectations." The young man's gratitude was matched, even surpassed, by McMillan's. Expressing "the deep thanks and gratitude of this organization," McMillan added, "Such action continues to give me assurance that you are destined to be one of our Great Senators." McMillan, as it turned out, became one of Cannon's biggest detractors on the Westside, running against him for reelection in 1964 because "he was just one of the 'good old boys' and he never did do anything for civil rights or black people that was visible." Sometimes gratitude is fleeting.

Archie became one of the mainstays of Cannon's patronage, completing his undergraduate studies (he decided to enroll at Howard University instead of Georgetown) in 1964 and enrolling in law school. During that time he worked in a clerical position in Cannon's office and as a Capitol policeman, guarding Senate office buildings on the graveyard shift.

The Westside's disappointment notwithstanding, the rest of Nevada seemed pleased with Cannon's committee assignments when they were announced on January 14. In addition to Armed Services, which was Cannon's first choice, he was named to the brand-new Aeronautical and Space

Sciences Committee, or Space Committee, and to the Senate's housekeeping panel, the Rules Committee. This body was concerned mainly with administrative functions of the Senate such as assigning office space and was not to be confused with the powerful House Rules Committee, which had the role of clearinghouse for legislation before it went to the House floor.

The *Sun* carried the committee news on its front page, reporting erroneously that Cannon was "the first freshman senator ever given a seat" on Armed Services. Senator Stuart Symington (D-MO) had actually been appointed to Armed Services when he came to the Senate after serving as secretary of the U.S. Air Force, and one of the new Alaska senators, Bob Bartlett, was appointed at the same time as Cannon. Interestingly, Bartlett had voted with Johnson on the Anderson tabling motion as well as Cannon.

The *Sun* editorialized a few days later that Cannon's position on Armed Services would allow him "to speak out in behalf of all military legislation as it affects Nevada." The Space Committee assignment, the *Sun* stated, would give him a role in shaping southern Nevada's role in "futuristic defense" represented by the Atomic Energy Commission's nuclear testing ground near Las Vegas and nuclear-rocket engine development conducted at Jackass Flats near the nuclear test site.

That was an accurate call, as Cannon took to the defense and rocket-testing challenges with enthusiasm. The new senator's take on space science had little to do with romantic visions of peaceful space colonies of the future. The launching of Sputnik by the USSR in 1957 was, to Cannon, the first shot in the space wars, and he was determined not to give the Soviets further advantage in this crucial area of national defense.

As important as the Armed Services Committee and Space Committee assignments would prove to Cannon, they were not his sole preoccupation in his freshman year. Showing the enormous energy that marked his twelve years in Las Vegas and would remain constant for another twenty-four years in the Senate, Cannon immersed himself in myriad issues, disputes, and legislative initiatives. The nagging question of his political identity—liberal or conservative?—colored these early entanglements. A rude awakening concerning the evanescent nature of past allegiances joined the conflict between these two poles in March 1959.

It seemed an innocuous, even fortuitous portent: a letter from Las Vegas title insurance executive Robert Jones informing Cannon that Jones had been named chairman of the Congressional Action Committee of the Las Vegas Chamber of Commerce. Not only was Cannon one of the chamber's poster boys for success because of his long association with the group (including the presidency in 1955), but Jones was also a former Utah resident, a Mormon, and a Democrat who had been active in Clark County politics during Cannon's rise to political power. Cannon could envision a friendly exchange of views with his Chamber of Commerce buddies. "We are enjoying our last beautiful spring weather and hope that the sunshine has also hit Washington, DC," Jones wrote. "The beautiful cherry trees should be out soon." In response, Cannon stated he would be happy to hear from Jones at any time and wished him and his family "the best of health." It was the last friendly exchange between the parties, and signaled the beginning of Cannon's battle with the conservative anti–federal government faction of Nevada politics.

In May and June, Cannon received letters from Jones expressing the chamber's opposition to a pending increase in the minimum wage from $1 to $1.25 an hour, and to legislation spelling out a formula of federal financial aid to local school districts. Cannon had indicated his support of the minimum-wage increase and was a cosponsor of the federal education bill labeled Murray-Metcalf after its two authors. He responded courteously and thoroughly to both of Jones's letters, spelling out his belief that because of income limits in the minimum-wage bill, most if not all Nevada businesses would be exempt. He added that paying a worker $1.25 an hour would provide an annual income of $2,500, an amount so low that anything less "would not even begin to provide adequate food and shelter for a family." As for the federal educational aid bill, Cannon took dead aim at what he considered the basic flaw of published opposition: an erroneous calculation of what Nevadans paid in federal taxes relative to what the state would receive under the Murray-Metcalf formula. Cannon's conclusion was that Nevada schools would receive $1.17 in federal support for every $1 paid in taxes. He so informed Jones, setting off a battle royal between himself and the combined might of the Las Vegas Chamber of Commerce and the influential Nevada Taxpayers Association that was carried out in the news and editorial columns of newspapers throughout Nevada.

Although circumspect and polite in his correspondence with Jones, Cannon was significantly more adversarial in his public comments on the dispute. He wrote letters to editors of several newspapers, accusing the taxpayers' group of "drawing their figures out of a hat," a tack that unsurprisingly enraged the group and provoked them to respond in kind. Although Cannon's actions in defending the minimum-wage increase and federal aid to education displayed a willingness to confront his critics and made his position perfectly clear, they also put him squarely in the crosshairs of the extreme conservative forces in Nevada. No matter how much Cannon reasoned, no matter how many facts and figures he and his staff dug up, they were not going to remove the deep-seated conservative belief that any funding from federal sources amounted to a dangerous incursion on states' rights and individual freedom.

Cannon's initial year in the Senate was not marked by controversy alone. He and Bible teamed up on a number of measures introduced for the general good of the state, emphasizing a concept of senatorial teamwork that was welcome in Nevada after years of McCarran's egomania and Malone's idiosyncratic view of what a Nevada senator should stand for. They cosponsored a bill authorizing "payments in lieu of taxes," a plan to reimburse areas such as Nevada—which was nearly 90 percent owned by the federal government—with large concentrations of untaxable federal lands; under Bible's leadership, they cosponsored what they called the nation's first legislation calling for research into the development of solar energy; and, in an effort that tried both senators' patience with their House counterpart, Representative Walter Baring, they introduced a bill calling for establishment of Nevada's first and only national park, the Great Basin National Park, south and east of Ely. Payment in lieu of taxes has become a well-established principle, returning millions to Nevada counties to shore up their tax bases; solar energy development is now a major component of alternative energy programs; and the Great Basin National Park today sits proudly in northeastern Nevada, some three hundred miles from Las Vegas. But the park is not part of the Bible-Cannon legacy, having been established only in 1986 thanks to the intransigence of Baring and his devotion to mining and stock-raising interests who opposed closing off any portion of Nevada that might someday yield mineral riches or contain grazing pastures.

One of the Bible-Cannon joint initiatives in 1959 opened Cannon's eyes to an additional means of assisting Nevada and its largest industry. At issue was the federal cabaret tax, a 20 percent levy on revenues generated by hotels or cabarets providing food and entertainment. The tax had been a thorn in the side of Nevada resorts since its introduction as a wartime revenue raiser, causing them to frequently appeal to the Internal Revenue Service that their gaming activities were separate from their food-and-drink operations. Given the fluid nature of the action at Nevada resorts—with patrons moving from bar to gambling tables to entertainment venues and back again—it was a never-ending source of concern for the resort industry.

Bible introduced with Cannon's cosponsorship a modest measure in January 1959 that would have cut the tax in half for tax-exempt organizations such as churches and charity groups. Such groups often held events at Nevada resorts, and reducing the tax would increase the resorts' profits from providing them food, drink, and entertainment. The cabaret tax was one of the rare instances when a Nevada concern was shared by other elements of American business, however, so a House bill introduced in 1959 went further than the Bible-Cannon bill—it halved the tax across the board, not only for nonprofits. For his part, Baring also introduced a bill to eliminate the cabaret tax completely, but the 10 percent measure was the one that advanced. It came over to the Senate in 1960, and Cannon went to work on members of the Senate Finance Committee, which would determine whether to pass it along to the full Senate. At Cannon's urging, the committee agreed to pass the legislation, prompting Cannon to hail the measure as "the most important piece of legislation for Nevada's economy to be enacted in many years." The shouts of joy from the gaming industry when the Senate joined the House in supporting the cabaret-tax reduction, and when President Eisenhower signed the bill into law in April 1960, were overwhelming. Cannon received letters from resorts throughout the state lauding his efforts on behalf of the reduction, with one stating, "This is probably the greatest single encouraging movement in our business by any governmental body in the past 15 years."

In succeeding years, Nevada's representatives continued to push for further relief from the cabaret tax. Cannon's activities on this issue revealed both the ongoing jostling for credit among Nevada's delegation and Cannon's behind-the-scenes methods of winning congressional support for legislation important to Nevada. Cannon's active public relations machine headed by former Las Vegas newsman Chet Sobsey issued news releases on the Senate Finance Committee's approval of the 10 percent reduction and on Cannon's urging of Eisenhower to sign the bill into law. Both releases found their way into Nevada newspapers. By 1964, when Congress was once again considering reduction or repeal of a host of excise taxes, including the cabaret measure, Cannon had taken the lead on the issue. Indeed, he was successful in winning Senate approval of an amendment to reduce the tax from 10 percent to 3 percent in June 1964. That measure was overturned in a House-Senate conference committee, but Cannon had positioned himself as the point man on securing the tax's eventual repeal.

It is unknown precisely when or how Cannon began courting the wily and much respected Senator Russell Long (D-LA), who was a high-ranking member of the Finance Committee when Cannon joined the Senate in 1959 and would soon become its chairman. But making friends with Long was a master stroke. That Cannon could win Long's ear was a testament to his personal qualities and to his acceptance by the southern Democratic bloc of senators who ruled over so much of the Senate committee structure. Cannon had established a relationship with the dean of southern leaders, Richard Russell of Georgia, by virtue of his membership on Armed Services, which Russell chaired. Mississippi's John Stennis, chairman of the Military Construction Subcommittee to which Cannon was appointed early in his first term, also took Cannon to heart. And then there was his relationship with majority leader Johnson, who had great sway with not only the entire Senate Democratic membership but also the southern senators. As a hardworking, low-key moderate, who did not veer too far to the left in the early civil rights battles, Cannon appealed to Johnson and to his fellow southern barons.

Establishing ties with Long paid off for Cannon and Nevada over and over through the years, as Cannon was able to follow up the cabaret-tax victory with measures to reduce the federal excise tax on sports wagers from 10 percent to 0.025 percent and to return to Nevada the proceeds from a federal tax on slot machines. These latter measures produced dramatic economic benefits to Nevada.

Cannon's education continued as he settled into the first hearing of the Military Construction Subcommittee, his initial assignment as a member of the Armed Services Committee. He had been warmly welcomed to the subcommittee by its chairman, Mississippi's Stennis, just before hearings were scheduled to begin on March 10, 1959, in the Armed Services Committee Room on the second floor of the Russell Office Building. The subcommittee had been expanded from three to six members in recognition of the growing size of the military establishment and the increasing importance of military construction in the postwar defense posture.

Cannon's handwritten notes from that initial hearing dealt with two items from the vast array of military building projects under the committee's jurisdiction: a $259,999 taxiway project at a military field near Reno, Hubbard Field, and $672,000 in projects for Nellis Air Force Base north of Las Vegas. It was as if he were reminding himself that the Defense Department had a lot of money to spend on military installations and Nevada had more than its share of such facilities. Just as his awareness of the possibilities of the space program for his home state was raised upon being assigned to the Space Committee, so, too, did he perceive a role for himself in the development of Nevada's military facilities.

Within a year, Cannon would be able to announce approval of nearly $3 million in military construction projects for Nevada. The figure would rise to nearly $6 million in 1961, by which time Cannon would be quoted as saying he was opposed to "placing a dollar sign over any part of the defense establishment." The price tag for defense spending in Nevada for fiscal year 1962, Cannon announced, was $62 million, including an annual payroll of $37.5 million for 8,701 active-duty personnel and $16 million for 2,777 civilian personnel.

As Cannon's early notes on the military construction budget showed, he had a keen eye for directing defense and space dollars to Nevada. It was not long before that instinct was directed toward a major opportunity to involve Nevada in the U.S. space program. Project Rover was an attempt to overcome the USSR's superiority in high-thrust rocket systems, the launch vehicles for space exploration, by developing a nuclear-powered rocket-propulsion system. The Nautilus submarine had demonstrated that military vessels could be powered by an onboard nuclear reactor, and Project Rover would put one in a space rocket. The effort had been under way in an area called Jackass Flats on the outskirts of the Nevada Test Site since the mid-1950s, and Cannon was determined to increase its importance, issuing numerous news releases on funding and other hopeful developments and proving a willing ally to a booster-minded media that was intrigued by the Rover program.

Nevada giddiness over the prospects for Rover reached new heights— lunar heights, one might say—with President Kennedy's historic challenge on May 25, 1961, for the United States to "commit itself to achieving the goal, before this decade is out, of landing a man on the moon and returning him safely to earth." Unreported by history, but making headlines in Nevada, was Kennedy's pledge within that same speech to seek from Congress an additional $23 million, on top of $7 million already appropriated, to "accelerate development of the Rover nuclear rocket." In words that gave credence to Cannon's enthusiasm for Rover, Kennedy described it as a "technological enterprise in which we are well on the way to striking progress, and which gives promise of some day providing a means for even more exciting and ambitious exploration of space, perhaps beyond the moon, perhaps to the very ends of the solar system itself."

There were no "Man on the Moon!" headlines in Las Vegas the next day, as the *Sun* revealed its priorities by exclaiming in orange one-inch type, "JFK Seeks $23 Million for Plan Here." The Kennedy speech made Cannon and his two-year proselytizing on behalf of Rover look like a prophet. The Rover euphoria continued for several years, buoyed by a Kennedy visit to the Jackass Flats facility in December 1962, but the bubble burst during the Johnson administration, as the new president encountered the problem of funding an escalating conflict in Vietnam while launching his Great Society programs. Thus, Project Rover faded from Nevada's dreams, although Cannon waged an energetic rearguard campaign to keep it alive.

Cannon's position at the spigot of federal dollars for defense and space caused a rethinking in the media about what were the key economic drivers of southern Nevada. In a March 1962 front-page story, *R-J* staff writer Jude Wanniski noted that expected federal spending in the coming year—in excess of $300 million—would exceed estimated tourist revenues (around $250 million). Wanniski, who would go from the *R-J* to become an editor at the *Wall Street Journal* and originator of the "supply-side economics" phrase that epitomized the Reagan administration before his death in 2005, cited Cannon as the source of his story. Thus, Cannon, following in the footsteps of McCarran, who also ardently sought federal dollars for projects beyond mining, was positioned as a spokesperson for a spending dynamic that was dependent not on the roll of dice by visiting gamblers but on an equally risky roll of dice on federal outlays.

Wanniski's conversion from chronicler of this shift to an active participant in the movement to curtail federal spending was indicative of a division of opinion among Nevadans. The electorate was divided between grateful acceptance of federal spending for such things as military or space programs and wariness over its effect on income taxes and general growth of government, a division that would manifest itself throughout the rest of Cannon's political career.

In addition to his spadework on the Armed Services Committee, Cannon forcefully advanced the notion of a greater U.S. emphasis on military uses of space. He was not blazing a trail here, as others had also railed at the defense establishment for thinking of space solely in peaceful terms. But Cannon broke from the pack in August 1962 after one of the numerous Soviet breakthroughs in space. The Soviets had launched two spacecraft, Vostok III and IV, and maneuvered them into close proximity with each other while in orbit. The feat far surpassed U.S. capabilities of the time and provided a backdrop for a Senate floor speech by Cannon on August 20. "I see no evidence that there is a national, authoritative intent to accelerate the earliest practicable development of urgently needed [space] capabilities," he said. "Where, for example, is the necessary project to develop a means of intercepting, inspecting and destroying, if necessary, hostile satellites that could bear super-megaton bombs down on us?" In this call for a space-based defense capability, Cannon was jumping the gun on President Reagan's much-criticized "Star Wars" plan announced years later. Cannon's speech was widely and favorably covered, the *Omaha World-Herald,* for example, saying, "No speech by a comparative political newcomer in some time aroused as much attention as did that Monday by Nevada's Senator Howard W. Cannon." On the Wednesday following the address, the *Washington Star* editorialized favorably on Cannon's call to arms, stating, "We think this was a very significant speech and that it dealt with a very real threat to the future security of the United States."

Cannon's outburst on August 20 was not an isolated act, as he had been calling for his own "crash program" to overcome the Soviets' lead in space for some time. He combined his warnings about conceding space superiority to the Soviets with another concern of his, the lack of technical preparation provided by U.S. schools and colleges.

Cannon's speeches, writing, and other efforts did not result in an apparent change in Pentagon policies concerning space, nor a crash government program to increase the number of engineering and other technical students produced by America's colleges. But it was a worthwhile effort, an example of using the Senate as a "bully pulpit" to prod the government and public to a different course of action. The attention and respect his remarks generated stood in stark contrast to the chamber-clearing perorations of Molly Malone on the dangers of free trade.

That Cannon was finding an audience beyond the Senate was obvious by the many articles in military and space publications that he either wrote or in which he was quoted. And, in his biggest public breakthrough since coming to the Senate, Cannon authored an article titled "Are We Being Too Peaceful in Space?" for the June 15, 1963, edition of the *Saturday Evening Post*. "A perilous notion grips Washington" was the ominous overture to the article, which was placed ahead of all other editorial content. Along with the *Post's* gentle fiction, "Hazel" cartoons, and articles on such topics as "Jean Seberg's Cinderella Career," Cannon gave his most detailed account of the problems stemming from overlooking military uses of space and his suggestions for reversing course. To reverse America's errant course, Cannon suggested a four-part program, which is notable because of how much of it was eventually incorporated into the U.S. space program.

He called for "speedy development of orbiting vehicles able to rendezvous with, inspect and, if necessary, disable potentially hostile spacecraft." Today, U.S. astronauts routinely dock with Russian cosmonauts, although their mission is not to disable their spacecraft. Cannon also wanted the U.S. Air Force to launch its own space vehicles independent of NASA, his most blatantly overlooked suggestion. Another proposal, development of a "space station large enough for 20 to 30 crewmen," is also under way today. Finally, Cannon called for stepped-up development of rocket boosters that could be recovered after launch and used again—à la the current space shuttle program. Clearly, Cannon saw the future outline of America's space program, although he called for a more direct military influence than is present today.

The *Saturday Evening Post* was a venerable magazine perhaps best known for its Norman Rockwell covers. But the seemingly whimsical, upbeat world of Norman Rockwell was at odds with the stark message of Cannon's article. Indeed, the fearsome implications of Cannon's position may have explained why no national groundswell formed behind him. The nation was beset with worries, from the ominous threat of communist expansion to fears of nuclear fallout and mass annihilation. President Kennedy judged the public mood better than Cannon by couching space exploration in terms of a challenge to American ingenuity and competitiveness. The public was content to let its dynamic president figure out how to ensure that space didn't become just another military battleground with the Soviets.

Cannon's assignment to the Senate Rules Committee provided him a different perspective on Senate life than did the Armed Services Committee and Space Committee positions. Officially designated a minor committee, the chief function of the Rules body was to oversee operations of the Senate and official functions such as presidential inaugurations. It also approved budgets for other committees and had the final word on office-space assignments, enlargements, and furnishing. In that light it offered its members an opportunity to insinuate themselves with their colleagues, even to exercise a fair degree of power over the essential, if hidden, day-to-day concerns of senators. Cannon's efficient and accommodating approach to service on the Rules Committee provided him his first subcommittee and full-committee chairmanships and an opportunity to make himself known—and useful—to every other senator.

It also offered him his first chance to shine as a national legislator. The only substantial legislative purview of the Rules Committee was the nation's election laws, including the minefield that was campaign finance. Then, as now, campaign-finance laws were a battleground among reformers, stand-patters, and the U.S. Constitution. In Cannon's first year in the Senate, the Rules Committee chairman, Senator Tom Hennings of Missouri, was sponsoring a bill to revise the primary statute that covered federal elections, the 1925 Corrupt Practices Act. As had several previous legislative attempts, the Hennings bill would have required more detailed reporting of campaign gifts and spending, and would have raised the overall expenditure ceiling to $50,000 from $10,000 for senatorial candidates. Cannon knew from his own experience how unrealistic the $10,000 limit was, and overcame it by utilizing the same loopholes as others.

The Hennings bill passed the Senate in January 1960, but died in the House. Cannon would inherit the issue when he became chairman of the Privileges and Elections Subcommittee in 1961. Cannon's subcommittee conducted hearings on the various measures during May and June 1961, then reported a "clean bill," s2426, to the Senate floor in August. Senate debate began on September 14, with Cannon assuming the role of floor manager for the first time in his career.

A bill's floor manager is responsible for explaining the legislation, considering amendments, controlling debate, and guiding the bill to passage. s2426 was considered "far weaker" than bills that had been passed by the Senate in previous years, but those bills had died in the House. In urging defeat of strengthening amendments to s2426, Cannon called attention to those previous doomed efforts, adopting the strategy of half a loaf being better than no loaf at all. Although critics considered s2426 weak, Cannon received praise from his colleagues for his handling of the bill. Most generous was majority leader Mike Mansfield of Montana, a moderately liberal westerner like Cannon, who said upon passage on September 15, "I think this is a red-letter day, and a great bill, and that a great senator has brought it to passage in the Senate." That this was more than the usual extravagant Senate courtesy was indicated by a letter Mansfield sent to Cannon less than a month later. Thanking Cannon for his contribution to the Senate's work during the just-completed session, Mansfield added a handwritten note at the bottom: "Howard, Solid & dependable. A magnificent job on the election bill."

Mansfield's support paid off shortly after Congress reconvened for its Eighty-eighth two-year term in 1963. As Senate majority leader, Mansfield also chaired the Democratic Steering Committee, which controlled committee assignments. Following its first meeting of the year, the Steering Committee announced that Cannon had received a prestigious assignment to the Interstate and Foreign Commerce Committee and its Aviation and Surface Transportation subcommittees. Furthermore, Cannon would not have to give up any of his previous committee assignments, making him the only senator to serve on four legislative bodies.

Winning the Commerce post was a significant milestone in Cannon's career for several reasons. For one, it enabled him to assume a direct role in shaping U.S. transportation policy, a role that he would utilize to accomplish the most sweeping overhaul of transportation regulation in the nation's history by the end of his Senate service. For another, it continued Cannon's record of working closely with the Senate majority leader, a knack he demonstrated with LBJ in receiving his initial appointment to the Armed Services Committee.

With jurisdiction over U.S. aviation legislation, as well as the regulatory and safety bodies, the Civil Aeronautics Bureau and the Federal Aviation Agency, the Commerce Committee was Cannon's first direct link to the aviation policy matters that had been a large part of his life since winning election as Las Vegas city attorney in 1949. It was also another link to the McCarran era, as McCarran was influential in obtaining federal dollars for early aviation efforts in Las Vegas, as demonstrated by his name adorning Las Vegas's vital connection to tourists around the world, McCarran International Airport.

Cannon's diligence in the cause of air service to Nevada extended beyond attempts to keep federal dollars flowing. Just as he had done as city attorney, he participated in numerous CAB hearings on improved air service to cities throughout the state: on behalf of Reno in a case involving service between San Francisco and Reno by way of San Jose, Stockton, and Sacramento; in favor of a Western Air Lines proposal for service from Hawaii to Las Vegas and Los Angeles; in favor of a Boise to Las Vegas link that would have included stops in the isolated Nevada towns of Ely and Elko; supporting service to South Lake Tahoe; and pleading various causes on behalf of the Hacienda Hotel in Las Vegas, which had launched its own air service for high rollers throughout the country to transport them directly to the Hacienda gaming tables.

Cannon was on the winning side of some of these cases, and on the losing side for many more, as the CAB retained its bureaucratic resistance to most of the expansion requests it heard, usually on the grounds that new service would disrupt the so-called competitive balance. He clearly knew many cases were hopeless, even though he never refused to make a personal appearance on a Nevada request to the CAB. And each numbing denial by the CAB planted seeds of doubt in Cannon's mind about the elaborate, costly, and time-consuming procedure whereby solvent companies sought permission to provide better service to a transportation-dependent state and make more money for their shareholders.

By slowly and surely winning respect and admiration for his hard work and solid achievements, Cannon was following the path he first walked as city attorney. His legislative victories, promotion to brigadier general in the Air Force Reserve by President Kennedy in April 1961, leadership on the issue of militarization of space, and appointment to the Interstate and Foreign Commerce Committee were signs of his growing influence and stature. A May 27, 1963, column by syndicated Washington reporters Rowland Evans and Robert Novak gave startling evidence of how far Cannon had progressed. "An obscure first-term Senator from Nevada named Howard Walter Cannon is quietly being groomed by the Democratic oligarchs of the Senate as the next majority leader," wrote the nationally known columnists. That Cannon would be mentioned in the same company as the towering Johnson and then–majority leader Mike Mansfield was probably puzzling to many of the column's readers throughout the United States who had never heard of him. But the Evans and Novak report fleshed out the development in a way that was understandable to close followers of Cannon's career.

The person suggesting Cannon for the post was Richard Russell, the once-revered but now fading sixty-five-year-old chairman of the Armed Services Committee, a leader of the powerful southern bloc that dominated the Senate, and an unsuccessful candidate for the 1952 Democratic presidential nomination. Russell's strategy in touting Cannon as "a comer of leadership timber" was to ensure that the liberal Hubert Humphrey would not have a shot at the majority leader's role. Mansfield was up for reelection in 1964, and, if he should lose, Humphrey might seek to consolidate liberal power in the majority leader's office. For Russell, who had cultivated, promoted, and reveled in Johnson's use of the office to thwart any meaningful civil rights legislation, envisioning Humphrey in that position would validate his worst dreams of southern humiliation.

Russell had ample opportunity to view Cannon's work ethic and conservative defense principles from his position as chairman of Armed Services. And Cannon had given Russell many opportunities to judge him as more moderate on civil rights than Humphrey and his supporters. As a Nevadan, Cannon constantly had to balance his desire for federal dollars with concerns about federal control over gambling and his constituents' general opposition to federal interference. Not possessing a crystal ball that would have predicted Cannon's historic pro–civil rights vote a little more than a year later, Russell in May 1963 would have considered Cannon a safe alternative to Humphrey.

The possibility of Cannon as majority leader was not great, as Mansfield was reelected in 1964 and served as leader until he left the Senate in 1977. And Cannon would have faced strong opposition from the liberals who were aware of his pre-1964 stance on civil rights, Evans and Novak reported. Those liberals were planning to oppose Cannon through a smear campaign directed at the weakness of any Nevada senator—that he was "the representative of legalized gambling and divorce." The sin-and-greed reputation of Las Vegas would have proved a difficult obstacle for Cannon to overcome.

That Cannon had arrived at a pinnacle in mid-1963 was underlined by the closing words of the Evans and Novak column: "But even if he never becomes floor leader, Cannon is a growing power in the Senate—and a fixture there." He proved worthy of that accolade within a few months' time, leading Senate passage of a monumental military pay-raise bill urgently sought by President Kennedy in the closing days of the 1963 congressional session.

The bill, calling for the pay increases to go into effect on October 1, was guided through Congress by Cannon and sped to the White House, where President Kennedy signed it "with a good deal of pleasure" on October 2. The traditional White House bill-signing ceremony was attended by House and Senate leaders, including Mansfield, Russell, and, beaming among the others, Cannon. Kennedy presented Cannon the pen with which he signed the bill, a moment recorded by a White House photographer and dispatched by Sobsey to every newspaper in Nevada. That Cannon and Kennedy would work successfully together on major legislation was not an aberration, as the two had proved to be politically similar both as fellow senators and with Kennedy in the White House. Cannon supported then Senator Kennedy solidly on a 1959 labor-reform measure, and Cannon's support of federal aid to education mirrored Kennedy's. Although it took President Johnson to finally break through resistance to an expanded role for federal aid and win passage of a general aid measure for elementary and secondary education in 1965, Cannon had sided with Kennedy in several failed attempts.

Their working relationship was enhanced by several gestures of personal friendship, beginning with Kennedy's one thousand–dollar contribution to Cannon's initial Senate race in 1958, which Cannon never forgot. Kennedy also presented Cannon with a personally inscribed copy of his Pulitzer Prize–winning book, *Profiles in Courage*. Cannon kept the volume all his life, and it is still in his daughter's possession, along with a personally inscribed copy of the flight manifest from a trip Cannon took with the president aboard the presidential aircraft. "To Nancy Lee—warm regards, John Kennedy," the president scrawled along the top of the document.

In June 1961, both the Cannons and President Kennedy were attending graduation ceremonies at the Naval Academy in Annapolis, thirty miles from Washington. The president hailed Senator and Dorothy Cannon from the crowd and offered them a ride back to the White House in the presidential helicopter. Dorothy told a reporter than even more thrilling than the ride was landing on the White House lawn and seeing the president's daughter, Caroline, waving from the balcony. The president presented Dorothy with one of the midshipmen's white hats that he had caught when it was flung in the air in celebration.

Cannon was intimately involved with a Kennedy visit to Las Vegas on September 28, 1963. The final stop on a ten-state, five-day tour of western conservation areas, Kennedy's visit included a motorcade from McCarran International Airport to the Convention Center, where the president addressed an overcapacity crowd of some eight thousand excited Nevadans. It was the first visit of a sitting president to Las Vegas since 1935, when FDR came as part of the dedication ceremonies for Hoover Dam. The timing of Kennedy's visit emphasized the growing ties between the two. The Senate had ratified the Nuclear Test Ban Treaty on September 24, only four days before JFK's visit. Cannon had supported it, but it was the most difficult vote he had cast in support of the president.

A few days after the Las Vegas appearance, Cannon was at the White House to receive Kennedy's praise—and a presidential pen—for the military-pay bill. Pending a vote in the Senate was the president's historic eleven billion–dollar tax cut, which Cannon also supported (it was enacted in February 1964). These overlapping events created a momentum for Kennedy and Cannon, both of whom seemed headed for reelection in 1964. Cannon's stock in the Senate had risen, and Kennedy was showing signs of shaking off the effects of the Bay of Pigs fiasco and some bruising encounters with the Soviets on international issues and gaining his footing in the White House. Cannon had already been the beneficiary of two presidential trips to Nevada and could perhaps envision another one as he sought his second term in the coming year.

Those pleasing thoughts were obliterated a few weeks later by Oswald's bullets. Cannon may have wondered about the effect of the president's death on his reelection, perhaps remembering the thrill of riding in the presidential limousine during Kennedy's Las Vegas visit as he watched the grim footage from Dallas. The strong political alliance, the growing personal ties, and his and his wife's memories of favors from the president and Jacqueline Kennedy were all shattered on November 22. Cannon could only utter the same insufficient words of shock as others following the assassination, calling it a "dastardly event" and "one of the greatest tragedies in the history of our country." Not only was Kennedy a great president, Cannon said, but he was also "a close personal friend."

Of all the unfinished items on the Kennedy agenda that were realized under President Johnson, none was more significant to Cannon's career and reputation than the Civil Rights Act of 1964. Most of Cannon's encounters with civil rights issues in his first several years of office stemmed from initiatives by colleagues rather than the White House. He retained a perfect record of opposing cloture to halt filibusters against various civil rights measures, voicing the time-honored Nevada precept that small states needed the power of "unlimited debate" to ward off unfavorable legislative initiatives from larger ones. On noncloture issues, Cannon in 1960 voted with comfortable majorities to slightly amend the weak Civil Rights Act of 1957 to provide African Americans some assistance in registering to vote (it passed 71-18), and to approve the Twenty-third Amendment to the Constitution to give the mostly African American population of the District of Columbia the right to vote in presidential elections (approved by a vote of 70-18). He also voted for an extension of the largely ineffective Civil Rights Commission in 1961 (passed 70-19), but opposed four amendments that would have strengthened the body.

The pattern continued throughout 1961 on a series of measures advocated alternatively by Senate civil rights advocates to test the barriers against sweeping reform and southern segregationists trying to stamp out the growing civil rights fever. Cannon's back-and-forth votes on these measures—favoring some, opposing others—created confusion about his true feelings about civil rights, and his remarks from time to time further muddied the waters.

Cannon remained ambivalent about civil rights seemingly until the initiation of Senate debate on the civil rights bill on February 26, 1964, and possibly even after that. Kennedy's death, Johnson's wholehearted support of civil rights, and the bubbling cauldron of civil rights ferment throughout the country, as well as in Nevada, were arguing with his conservative social tendencies and the undoubted preponderance of home-state sentiment against the measure. The first skirmish over civil rights was whether to place the bill directly on the Senate calendar after its House passage and thereby bypass a certain bottleneck in Mississippi segregationist Senator James Eastland's

Judiciary Committee. Mansfield sought permission of the Senate to do this; Senator Russell, who would lead the southern forces against the bill, objected; and Mansfield moved to table Russell's objection. Mansfield succeeded by a vote of 54-37, but Cannon voted no, probably because he felt—as did many of his colleagues—that bypassing a committee with clear jurisdiction over a bill was a dangerous precedent.

After two months of debate, the crucial cloture vote was scheduled for June 10. Russell's strategy in opposing the civil rights measure was built completely on the cloture vote, as he had disdained negotiating over particulars of the bill. It was an all-or-nothing strategy, one that increased the already historic import of the cloture vote. He was counting on the consistent failure of the Senate to muster two-thirds plus one in favor of ending debate, a history that included Howard Cannon prominently in its annals. Conventional wisdom dictated that Cannon would continue his perfect record in opposing cloture, and he did nothing to dispel that.

As the vote unfolded, however, the conflicting currents of Cannon's mind led to a startling departure from his past behavior: He voted "yea" to invoke cloture and joined the unprecedented action of the Senate to end a filibuster on a civil rights issue. The final vote was 71 in favor of cloture and 29 against; with all 100 senators present and voting, it took 67 votes to invoke cloture. The only blemish on Cannon's bold and surprising move was the fact that he did not answer when his name was originally called, but came onto the Senate floor as the roll call was under way to cast his vote. Critics would maintain that he waited until the matter was resolved before voting, but Cannon denied that charge. He had been on the telephone when the roll call began, he said, and had no idea how the vote was going when he entered the Senate chamber to cast his vote. He was the first senator to vote when the clerk repeated the roll call to catch those, like Cannon, who did not vote the first time around.

The official Senate historian revealed that, indeed, the matter had been resolved before Cannon cast his vote—69 senators had already voted in favor. Only Cannon and Senator Francis Case were recorded in favor of cloture after the initial vote tally. The historian could not tell, however, whether Cannon was aware of the vote count when he cast his "yea."

That issue aside, Cannon's vote was hailed in Nevada as a courageous and just act. "Anyone who knows the situation in Nevada, where a state civil rights bill has been steadfastly rejected by the Nevada legislature, realizes that it took a lot of courage for Sen. Cannon to act as he did," editorialized the *Sun*. "His situation is complicated by the fact that he is up for reelection this year and continuing racial strife through the summer could become a dynamite-laden issue in the fall voting." Cannon's colleague, Senator Bible, voted against cloture, and the state's only congressman, Walter Baring, had voted against the civil rights bill in the House, further emphasizing the leap that Cannon had taken.

In a prepared statement explaining his vote, Cannon underplayed its significance, both in historical terms and in its impact on the beleaguered citizens of West Las Vegas. "I finally decided the work of the Senate had been held up long enough," he said, as if the matter were merely procedural. "The bill had been debated until there was little else to be said about it. In good conscience, I had to vote to bring debate to a stop and get on to the other important business." This was typical Cannon, to downplay an action of obvious historical importance. Part of his motivation was his natural reluctance to crow about personal achievements, an admirable trait. But part of it was political calculation, as Cannon clearly understood the unpopularity of the civil rights movement in Nevada. He did not want to give his critics any more ammunition to use against him than the cloture vote provided, as he faced a bruising campaign for reelection to a second term.

Cannon, bandleader and clarinet player, with the Howard Cannon Dance Band in the 1930s. Courtesy Nancy Cannon Downey Collection.

Cannon and Krebs at the hidden underground shelter they occupied for the last three days of their forty-two-day evasion of the Nazis in 1944. Courtesy Nancy Cannon Downey Collection.

FACING PAGE:
Top: Cannon (*right*) and commanding officer Francis X. Krebs in the cockpit of the C-47 troop carrier plane they flew through World War II. Courtesy Nancy Cannon Downey Collection.

Bottom: Cannon in the peasant garb he donned during his escape from Nazi-controlled Holland in 1944. Courtesy Nancy Cannon Downey Collection.

Cannon receiving the Croix de Guerre from a general in the French air force in recognition of his contributions to the liberation of France, Chartres Cathedral, July 1945. Courtesy Nancy Cannon Downey Collection.

Krebs and Cannon standing beneath their wartime images in a painting commemorating their escape from the Nazis. The painting hung in Cannon's Senate office, where Krebs served as a legislative assistant after leaving the service. Courtesy Nancy Cannon Downey Collection.

The Senate candidate and his wife during the 1958 campaign. Courtesy Nancy Cannon Downey Collection.

FACING PAGE:

Top: Dorothy Pace Cannon. Courtesy Nancy Cannon Downey Collection.

Bottom: Cannon, Alan, Nancy, and Dorothy out to dinner in Las Vegas in the late 1950s. Courtesy Nancy Cannon Downey Collection.

Cannon and LBJ enjoyed a close working relationship during Johnson's presidency. Johnson campaigned on behalf of Cannon in both Las Vegas and Reno in 1964, and his visit might have been the difference in a tight race. Courtesy Nancy Cannon Downey Collection.

FACING PAGE:

Top: Cannon (*standing*) with fellow members of the Nevada congressional delegation after the 1958 election. Although both Cannon and Senator Alan Bible (*right*) seem pleased to be in the company of Representative Walter Baring (*with phone*), the senators soon tangled with the independent-minded Baring. Courtesy Nancy Cannon Downey Collection.

Bottom: Although Cannon's daughter, Nancy, tired of the Washington political scene by the time she graduated from high school, she did receive some Washington perks— such as a kiss from Vice President Lyndon Johnson—during her time there. Nancy was representing the Girl Scouts during the organization's fiftieth anniversary celebration. Looking on are proud dad, Howard, and Lady Bird Johnson. Courtesy Nancy Cannon Downey Collection.

Aboard Edgewood Sunrise, a prizewinning Palomino stallion he acquired early in his Senate career, Cannon rode in innumerable parades throughout Nevada and elsewhere, sometimes with daughter Nancy. Courtesy Nancy Cannon Downey Collection.

FACING PAGE:

Top: Cannon (*right*) and then attorney Harry E. Claiborne are all smiles as Claiborne visits Cannon's Washington office in 1961. Three years later Claiborne challenged Cannon in a nasty primary battle that Cannon won. Courtesy Nancy Cannon Downey Collection.

Bottom: Vice President Nelson Rockefeller dropped by Cannon's Senate office in 1974 just before being sworn in to the nation's second-highest office. Rockefeller appreciated the fair way Cannon conducted hearings on Rockefeller's nomination. Courtesy Nancy Cannon Downey Collection.

Cannon looks over President Carter's right shoulder as Carter signs the Airline Deregulation Act that Cannon authored and steered to passage in 1978. Courtesy Nancy Cannon Downey Collection.

Cannon and Jim Santini buried the hatchet at a luncheon following their bitter 1982 primary election fight, which Cannon won. Santini vowed to help Cannon win the general election against Chic Hecht, but his efforts were not sufficient. On Santini's right was unsuccessful congressional candidate Mary Gojack, and on Cannon's left was Harry Reid, who won the House seat vacated by Santini to begin his Washington career. Courtesy Nancy Cannon Downey Collection.

Howard and Dorothy in 2000 at the dedication of the Howard W. Cannon Aviation
Museum at McCarran International Airport in Las Vegas. Courtesy Nancy Cannon
Downey Collection.

CHAPTER 5

Conflict and Challenge

"But even if he never becomes floor leader, Cannon is a growing power in the Senate—and a fixture there," reported syndicated columnists Evans and Novak in noting that Cannon was being groomed as a possible candidate for Senate majority leader. To borrow from Mark Twain, reports of Cannon's "fixture" status proved to be greatly exaggerated. Indeed, his 1964 reelection campaign became one of the most contentious and dramatic in Nevada history and, ultimately, the closest Senate contest in U.S. history.

Evans and Novak's assessment of Cannon's status with Nevada voters *should* have been correct. By many standards he had achieved much more than a first-term senator could hope for: prestigious committee assignments, solid legislative achievements, and favorable attention from not one but two popular presidents. Moreover, he had demonstrated in Washington the same high energy he displayed as Las Vegas city attorney, going beyond the normal requirements of a senator to tend to crucial Nevada businesses such as aviation and development of the Nevada Test Site.

He had capped an eventful first term by casting an unprecedented vote for cloture on the Civil Rights Act of 1964, a move that proved momentous to the growing African American population in southern Nevada. But, just as there would be eighteen years later surrounding Cannon's stunning defeat by political lightweight Chic Hecht, there were numerous questions about his shaky 1964 showing. Did Cannon veer too far to the left in his support of such issues as federal aid to education and civil rights? Did his vigorous quest for federal dollars rub independent Nevada voters the wrong way? Did he appear too much as a remote Washington figure, content to let his aides, particularly the strong-willed Conlon, handle Nevada issues for him?

The Conlon factor is certainly one of the most intriguing. Cannon's most trusted aide had the background and the predilection for political conflict that would lead him to take an active role in Nevada politics even from Washington. While a student at the University of Nevada–Reno in 1932, Conlon was elected president of the college's Young Democrats organization. He was involved in Senator McCarran's first campaigns and later helped strategize Edward P. Carville's successful election as governor in 1938. He followed Carville to Washington when the governor was appointed to fill out the U.S. Senate term of James Scrugham, who died in office. After Carville's bitter primary defeat in 1946, Conlon moved to Las Vegas. He operated several businesses, including at least two bars, became active in Democratic Party politics, and managed various political campaigns. Personally, he was charismatic and compelling, affecting a no-nonsense leadership style softened by his penchant for a drink and an Irish song or story.

Conlon's role in Cannon's 1958 victory and stewardship of his Washington office in the first term contributed greatly to Cannon's success. Moreover, all observers agreed that Conlon continued to earn Cannon's admiration and friendship. In at least one instance, however, his meddling in Nevada political affairs had adverse consequences for his boss. Conlon had never gotten over his animosity to Berkeley Bunker, the Las Vegas gas station and mortuary owner and former House and U.S. Senate member who opposed Carville for the Senate nomination in 1946 after Carville had spent two years in the Senate. That Bunker defeated Carville for the nomination, an event that so split Democrats that Molly Malone sneaked into the Senate, made matters worse.

In addition to Bunker, Conlon viewed another Nevada politician, Governor Grant Sawyer, with skepticism. Sawyer, Conlon believed, was using the governorship to maneuver for a run for the Senate against Cannon. These twin forebodings of Conlon's came to a head in the 1962 Nevada elections, when Sawyer had a chance to enhance his position by supporting a new lieutenant governor to succeed the popular Republican Rex Bell, who bucked the Democratic tide in 1958 to win the lieutenant governorship but died suddenly in 1962. For Sawyer, this was a chance to help elect a lieutenant governor of the same party, and after careful deliberation, he decided on Bunker as his choice to succeed Bell.

A neutral observer might easily conclude that Sawyer was simply making his political life easier by supporting a lieutenant governor of his party—one who would owe allegiance to him. To Conlon, however, Sawyer was making it easier for himself to run against Cannon in 1964 by putting a reliable ally in the lieutenant governorship. With Republican Bell occupying the position, Sawyer would be loath to run for the Senate. With Bunker in place, however, Sawyer could take on Cannon in the 1964 primary knowing that the governorship would remain in Democratic hands.

"Conlon was relentless," remembered Ralph Denton. "Jack always viewed Sawyer as a potential opponent of Cannon's, assuming he would run for the Senate when he left the governor's office. Jack was an old-time political figure, had been in campaigns a long time, and he believed you ought to knock down, whenever you can, anyone who might be a potential opponent." Therefore, according to Denton, Conlon reached out from Washington to rally Democrats against Bunker when he ran for lieutenant governor in 1962. "Jack took the lead in getting Carville people to say, 'We're going to show Bunker!'" Denton recalled. "In droves, old Carville Democrats voted against Bunker in the general election. I could just hear them: 'Do you realize Bunker bit the hand that fed him?'"

Although this tactic was successful in helping deny Bunker the lieutenant governorship, it created a far greater problem for the Cannon-Conlon team. That's because the man who won the lieutenant governorship in 1962 would prove to be a formidable Cannon adversary from that point to Cannon's final Senate race in 1982. That man was Paul Laxalt.

Standing more than six feet tall, handsome, and looking younger than his forty-one years, Laxalt combined strains of rugged individualism with a western persona that included highly polished cowboy boots (although Paul affected the cowboy look, he was reportedly afraid of horses). As lieutenant governor, Laxalt, as Bell had been, was the only Republican to hold state-wide office. Unlike Bell, however, Laxalt was on a mission to rebuild the Republican Party in Nevada. He drew on his personal charm, his family's status, a thriving law practice, and a fervent belief in the Goldwater strain of conservatism to achieve his goal.

Laxalt had formerly served as Ormsby County district attorney and city attorney of Carson City. He had married well, choosing Jackie Ross, the daughter of widely known and respected lawyer, Republican leader, and, later, federal judge John Ross. His parents, Dominique and Theresa, were beloved figures in northern Nevada, partly because of a glowing, nostalgic book called *Sweet Promised Land,* written in 1957 by Laxalt's brother Robert. It recounted the Laxalt family's roots as Basque sheepherders in the French Pyrenees, a tradition Dominique continued by tending sheep in the Sierra Nevada around Carson City while Theresa raised the children (four boys and two girls) and operated a hotel-restaurant in town that was frequented by politicians of both parties.

Laxalt's inexperience may have diminished him as a threat in Conlon's eyes, but he turned out to be an ideal candidate to upset Cannon's reelection dreams. Although Sawyer had a certain boyish charm, with his crew cut and bow ties, Sawyer was basically a political soul mate of Cannon's. Sawyer's people saw him as more liberal than Cannon, evidenced by a friendship with President Kennedy and his impassioned calls for a civil rights statute in Nevada, and perhaps more dedicated to cracking down on abuses in the gaming industry. But he was still a moderate Democrat tied to the ruling forces in Washington. Laxalt, on the other hand, by positioning himself with the emerging policies of potential presidential candidate Goldwater, was solidly aligned against the sort of "big government" political solutions embraced by Cannon in his relentless pursuit of federal programs and dollars for Nevada.

Moreover, Laxalt won from the beginning of his political career something Cannon never achieved—genuine affection among the state's voters and media. Cannon was an excellent campaigner in small groups and one-on-one encounters. He had an encyclopedic memory of people and their families in every corner of the state. He would constantly remark, upon meeting someone in Wells or Moapa or innumerable Nevada byways, that, yes, he did remember them and their parents as well. His recollection was genuine, and those who met him were impressed.

But Cannon was a stiff and unimpressive public speaker and was not a smooth media performer. Of greatest concern was an instinctive dislike for reporters that they could sense and had a palpable effect on his relationship with them. Since one of Cannon's closest advisers, Chet Sobsey, was a former newsman, and since Cannon received mostly laudatory news coverage in his days as city attorney and U.S. senator, one would have expected him to embrace reporters. But, for some reason, he did not, instead regarding them as a necessary evil that accompanied his job.

With prodding from his staff, Cannon would do the required things: give interviews, call back reporters at the end of the day, even drop by newspapers and television stations when he was in Nevada for unrestricted questioning. He lacked an ease with reporters, however, a warmth that would make them feel he was leveling with them and letting them in on deep-felt convictions. Cannon's sessions with reporters were invariably stiff, with him relying on stock answers. He rarely ventured beyond the minimum requirements of an answer and rarely revealed a human side of himself to reporters.

Laxalt was just the opposite. He exuded warmth and graciousness to voters as well as reporters, traceable to a friendly, steady gaze that he aimed right at their eyes. He had also mastered the technique of shaking a voter's or reporter's hands with both of his and holding on to the interlocutor as if he or she was a member of his family. These characteristics and his rock-ribbed conservatism made him a potentially formidable Cannon opponent as the 1964 race approached.

As was the norm in Nevada politics, however, 1964's was a late-developing race. Although winning admiration throughout the state for his personal charm and steadfast belief in the Goldwater strain of Republicanism, Laxalt continuously fought off efforts to induce him to run against Cannon. Laxalt fever was stoked by his first major political address in Las Vegas in September 1963, on the eve of President Kennedy's much-anticipated visit. Speaking to three hundred Clark County Republicans, Laxalt raised twenty thousand dollars, reportedly the largest fund-raising event held by the Nevada Republican Party in an off year.

Even though the enthusiasm generated by Laxalt's Las Vegas speech turned up the pressure on the lieutenant governor to announce his future plans, within a month of that appearance he unequivocally took himself out of the race against Cannon. He replied "Absolutely not" when asked if he would run for the Senate, adding, "I am not in a position personally nor professionally" to run. A strong Republican candidate would emerge by the first of the year, he predicted.

That did not happen, and the comparative political calm throughout 1963 and well into 1964 might have lulled Cannon into a false sense of comfort. He had armed himself financially through a wildly successful testimonial dinner on April 20, 1963, that reportedly raised one hundred thousand dollars for his campaign. Organized by Ben Goffstein, the former bookmaker who had advanced under Gus Greenbaum's tutelage from righting the Flamingo's finances to a vice presidency of the Riviera Hotel, the event drew a sold-out crowd of nearly twelve hundred who paid one hundred dollars each for a cocktail reception and dinner at the Flamingo.

The dinner revealed a great deal about Cannon, the basis of his political support, and his sense of himself. First of all, it was a quintessentially Las Vegas event, from its sponsorship by Goffstein, a colorful reminder of the Mob-dominated Siegel-Greenbaum era in Las Vegas, to its lavish Strip hotel accommodations ("roast sirloin of beef, bouquetiere"), to its eyebrow-raising one hundred–dollar price tag. There had been nothing to rival the Cannon dinner before in Nevada politics, and the Las Vegas media responded in a manner reflecting the historic importance.

Cannon basked in the warm glow of the good wishes sent his way by the huge crowd and admiring speakers. The banquet setting proved a favored way of his to cement ties with supporters and raise money for campaigning, and he included one before his next two Senate reelection campaigns. Cannon's innate shyness made him uncomfortable raising money by telephone or personal solicitation, and a banquet sidestepped those methods. A third party, abetted by Cannon's staff, sponsored the events, and ticket solicitation was handled by sponsors instead of by Cannon. He could show up at the event appearing surprised and pleased at the turnout, no matter how preoccupied he may have been with its success.

At the initial testimonial, Cannon was moved by the genuine good spirits and favor evidenced by the size and glamour of the event. He truly was a favorite son that April night in his fifth year as Las Vegas's first senator, with attendant cachet as an intimate of the popular president, John Kennedy, and with many bruising personal and political battles still ahead of him. It was not a stretch for him to tell the crowd, "I feel more fortunate than my colleagues, for I have the privilege of working for you, the nicest people of them all."

But not everyone was enamored of Cannon, including some elements of his own party. While Laxalt was having trouble rounding up a Republican to oppose Cannon, two Democrats emerged to offer spirited and troublesome primary opposition. The first was a young city councilman from Sparks, the railroad community adjacent to Reno, named Bill Galt. Galt was a handsome, fresh-faced thirty-six-year-old with a wife and two small daughters, who called Cannon a "special agent . . . of powerful special interests" when he announced in late June 1964. The specific sin of Cannon he cited was a rebuke issued by the senator over the aggressive tactics that IRS agents used in closing down a Las Vegas bookmaker accused of taking illegal out-of-state bets. Galt added that "the big powerful special interests are reported to have made our junior senator nothing more than a special agent," and pledged to commit himself to "no one but the individual voter of Nevada."

More troubling to Cannon was the candidacy of friend and fellow attorney Harry Claiborne, who launched a quixotic, albeit short-lived, campaign for Senate at the last minute on July 15. In addition to his high profile in Las Vegas, which made him a greater threat to Cannon's base than Galt, Claiborne had a man-on-the-street appeal that Cannon couldn't match. Claiborne's primary campaign soon deteriorated into a piecemeal, uncoordinated exercise that almost all political analysts and journalists described as hopeless, but it did reveal a Cannon shortcoming that would become more pronounced in the general. The *R-J*'s Jude Wanniski neatly described the differences between the two: "Cannon has a solid voting record and a lengthy list of accomplishments, but somehow it sounds rather flat on television," Wanniski wrote. "It's all too polished and mechanical and far-removed from the voters, who still like to feel close to their elected representatives." Claiborne, on the other hand, "seems forceful, animated and determined—even if less organized. He bills himself as a fighter and he sounds that way. He mispronounces words here and there, and, for a lawyer, mangles the English language to an unbelievable extent. But it's all masculine and vigorous," Wanniski offered.

Like Galt, Claiborne initially cast his campaign in a typical political light, declaring that he was running because Cannon "has spent too much time trying to build a machine and take over the Democratic Party in Nevada"— a reprise of the criticism of Conlon. But his campaign, like Galt's, soon revolved around another issue that had bedeviled Cannon throughout late 1963 and all of 1964. The issue had both a name and a face: Robert Gene Baker of Pickens, South Carolina.

Bobby Baker was an outgoing, energetic, voluble young man who flourished in the Senate of majority leader Lyndon Johnson—"the Leader," as Baker referred to him. Coming to the Senate in 1943 as a fourteen-year-old page, Baker evolved into the perfect right-hand man for Johnson's brand of leadership. Part gossip, part legitimate information resource for Senate Democrats, Baker was unfailingly loyal to Johnson and personally ambitious beyond almost anyone's imagination—certainly beyond Johnson's. He abetted Johnson's voracious appetite for information about fellow senators, kept a close watch on all Senate business, provided information and favors for the Democratic majority, and did anything and everything else necessary to maintain Johnson's ironclad control of the legislative flow. For his efforts, Baker was awarded a heady job and title in 1955 at age twenty-six. Johnson named him to the position of secretary to the majority when he was elected majority leader.

By the time Baker resigned his position under fire in October 1963 rather than face a dogged Senate investigator in the person of Delaware Republican John J. Williams, he had accumulated a paper fortune of more than $2 million, a $125,000 home (worth at least ten times that amount today) in one of Washington's most exclusive neighborhoods, a motel in Ocean City, Maryland, a Capitol Hill town house for his girlfriend, and numerous other assets, partnerships, debts, and affiliations that were remarkable for someone who made less than $20,000 a year and supposedly worked for one of the world's great taskmasters, Senator Johnson. A cloud of scandal, corruption, and influence peddling hung over him.

To say that Baker's indiscretions posed a problem for Democrats in the Senate and elsewhere was a gross understatement. Senate Republicans who had been outmaneuvered and outvoted by Johnson and his Democratic counterparts for many years could scarcely contain their glee at finding skeletons in the closet of someone universally regarded as "Lyndon's boy." Some members of the Kennedy administration who never did warm to Johnson's selection as vice president looked at the Baker case as further evidence that LBJ might not make it on the second Kennedy ticket in 1964. Johnson had already proved an embarrassment through scandals involving Texas crony

Billy Sol Estes (no links with Johnson were ever found) and his top assistant in both the Senate and the White House, Walter Jenkins. Jenkins not only made headlines as one of the first Washington officials to fall victim to a homosexual charge but was also accused of aiding one of Baker's nefarious schemes. A full-blown Baker scandal would not be welcome news in the White House.

The concept of an independent counsel's office did not exist in 1963, nor did an official Senate investigatory committee. The only vehicle for an examination of Baker's wheeling and dealing was the little-known, moderately busy Senate Rules Committee, on which Cannon sat. Thus it was that the Baker investigation was dropped into the laps of Cannon and his five Democratic colleagues on the Rules panel, and it began its formal investigation on October 29. That meeting, and many others during the succeeding forty-five days of hearings over a sixteen-month period, was held in closed session, with the only witness being Baker's Javert, Senator Williams. When Baker himself was called to answer Williams's charges on February 19 and 25, 1964, again in closed session, he invoked his constitutional right not to answer questions. He pointed out through his counsel, the formidable Edward Bennett Williams, that he was already under investigation by the FBI and IRS. That investigation would lead to an indictment in 1966 and conviction in 1967 on eight federal crimes involving tax evasion and tax conspiracy. In declining to answer questions from the Rules Committee, Baker said, "I do not intend to participate as a defendant witness in a legislative trial which is governed by no rules of evidence, which denies me the right to cross-examine my accusers through counsel, which holds proceedings both in secret and in the open and which has provided me with no specifics of charges."

Self-serving as it was, Baker's defense did accurately portray some of the weaknesses of the Rules Committee investigation. It quickly developed into a fiercely political exercise, with Williams parading a series of charges against Baker and, by association, other senators, employees, and associates of Baker. The Democratic majority on the committee repeatedly found itself refusing to acquiesce to Williams's demands for more witnesses and more extensive investigations. The apparatus of the Senate at that time was plainly insufficient to conduct an investigation as thorough as Baker's exploits required. Further, the political nature of Baker's position cried out for an investigation separated from the Senate and its members.

Although Cannon's opponents would try to make the case that Cannon subverted the Baker investigation, that claim exaggerated the facts. In the first place, the issue was too big for a freshman senator lacking seniority even on the small Rules Committee (six Democrats, three Republicans) to significantly alter. Baker's indiscretions touched the White House and played into the tensions between President Kennedy and Vice President Johnson. Plus, they involved the time-honored ingredients of sex and corruption that were more powerful than Howard Cannon in his greatest moment. One of the most titillating aspects of the tale involved Elly Rometsch, a beautiful German call girl who often visited the Capitol Hill town house of Baker's secretary and girlfriend, Carol Tyler. Famed investigative reporter Clark Mollenhoff had broken the Baker-Rometsch story in October 1963, and Baker was soon on the covers of *Time, Life,* and other national publications.

As the torrent of news stories about Baker and the Senate investigation continued into 1964, it was inevitable that Cannon, like all Democratic members of the Rules Committee, would come under the unfriendly glare of national publicity. Although the catalog of Baker's financial dealings was vast, including a vending-machine firm, the Ocean City motel (the Carousel Motor Inn), another motel in North Carolina, a travel agency, an insurance agency, a law office, a real estate development firm, a private credit bureau, and a cemetery, none of them even remotely involved Cannon. The vending-machine company, Serv-U Corporation, which lay at the root of Baker's troubles, did include some Las Vegas gambling figures among its ranks, including at least one, Ed Levinson of the Fremont Hotel, who donated generously to Cannon's campaigns in 1958 ($650) and 1964 ($10,000). But there were no reported or suspected links between Cannon and Serv-U Corporation. The ubiquitous Cliff Jones was among a group of people who used Baker's help to bid on a gambling concession in Curaçao in the Caribbean, but Cannon had never joined Jones in his gambling pursuits.

But there was a link between Cannon and Baker that generated considerable publicity and caused considerable harm to Cannon's 1964 reelection. That link was forged at the Quorum Club, the Capitol Hill watering hole favored by Conlon, where one of his drinking buddies was Bobby Baker. "That's where that marriage was hatched," was Sobsey's wry recollection of Baker and Conlon swapping gossip at the Quorum Club.

Probably as a result of the Conlon-Baker friendship, Cannon agreed to attend the 1962 opening of Baker's Carousel Motel in Ocean City, Maryland, a four-hour drive from D.C., which was described as the "high-style hideaway for the advise and consent set." Cannon may have felt conspicuous as the only member of Congress who attended the Carousel opening, although Vice President Johnson and Lady Bird were there, along with Washington's "hostess with the mostest," Perle Mesta. On that occasion, Cannon posed for—or was simply caught in—one of the most bizarre, and regrettable, photographs of his life. Attired in a matched paisley top and swimming trunks, Cannon was pictured between Mesta on his right and Baker on his left. Both Mesta and Baker were dressed conservatively, further highlighting the oddness of Cannon's cabana attire.

Although that lapse in judgment occurred in 1962 when Baker was the fair-haired boy of the Senate, it became fodder for national news outlets in March 1964, as the Baker investigation was plodding through the Rules Committee. As one example, the *New York Herald-Tribune* used it in a Sunday feature on the Baker case, alongside some questions posed under the headline, "Explanation Wanted." "Are some democratic members of the Rules Committee acting as defense attorneys for Mr. Baker, notably Sen. Howard Cannon, Nev., Sen. Robert Byrd, W. Va., and Sen. Claiborne Pell, R.I.? By the nature of their questions they appear to be trying to discount the possibility of misbehavior on the part of Mr. Baker. Of the three, Sen. Cannon attended the champagne and caviar opening of Mr. Baker's Carousel Motel. He now sits in judgment on his host."

Creating the charge of soft-pedaling the investigation were reported snippets of Cannon's conduct during the hearings, once questioning the expenditure of additional funds on the case and at other times pooh-poohing some of the charges leveled by Senator Williams or others. Cannon's hometown paper, the *R-J*, noted the rumblings about a possible Cannon-Baker connection and lampooned it in an editorial cartoon by Ed Kelly on June 28, 1964. Titled "The Rover Boys," the cartoon showed a perplexed voter looking at Cannon and Conlon attired in Boy Scout–like uniforms. Cannon's shirt was emblazoned "Bobby Baker" Cannon, and Conlon's read "Quorum Club" Conlon. Both were shown with their fingers crossed under the statement, "We wuz good boys in Washington."

Cannon was further tarred by the Baker brush when word leaked out about some of the participants in the April 1963 testimonial dinner. A group of Washington lobbyists, including several airline representatives who were aware of Cannon's interest in aviation and his appointment to the Aviation Subcommittee, chartered an airplane from a small carrier named Riddle Airlines and flew to Las Vegas for the festivities. Despite a slightly sour smell caused by Washington fat cats going to such elaborate lengths to pay respects to a fast-rising senator, there was nothing initially troubling about the Riddle Airlines contingent. Until it headed back to Washington, that is.

For reasons never explained, Baker hitched a ride on the flight back. He had reportedly not attended the dinner, and never said how he happened to be in Las Vegas at the same time it was under way. To make matters worse, when Riddle presented a sixteen thousand–dollar bill for the plane rental, the bill went to Baker. This was explained as an honest mistake, and the bill was passed along to one of the flight's organizers. As an embarrassing side note that guaranteed maximum exposure of the incident, it was revealed that Washington's muckraking columnist Jack Anderson, a recent addition to the board of Riddle Airlines, had suggested sending the bill to Baker. It seemed that everybody in Washington was somehow connected with Bobby Baker, and to many it must have seemed strange that Anderson assumed Baker would pick up the check for the junket.

Years removed from the 1964 contest and not long before his death, Claiborne recalled that he was recruited into the race by Democratic Party activists concerned that the "Baker thing" would defeat Cannon. Giving credence to rumors concerning Galt's candidacy, Claiborne said he believed "there was ample proof" that the people who asked him to run also recruited Galt.

The combined effect of the Galt and Claiborne campaigns, along with that of activist James McMillan, a dentist and Westside resident who became the first African American to run for the Senate in Nevada, provided Laxalt much of what he would have desired in a Republican opponent to Cannon: repeated attacks on the incumbent's record. Thus, when he could not convince another up-and-coming Republican, Washoe County District Attorney William Raggio, to take Cannon on, Laxalt reversed himself and entered the Republican primary on July 5.

Reflecting a campaign that was assembled at the last minute, Laxalt had a mixed bag of messages as he prepared to overtake the Democratic Party's two-to-one registration edge statewide and Cannon's seemingly impregnable position in Clark County. The issue that pushed him over the edge, he said, was a recent U.S. Supreme Court decision requiring states to reapportion their legislatures according to "one man, one vote" principles. In Nevada, this would end the lopsided representation of small counties and the disenfranchisement of the rapidly growing colossus in Clark County. Whether the average voter worried about such things or not, Laxalt had another problem in making the issue stick in a campaign against Cannon: Cannon agreed with him. Not only was he on record as opposing the Supreme Court's decision, but he had voted for a two-year delay in implementing it. The only charge Laxalt could make against Cannon was that the senator opposed direct congressional action to overrule the Supreme Court, which, Cannon believed, would violate the separation-of-powers principle underlying the U.S. Constitution and create untold legal and political turmoil. Laxalt settled for distorting Cannon's record on the issue and claiming that he "sold out to Big Government."

This, at least, had the value of consistency, as Laxalt's best issue against Cannon was the senator's wholehearted embrace of federal programs and solutions for Nevada's problems. Laxalt countered with his defense of rugged individualism as exemplified in the campaign of Barry Goldwater to win the Republican presidential nomination. Laxalt was drawing a sharp contrast between himself and Cannon, and Cannon was only too willing to play his part in the drama.

Cannon built his campaign around two basic ideas: that he had "delivered" for Nevada in terms of federal spending in the state and that Laxalt's opposition was an example of right-wing extremism. Cannon's main campaign brief revolved around his advantageous Senate committee assignments and the goodies they meant for Nevada. Among the figures he cited were one billion dollars in military, space, and Commerce Department spending in Nevada during his first term and the fact that his three major committees had jurisdiction over 99 percent of federal activities in Nevada. What Cannon may not have realized, but Laxalt surely did, was that if you set yourself up as the person responsible for the state's welfare to the extent Cannon did, it makes you vulnerable to criticism whenever the least thing goes wrong.

Cannon and Laxalt sailed through their respective primary contests easily, although the more serious opposition Cannon attracted reduced his margin of victory to 59 percent while Laxalt triumphed over much lesser competition by an 88 percent margin. Claiborne's energetic but disorganized campaign turned out not to be much of a threat to Cannon, as he received only 10,807 votes statewide, trailing even Galt, who received 12,054. True to his mercurial nature, Claiborne raced over to Cannon campaign headquarters as the vote totals came in on primary night, congratulating the victor and pledging to help in his campaign. "Howard Cannon is a fine man," Claiborne proclaimed. "I know he can serve us better than his opponent." Looking back at the campaign nearly forty years later, Claiborne recalled simply, "I misjudged the Baker factor. I thought it would defeat Howard."

Cannon's victory statements mirrored his main theme, as he hailed "progressive moderation, which must be the course for Nevada and the nation." Goldwater had captured the Republican presidential nomination in July, and Cannon was clearly not going to stop contrasting his version of government with the Goldwater-Laxalt version. Laxalt shifted emphasis after trouncing his little-known competition, bringing the Bobby Baker issue back into focus, although with an ominous-sounding twist. "It definitely won't be on a name-calling basis, and it won't be on any basis of guilt by association," Laxalt said. "It will be the development of the record as we found it." Laxalt and his campaign aides had been busy investigating the Baker charges to find any bombshells they could launch in the general election contest, it turned out.

Toward the end of the campaign, a Reno newspaper reported that "two leading Republicans, one of them with extensive investigative experience," had been digging around the Baker case in Washington. Their goal was the passenger manifest of the Riddle Airlines flight, which, according to another account, had the status of the Holy Grail among Laxalt's campaign team. Laxalt's literary brother, Robert, included a fictional account of the Cannon-Laxalt race in his 1994 novel, *The Governor's Mansion.* Although some elements of the Cannon-Laxalt contest were altered in the novel—Laxalt is the sitting governor and Cannon a three-term incumbent—it provides insight into just what the Laxalt team thought it had discovered. Written as a novel, it is a roman à clef, that is, a "novel with a key," and the key isn't hard to interpret. Some people in the novel are identified by their real names, and some are thinly disguised. Paul Laxalt is Leon Indart and Cannon is Senator Jack Horner ("Little Jack Horner" perhaps, a dig at Cannon's height compared to Laxalt's?).

By novelizing certain elements of the 1964 Cannon-Laxalt race, Robert Laxalt was able to exaggerate its David versus Goliath nature. As mentioned, Senator Horner is described in Robert's book as a three-term senator who "had been doing favors for the financial and political giants for a long time." The single Riddle Airlines charter to Cannon's Las Vegas testimonial is referenced in equally exaggerated terms: "The giants were being flown into Nevada by chartered airplanes. There were so many of them they resembled an endless squadron of B-29s in a World War II bombing raid."

Robert describes the Washington investigatory trip mentioned in the newspaper account in James Bond–like terms. "Leon's" operatives are bent on retrieving an unedited transcript of the Baker investigation hearings before it is permanently destroyed, according to Laxalt. "But neither Abner nor I nor Leon nor anyone else was ever to find out how Skinner (all fictional names) managed to pirate the original uncut transcript of the Senate hearing out of the records. We did not hang around in Washington long enough to examine the transcripts."

The Governor's Mansion describes how Laxalt's minions pored over the transcripts for two weeks, virtually locked in a hotel room, to produce a television script "aimed at the heart, head and tenure of U.S. Senator Jack Horner." Judging from the script described in the book—and Paul Laxalt's actual television broadcast aired on October 21—the campaign aides might as well have saved the airfare to Washington. Almost everything contained in the book and Laxalt's address was available either in news reports or in the Rules Committee's official report on the Baker investigation released on July 8, 1964, and available from the Government Printing Office.

In *The Governor's Mansion,* Leon/Laxalt's brief against Senator Horner is basically that Bobby Baker was a bad person and Horner knew him. Most of the script recounts the litany of Baker's shady business dealings. Finally getting to Horner/Cannon, the script states, "Very soon, suspicion revolved around the actions of one man in particular—Senator Jack Horner of Nevada." It then includes the information gleaned from the real Laxalt campaign investigation, the passengers on the Riddle Airlines flight, describing them as "influence peddlers, lobbyists, special interest boys and government agency fixers." Of seventy-four names on the list, twelve of them were "mentioned" during the Baker hearings, the script adds. "Ask yourselves in your own mind how deeply Senator Jack Horner was involved in the Bobby Baker scandal . . . ," the book reads. "The record is absolutely clear that many of the passengers on Jack Horner's money-raising flight to Las Vegas were close associates of Bobby Baker." Laxalt's actual address was couched in similar terms, claiming that Laxalt had uncovered business ties between Baker and passengers on the Riddle Airlines flight. But in linking the Baker scandal back to Cannon, Laxalt could offer as proof only his unsubstantiated charge that Cannon had covered up for Baker in the Rules Committee investigation.

Laxalt's dramatic escalation of charges against Cannon, delivered in a much-publicized television address just two weeks before the November 3 election, changed the dynamic of the campaign, not by the "facts" presented but by the nature of the direct challenge to Cannon's integrity. Cannon could have easily refuted Laxalt's charges and exposed his Baker revelations as amateurish and without merit. His innate distrust of the media, however, combined with Conlon's hardheaded campaign stance of never answering charges from an opponent, left Laxalt's accusations—flimsy as they were—out in the open.

That he sustained damage by Laxalt so close to the election was even more puzzling because of the lift Cannon's campaign had received from a visit by President Johnson just a week before Laxalt went on TV. Cannon had been lobbying the former majority leader since at least August to make a Nevada stop as part of his own reelection campaign, and he was finally able to deliver the word about Johnson visits to Las Vegas and Reno on Saturday, October 10. The news was all good for Cannon and his supporters, as Johnson would arrive the following Sunday evening, ride in a motorcade to the Convention Center, and deliver what was called a "major address." He would then spend the night in Las Vegas before departing for Reno on Monday morning. By including the overnight stay, Cannon's campaign was able to pronounce Johnson's visit the longest in his current campaign swing.

Johnson's reception in Las Vegas was tumultuous, and the Convention Center crowd that gathered to hear him lambaste Goldwater and praise Cannon was equal to the eight thousand that had greeted the late President Kennedy the year before. But an even more enthusiastic welcome awaited him in Reno, the more Republican-leaning of the two largest Nevada cities and the heart of Laxalt's support. Johnson, a veteran campaigner who was used to campaign ups and downs, was genuinely moved by the Reno crowds.

Told of a police estimate of fifteen thousand for the crowd awaiting his speech in a Reno park, Johnson remarked that it was "the largest crowd of 15,000 I have ever seen." City officials quickly revised their estimate to fifty thousand, and Cannon called the scene "the biggest, most enthusiastic, most sincere welcome ever given to any man in the history of northern Nevada." As Johnson's motorcade wound through town, it made an unscheduled stop that would have been unusual even if President Kennedy's assassination in a motorcade less than a year earlier wasn't fresh in everyone's mind. Johnson and Cannon climbed out of Johnson's bulletproof limousine and stood atop a bus-stop bench so Cannon could point out a Johnson billboard proclaiming, "Hello, Lyndon. Nevada is NOT Goldwater Country." A showgirl wearing a ten-gallon hat was rendered above the message on the billboard's top edge. Speaking to the crowd through a portable microphone, an animated Cannon said, "I just wanted the President to see this sign. Nevada has voted for the winner for the last 52 years, and this year it's going to do it again . . . a landslide for Johnson."

Adding to the drama and excitement injected into the Cannon-Laxalt race by the presidential visit and the Baker charges, Robert Brown, editor of the *R-J*, resigned suddenly because of an alleged bias toward Cannon in the paper's election coverage dictated by the paper's owner, Donald Reynolds. Another member of Reynolds's team, *Nevada Appeal* editor Ed Allison, resigned from that Carson City newspaper on October 25. Both claimed Reynolds's insistence that his newspapers endorse Cannon was the reason they quit, with Allison having a more concrete example to offer than Brown: Reynolds had ordered an Allison-written editorial supporting Laxalt pulled from the *Appeal*'s October 21 edition, causing a blank space to appear where the editorial would have been. Both men joined the Laxalt campaign after their resignations, indicating they had strong political motivations for their actions.

Ralph Denton, who was challenging Walter Baring for the Democratic nomination for Nevada's lone congressional seat in 1964, remembers an encounter with Brown that indicated the editor had more independence than he claimed. Responding to Denton's request for the *R-J*'s editorial support, Brown replied, "We could support you if you'd run against Cannon." Denton recalls it took him some time before he figured out what Brown was intending. "I didn't smell wolf manure for a while, that Bob had his own agenda. He was thinking if I beat Cannon, or had a big Democratic fight and weakened Cannon, Paul Laxalt would have an easier time. I think subsequent events proved how close he was to Laxalt," Denton said.

Reynolds made no secret of his support for Cannon, which was tied to a larger agenda concerning President Johnson's reelection campaign. Reynolds was seeking an ambassadorial appointment to Australia, and would use Cannon as his key Washington contact. Sobsey recalled how Reynolds ordered that his significant billboard operations in Las Vegas and Reno be turned over to enthusiastic welcomes to the campaigning president. In a postelection letter to Reynolds, Cannon thanked the publisher profusely for "the splendid editorial support your media accorded me in Nevada." He said he had contacted the White House and the State Department "on the matter about which you wrote" (the Australian ambassadorship) and planned to speak with President Johnson personally when he returned to Washington.

According to people involved in the 1964 race, Johnson's pressure on the *R-J* to support Cannon was direct and effective. In a eulogy for Brown following his death in 1984, former *R-J* columnist Wanniski said that Johnson's message to Reynolds to support Cannon may have included threats to Federal Communications Commission licenses for his television and radio stations. The result was a "virtual shutdown of coverage of Laxalt."

The televised Baker charges reinvigorated what had been, according to news accounts, a "relatively quiet" campaign, and rendered its outcome unpredictable. It had been considered close before Laxalt's claims of a Baker cover-up, and the resulting furor tightened it even more. Merely relaying the vote totals, however, does not reflect the drama of the Cannon-Laxalt race. A back-and-forth vote count throughout the evening of November 3 led both candidates to savor victory at different points and for the outcome to be unclear as Wednesday, November 4, unfolded. By around noon Wednesday, the general consensus was that Cannon had won by some 165 votes, but all sides agreed the matter was too close to consider final until all seventeen Nevada counties conducted an official canvass of the vote. Much posturing, name-calling, hints of election-day misdeeds, and shortness of temper ensued before that could happen.

As the vote was counted on Tuesday, Cannon initially established a lead ranging from 5,000 to 6,500 votes. But Laxalt continually whittled away at that margin, until it had shrunk to around 2,500 near midnight. At that point, Cannon declared victory, an event Sobsey remembered clearly nearly forty years later. The scene was Cannon's reelection headquarters in a new shopping center on Sahara Avenue just east of the Las Vegas Strip. Watching the results come in were Cannon, Conlon, Sobsey, and two characters closely entwined with Las Vegas's gambling culture, Jimmy "the Greek" Snyder and Ben Goffstein. Snyder had made a national name for himself by posting the odds on sporting events, capitalizing on the fact that betting on such events was legal only in Nevada. Goffstein, of course, was the former bookie who had achieved greater status as the Las Vegas gambling culture grew, advancing to an executive position at the Riviera Hotel-Casino on the Strip.

There was much discussion among this coterie, gathered in a private office shielded from the crowd of campaign volunteers and newspeople, about what Cannon's declining margin boded for the final result. As the tension among Cannon's campaign staff and assembled media representatives grew, Conlon assumed the combative stance he was known for and issued an ultimatum to Cannon. "Go out there and claim the victory!" Conlon demanded, pointing dramatically to the crowd of supporters and newsmen. Cannon followed Conlon's advice, for all the good it did in the resulting confusion.

Laxalt was undergoing a similar bout of nervousness as he monitored the returns from "Momma Laxalt's," the family home in Carson City. In his memoir, Laxalt recalled the moment during the morning hours of November 3 when the official media election reporting service declared him the winner by some 800 votes. "When the news came, I went to the bathroom and proceeded to heave my guts out. I had never come to grips with the fact that we might win!" he wrote. In keeping with the nerve-racking events of the night, Laxalt's margin quickly dwindled to 10 votes, then went back up to a reported 18. In the morning he boarded a plane to fly to Las Vegas, where the battleground over the balloting would be most hotly contested. Shortly after arriving, he received news that his "victory" might be premature. Clark County Clerk Helen Scott Reed had discovered a mistake in the count reported after the polling places were closed Tuesday night, and revised the Clark County total for Cannon upward, resulting in an unofficial 165-vote margin for Cannon reported throughout the state on Wednesday.

The seeming mystery of Clark County's changing vote count rankled the Laxalt forces mightily, and undoubtedly some of them still harbor suspicions—or moral certainty—that something fishy happened. Again using the fictitious *The Governor's Mansion* as a mirror into their souls, Robert Laxalt's words speak for those people. He recounts an alleged Laxalt spy watching on election night as unnamed persons in the County Clerk's office burned papers in a potbellied stove. "We don't need to be clairvoyant to guess they were burning absentee ballots cast for you," a character tells Indart/Laxalt.

The canvass involved election officials and the elected county commissioners in each county carefully checking vote totals before reporting official results to the Nevada Supreme Court for certification. All "results" reported before the canvass were unofficial, although in most elections the few discrepancies unveiled in a canvass hardly matter. In the Nevada Senate race they mattered a great deal. Various results were reported as the counties compiled their official totals: Laxalt picked up votes in some areas and Cannon in others. Clark County was the last to complete the canvass, and its results were anxiously awaited because of the revision of totals announced by Reed on November 4.

When the Clark County totals were reported on November 13, the result was a razor-thin margin of 48 votes for Cannon statewide out of nearly 135,000 votes cast. Laxalt had picked up 14 votes in the Clark County canvass, not enough to reverse Reed's postelection finding in Cannon's favor. Cannon had exceeded his own predictions by beating Laxalt by more than 13,000 votes in Clark County, but won only four other counties. Laxalt trounced Cannon by nearly 8,000 votes in Washoe County, and in two other northern Nevada counties surrounding the Reno–Carson City area where the Laxalt name was most revered, Douglas and Ormsby, he won by more than a two-to-one margin. President Johnson swamped Goldwater statewide by more than 22,000 votes, meaning that many Johnson supporters voted for Laxalt for the Senate over Cannon.

Another remarkable result was Cannon's overwhelming margin of victory in the Westside, an area where Laxalt immediately focused suspicion of wrongdoing. Not only did Laxalt quickly announce he would seek a recount—a logical move considering the extreme closeness of the race—but he also demanded that Reed provide official tallies, poll books, and affidavits of registration for some of the Westside precincts. Showing that his zeal to reverse the precarious outcome was boundless, Laxalt said he would summon a handwriting expert from Los Angeles to pore over the Westside documents. The Laxalt team obviously believed there was some tampering with the African American votes, which went to Cannon by such margins as 195-5, 167-1, 228-8, 185-8, 169-7, and in one precinct a total blanking of Laxalt, 137-0.

Cannon, who had drawn on resources available to him as chairman of the Senate's Privileges and Elections Subcommittee, was determined to bring the contested Nevada election back to Washington. He staunchly believed that the Constitution vested the Senate with ultimate authority to decide its own membership, including the power to decide disputed elections. James Duffy, a staff member of the Privileges and Elections Subcommittee, came to Nevada shortly after the election, making veiled references to "possible irregularities" that ruffled the feathers of Laxalt's camp. Laxalt, falling back on the Nevada-first theme he sounded throughout the campaign, accused Cannon of taking the election away from the people of Nevada. Both sides had a point.

Cannon sought to block a recount by asking the Nevada Supreme Court to prohibit it and declare him the winner. In one of the more humorous moments of the postelection maneuvering, Cannon demanded that Laxalt, as lieutenant governor, sign the election certificate declaring him the winner because Governor Sawyer was away from the state. Laxalt, who received Cannon's demand on Thanksgiving Day, thanked him for his "humorous . . . wire," which "enlivened our family gathering considerably." Rather than grant Cannon's request, Laxalt said he was "seriously considering certifying myself the winner."

The Supreme Court refused to stop the recount, which set off the second stage of legal maneuvers and high drama. The crux of a recount, as Americans learned painfully following the 2000 Bush-Gore race for president, is examining paper ballots for any irregularities. With a fragile 48-vote margin, Cannon could scarcely stint on defending the status quo, notwithstanding his belief that the whole matter should be determined by the U.S. Senate. Sobsey remembers that Duffy, the Senate staff member who angered many people by his presence in Nevada, issued a telling request of the Cannon staff: "Give me just one vote, and I'll make it stand up [in the Senate]," Duffy said. To which Conlon replied, "If I had one vote to give you, I would."

Demonstrating his ability to set aside personal grievances in favor of the ultimate objective, Cannon named erstwhile bitter primary opponent Harry Claiborne to lead a team of lawyers to oversee the recount in each of Nevada's seventeen counties. It would be their job to argue for or against accepting paper ballots that seemed vague or improperly filled out. It wasn't "hanging chads" that would draw their attention, but "crosses in unauthorized locations . . . irregular use of stamping device . . . blurred spots . . . erasures and scratches," or "ballot improperly folded or creased," according to a twenty-six-page legal brief Claiborne prepared for the attorneys under his command. Never one to hide his candle under a bushel basket, Claiborne recalled the brief nearly forty years later as "brilliant."

The examination of paper ballots unfolded throughout the state in scenes familiar from the 2000 presidential race: Lawyers scrunched their faces, examining suspicious marks on questionable ballots, while county clerks and their assistants huddled around stacks of ballots to ensure their sanctity. The seriousness of the process was illustrated by which precincts the key players focused on. Claiborne, for instance, who declared himself a recount expert, went to Laxalt's home turf, Ormsby County, where Paul Laxalt was represented by his brother Peter. Describing the "long, slow, tedious process," a local paper noted that each ballot was examined first by county election officials and then by the legal representatives, who could not touch the ballots.

Cannon scored a major victory in the Clark County recount when the embattled county clerk, Helen Scott Reed, announced there had been a 100-vote mistake in tabulating his votes on election day. Coming in a Westside precinct already labeled suspect by Laxalt's team, the mistake was made by a clerk entering the results from a voting machine into official voting records. The clerk credited Cannon with 32 votes, whereas the machine actually registered 132. Buttressing her finding against challenges from the Laxalt forces, Reed said the same mistake was made in the presidential contest. It must have been an excruciating blow to Laxalt, who commented, "At this point, 100 votes looks like 10,000."

Indeed, Laxalt's insistence on a recount proved more advantageous to Cannon, as the final result announced on December 2 was an 84-vote Cannon victory instead of the 48-vote margin he held after the canvass. The recount had actually moved one of Cannon's victorious counties, Mineral, into Laxalt's column, giving Cannon victory in only four of the state's seventeen counties. As it had in Cannon's narrow 1958 primary win over Dr. Anderson, the number of counties paled against Cannon's strength in Las Vegas. And crucial to that strength was the overwhelming support Cannon received from the African American community. The twenty Westside precincts went with Cannon by an astounding margin of 3,583 to 183, making his cloture vote only five months earlier the most crucial vote he cast in his entire twenty-four-year career.

To Claiborne, the recount proved that his group of lawyers was sharper in finding reasons to reject Laxalt ballots and defend Cannon ballots than Laxalt's team. Whatever the reason, it was not enough to convince Laxalt to concede defeat, as he decided to challenge the results in the Nevada Supreme Court the next day. But Cannon was ready for the challenge, having had nearly a month since the election to polish his legal arguments that state courts had no jurisdiction to overturn a federal election.

The Supreme Court decision only a week later was a straightforward victory for Cannon and his team, as the court dismissed Laxalt's suit on the grounds that it had no jurisdiction to overturn the election results. The court reached its decision on the same day, December 10, that it heard arguments in the case, indicating how clear-cut the matter was to them. Claiborne made sure Cannon realized who had led the successful fight against Laxalt's legal challenge, sending Cannon the printed copy of the Supreme Court's decision. And, in recognition that no good deed should go unrewarded, Claiborne reminded Cannon that he and his client Benny Binion, owner of the Horseshoe Club in downtown Las Vegas, would be in Washington after the first of the year to discuss Binion's application for pardon from an income tax–evasion conviction. Thus, Cannon's ties with the colorful postwar community he decided to call home would continue to resonate with the now reelected senator from Las Vegas.

At the April 1963 testimonial dinner in Las Vegas, Cannon's colleague Senator Bible said he had never seen a senator who "took hold so quickly and so firmly" as Cannon. He may not have proved his worth convincingly to Nevada voters in 1964, but his opponents would never doubt the firmness of Cannon's grip on a job he loved. There is no simple answer to the question of why Cannon narrowly escaped from the Laxalt threat, as it involved issues of politics—Cannon's liberalism on federal spending versus Laxalt's proclaimed conservatism—personal appeal, and campaign tactics. The Bobby Baker issue added spice to an already enticing political brew, and Cannon stumbled to the finish line by calling on every trick, ally, and personal favor he could muster. It wasn't a glorious result as the '58 campaign had been, but it was a win, and Cannon could hope for better results in the years ahead.

CHAPTER 6

Moving On

If the Howard Cannon Senate office were a corporation, the first item of business following the 1964 election would have been a meeting of the board of directors. Clearly, something had gone wrong with market acceptance of the product. From a resounding upset of a two-term incumbent in 1958, Cannon, Inc., had stumbled into a hair's-breadth victory over a political neophyte. Laxalt's political agenda, judging from the drubbing handed Barry Goldwater who personified it, was not widely accepted by Nevadans. Yet the state was almost equally divided in its opinion as to who should represent it in Washington, Cannon or Laxalt.

But politics is not business, and there was no leadership meeting to discuss what Cannon had done poorly either in the election or in office, according to two members of the Cannon staff, Lee Walker and Chet Sobsey. Business in suite 259 of the Russell Senate Office Building (the office had moved upstairs from room 142 early in 1961) continued as if Cannon had defeated Laxalt by eighty-four thousand votes instead of just eighty-four.

There was concern, as evidenced by Cannon's perusal of several postelection news stories, with his comments "Check this out" or "Is this true?" written on several. And Jack Conlon was fixated on why Cannon did so poorly in Reno–Washoe County and, perhaps more important, why the campaign was so unaware of his slippage among voters there. The campaign's polling company, John F. Kraft of New York, bore the brunt of this concern.

Kraft was having trouble collecting a final payment of twenty-five hundred dollars from the Cannon election committee. In a December 1964 letter to Conlon, Kraft said he had heard from another party "that you are mad at us," with the result being that Conlon was debating whether to pay the twenty-five hundred dollars. In a series of increasingly dramatic appeals that dragged on into May 1965, Kraft continued to ask for payment, admitting some shortcomings in his work but insisting that his company had provided good value for the money charged. But Conlon *was* upset over the work done by Kraft in the campaign, as he revealed in a letter of his own about the same time that Kraft began asking for payment. "[Kraft] places a lot of blame on intangibles . . . but it's specifics that we are interested in finding," Conlon wrote. "He says ' . . . we'd have argued for a continuing intensive effort . . . in Washoe.' I pleaded with this Bum to stay in the state and concentrate on Washoe during the last ten days. He has evidently forgotten this part of our conversation," Conlon concluded. Kraft had, indeed, decided against sending staffers to Nevada, arguing that he could monitor events better—and cheaper—from his New York headquarters.

Kraft missed the dynamic in Washoe by only a few percentage points, but that percentage took on added importance in a close race. His final preelection polling showed Laxalt ahead of Cannon by 48 to 44 percent, while Johnson was comfortably ahead of Goldwater, 58 to 38 percent. In actuality, Cannon received only 39.7 percent of the Washoe County vote, losing to Laxalt by nearly eight thousand votes, while Johnson's margin remained close to Kraft's prediction. The difference between 44 percent and 39.7 percent in Washoe was more than sixteen hundred votes, obviously a huge sum in a contest decided by fewer than one hundred votes statewide.

Hindsight is, famously, always 20-20, but Kraft's postelection analysis of his interview results in Washoe County was illuminating. Remarks about Cannon had a "bland, unenthusiastic air about them," Kraft said, which, on reflection, should have been counted a "very mild intention" to vote for him. By contrast, "an awful lot of Washoe people reported having met Laxalt," Kraft said, a comment that pollsters normally discount. "But it now appears that in Washoe an awful lot of people did indeed 'know' him through having shaken his hand, met his wife, seen his children, and so on," Kraft said. "We gave our 'normal' weight to such responses which means that perhaps we underweighted them."

In dredging through the ashes of Cannon's disastrous result in Washoe County, Kraft found one more sign that the Cannon reelection campaign misfired. "Baring carried more weight than we thought," Kraft reported on Nevada's lone congressman, who cruised to reelection after narrowly defeating Ralph Denton in the Democratic primary. Cannon had joined in the general criticism of Baring emanating from both the White House and Bible's office concerning the Great Basin National Park, and even added some fuel of his own by appearing to criticize Baring in a speech at the 1962 Democratic State Convention. Since Democrats had pointedly omitted Baring's name from a resolution praising the Nevada congressional delegation, Cannon's remark that "those of us who do not like the Democratic program can get out of the party and go find another program" was taken as a slap at Baring. Cannon insisted that he was speaking of southern Democrats who had been opposing Kennedy administration policies, but the damage had been done.

Tension between Cannon and Baring was exacerbated by reports throughout 1963 that Baring was considering running against Cannon for the Senate. Baring scotched those rumors in September by announcing his decision to seek reelection to the House, but, again, the possibility of a rift between Cannon and Baring was highlighted. "I found a lot of people who indicated their support of Baring with real enthusiasm, leaving no question of their support, who at the same time indicated little more than mild support for Cannon," Kraft wrote. "And on call-backs we now find that some of those people now claim they did vote for Laxalt." Baring, of whom it was often said, "No one likes him except the voters," thus proved to have had a radioactive effect on Cannon's reelection: touching him carried grave risks. Cannon was lukewarm toward Baring, and Baring felt the same toward Cannon, adding more impetus for voters to split their tickets in both Washoe and Clark counties.

Veteran observer Al Cahlan, who had left the *R-J* and was writing a column for his former archenemy, Hank Greenspun at the *Sun,* found particular significance in a snub of Baring during President Johnson's campaign visit to Las Vegas. "There is no question at all but that the apparently calculated snub of Rep Walter Baring in the Las Vegas meeting deeply affected thousands of Baring supporters, not only in southern Nevada but in the rest of the state, because the word got around," Cahlan wrote. "The fact that Baring got more votes than the President suggests that the Las Vegas incident hurt Cannon and actually aided Baring." The bottom line for the Cannon team was that they simply did not understand the northern Nevada electorate and, even if they did, did not have a candidate nearly as popular as the charming local boy, Paul Laxalt. The north-south split in voter sentiment was thus solidified by the 1964 senatorial contest.

Regardless of how he may have felt about his close race with Laxalt, Cannon's basic political instincts were not altered. Back in August 1964, Cannon had issued a strong statement of support for President Johnson's "War on Poverty," enthusiastically voting for the nearly one billion–dollar package of federal aid that encompassed it. "This program will be a milestone in our continuing search for a better life for all Americans," he said. "I have and will continue to support it by every means available at my command and I urge every public official and private citizen to join me." Since it is difficult to imagine Laxalt becoming a foot soldier in the War on Poverty, Cannon had staked out a position very different from his opponent's, and he held to it.

And Cannon was far closer to the national political mainstream than Laxalt. In the 1964 election, Johnson routed Goldwater, and every other member of Cannon's "Class of '58"—the twelve Democrats elected along with him—was reelected. This rare occurrence seemed to underline the move toward progressive politics first noticed in 1958 and emphasized by Kennedy's election and then Johnson's. The tide of public support combined with Johnson's latent desire to assist the underdog created a momentum that was reflected in the historic actions of the Eighty-ninth Congress. Medicare, aid to primary and secondary education, immigration reform, voting rights, rent subsidies to low-income families, even a national foundation to encourage and subsidize the arts and humanities came pouring out of the heavily Democratic Congress. Combined with the previous year's action in passing the Civil Rights Act, the income tax cut, and the War on Poverty program, the first two years of Johnson's administration compared favorably to the rush of legislation enacted in 1933–1934, the first two years of FDR's New Deal.

Cannon supported the bulk of Johnson's program, resisting only the proposal for rent subsidies for the poor. He also showed sensitivity to Nevada concerns by voting to support a constitutional amendment to reverse the Supreme Court's "one man, one vote" decision on state reapportionment (the measure failed to win the required two-thirds majority in the Senate). On another bedrock Nevada issue, repeal of the "right to work" provision of the Taft-Hartley Act (Section 14-B), Cannon also went against Johnson and sided with strong home-state sentiment opposing repeal.

The brief possibility of Cannon's consideration for a Senate leadership position dissipated in his second term. The 1963 insurance-policy theory of Senator Russell—that Cannon should be considered for majority leader in case Senator Mansfield was defeated in 1964—proved unnecessary. Mansfield cruised to reelection with 64 percent of the vote and was firmly established as one of the most respected—and electable—politicians in Montana history. Another boomlet for Cannon—this time as a prospective majority whip—had surfaced just before the 1964 election, when speculation about the position was engendered by Senator Humphrey's decision to seek the vice presidency under LBJ. "Nevada Sen. Howard Cannon, a church-going Mormon and middle-road Democrat, is expected to be Sen. Hubert Humphrey's successor as Democratic whip," reported Drew Pearson at the end of a late-October column. If Cannon were actually interested in the position, however, this interest did not translate into action. Louisiana senator Russell Long defeated two other opponents in a close election, and Cannon's name did not surface again as a possible candidate for a Senate leadership post.

Even so, Cannon became a major political force during his second and third terms. He had to shake off the cloud of suspicion that clung to him after the Rules Committee investigation of Bobby Baker in 1964, but he nevertheless consolidated his committee power, earned increasing respect from his Senate colleagues, and honed his pragmatic political skills. By the end of his third term, he had compiled an impressive record of legislative victories, taken a leading role in reforming campaign-finance rules, begun the process of deregulating the aviation industry, and attained the national spotlight in the confirmation of two appointed vice presidents, Gerald Ford and Nelson Rockefeller. Reforming the federal campaign-finance laws was arguably one of Cannon's most important and lasting legacies. The major components of the reform wouldn't become law until after Watergate—well into Cannon's third term—but he spent much of his second term doggedly building the groundwork for their eventual passage. In 1965 Cannon held hearings on a bill, s2541, that resurrected the mild election-reform bill he had steered to Senate passage in 1961 but which had died in the House. By year's end, he was convinced that the bill represented the limit of what Congress was willing to enact at that time.

Then early in 1966, President Johnson raised eyebrows in his State of the Union Address by calling for campaign-reform measures going far beyond what Cannon considered possible. The nonpartisan, nonjudgmental *Congressional Quarterly* dryly noted, "The President's interest in campaign finance reform came as a surprise to many Washington observers." Cannon was undoubtedly one of the more surprised of those observers. Nevertheless, he had to consider the president's proposals as he calculated his subcommittee's strategy in advancing s2541 in 1966.

A staff memo in March 1966 acknowledged that the Rules Committee would have to consider a Johnson-inspired bill if it was introduced in Congress. Moreover, the memo stated, "it will present trouble (1) if it comes soon and (2) if LBJ puts pressure on." As things turned out, the Johnson measure did not emerge very quickly (it was introduced in June), and the president did not contact Cannon to express his interest in having it enacted. Therefore, Cannon moved ahead on s2541, much to his eventual regret. Although the Johnson measure was introduced by a fellow member of Cannon's Rules Committee, Democratic reformer Joseph Clark of Pennsylvania, Cannon did not consider it in his subcommittee, instead pushing his own measure to consideration by the full Rules Committee in August 1966. The Cannon bill, s2541, was approved by only a 5-4 margin, touching off a series of harshly critical senatorial and media rebukes.

This unpleasantness was put behind him the next year, however, when Cannon himself introduced a new version of Johnson's election-reform measure. Johnson had reconsidered his tactics on the bill and sought Cannon's counsel and support the second time around, even agreeing to drop a provision calling for disclosure of outside income and gifts to members of Congress. Cannon had told the president that the provision would create too much opposition to the bill for it to be successful. Cannon's Privileges and Elections Subcommittee opened hearings on the Johnson-Cannon measure in June 1967.

Understandably, Senator Clark testified that the 1967 measure was weaker than the one he supported the year before, specifically citing the gift- and income-disclosure provision. But Clark was a reformer while Cannon was a pragmatist, and Cannon moved the bill to unanimous approval by the sub-committee in July and by the full committee in August. The remarkable ease with which the bill moved through Rules, in contrast to the bare margin of support for the weaker Cannon bill the year before, was a lesson in legisla-tive tactics and the power of a popular president to shape national opinion. By winning Cannon over, Johnson created a strong ally with the power to influence his fellow committee members. And by showing his resolve to achieve passage of the election-reform bill, Johnson created a media and public opinion groundswell that emboldened Congress.

Cannon maintained his command of the election-reform bill as it moved to the Senate floor on September 11. The bill was approved by a unanimous 87-0 margin on September 12, but died in the House. Cannon's rationale for supporting his "weak" bill in 1966 was vindicated: The House was not ready to support sweeping election reform. A measure similar to the 1967 Johnson-Cannon bill was again reported by the Rules Committee in 1970, but died in the full Senate. It wasn't until 1971 that the principles first out-lined in Johnson's 1966 State of the Union Address were passed by the Senate, accorded favorable consideration in the House, and signed into law.

Cannon's role in election reform—cautious, attentive to the concerns of his fellow senators, unwilling to challenge perceived limits—formed a major part of the legislative accomplishments of his second term, and, eventually, of his third as well. But his main concerns in his second term continued to be improvement of the nation's aviation infrastructure and strengthening of national defense, particularly the portion known as tactical airpower. And he never let slide his attention to key state concerns such as relief from gambling taxes, the Southern Nevada Water Project, and the beleaguered Project Rover. In civil aviation and defense, Cannon moved inexorably up the Senate power ladder by virtue of his increasing seniority, intelligence, energy, and favorable committee assignments.

In April 1969, Cannon was named vice chairman of Commerce's Aviation Subcommittee. By this time, his obvious love of aviation and his unflagging desire to advance the industry had already marked him as a powerful force. "Look for Sen. Howard Cannon to have an active role in directing the Senate

Aviation Subcommittee as vice-chairman," wrote industry newsletter *Aviation Daily*. Cannon would wear the vice chairman label for only another two years, being named chairman in January 1971, after winning reelection to a third term.

Cannon assumed a leadership role in aviation policy just as the White House and Congress were nearing agreement on a method to replace the 1946 federal Airport Act, which doled out matching grants for airport improvements. A hit-or-miss approach to airport expansion, the grant program was subject to presidential or congressional cutbacks, and also forced airport executives to go through a tedious, bureaucratic grant-application process each time they desired to make substantial improvements in their facilities. Aviation boosters sought a consistent, less cumbersome program for delivering federal aid for airport expansion, while the White House sought a way to control the cost of developing the rapidly growing national airline infrastructure. Johnson, therefore, proposed in 1968 to substitute a direct-loan program for the matching-grants system. And, in a key policy recommendation, he wanted aviation users rather than the general public to pay for a greater share of airport costs through major increases in user taxes on passenger tickets and aviation gasoline.

The major air carriers had a rival proposal that called for creation of an Airport Development Trust Fund patterned after the Highway Trust Fund, which had provided major federal support for the U.S. interstate highway program. Under the trust-fund concept, user taxes would be placed in trust and doled out yearly to airports seeking improvements. User taxes were also a key ingredient in this rival proposal, but they were slightly less onerous than the administration's proposal: a 7 percent tax on passenger tickets instead of 8 percent, and a two-dollars-per-person tax on foreign travelers.

Thus, when Cannon assumed the vice chairmanship of the Aviation Subcommittee in 1969, the outlines of a new plan for aviation development were set. Cannon would find himself in the hot seat on one of the most contentious aspects of the plan, the higher taxes on aviation fuel private pilots would have to pay. Since he was well known as an active private pilot himself, general aviation enthusiasts turned to him to soften this blow to their pocketbooks. Cannon would keep their concerns in mind as the final elements of a major airport development bill were implemented. Although the bill represented spadework done primarily by others, Cannon was floor manager of the Airport and Airway Development Act when it came to the Senate floor in February 1970.

The bill had widespread support and was approved unanimously by the Senate after two days of debate. The most interesting amendment debated was Cannon's, which sought to lower by one penny the seven-cents-per-gallon tax on private airplane fuel approved by both his own Commerce Committee and the Senate Finance Committee, which had a major role in the bill's taxation portions. Cannon's decision to go against not only his own committee but also the formidable might of Finance Committee chairman Russell Long indicated how much he wanted to achieve even a partial victory for the general aviation community. Cannon prevailed in the Senate floor fight, as his amendment was approved by voice vote, but he was not so lucky in negotiating with House members who served on a conference committee appointed to iron out differences between House and Senate versions of the bill. The seven-cents-per-gallon tax was approved and signed into law by President Nixon. The May bill-signing ceremony in the Cabinet Room of the White House provided Cannon his third straight presidential pen (Johnson had awarded him one for leading passage of a supplemental military authorization bill in 1966), and a photo of the event was sent to newspapers throughout the state.

Cannon's role in securing passage of the Airport and Airway Development Act, and his determined but losing fight to secure federal funds for development of the supersonic transport jet, did not deter him from attending to Nevada's continuing concerns over air transportation. Not only did he consistently intervene with the Civil Aeronautics Board on behalf of several applications for better service to Las Vegas, but he also concentrated heavily on service to Nevada's smaller cities, Reno and the Lake Tahoe area among them. Cannon had plenty of incentive to help the Reno–Lake Tahoe area because he had done so poorly among voters there, but his career-long efforts on behalf of northern Nevada availed him little in terms of popular support.

Shortly after Cannon, through seniority, advanced to vice chairman of the Aviation Subcommittee, he garnered another subcommittee chairmanship on the Armed Services Committee, but this one was gained through merit. Senator John Stennis, the courtly Mississippian who chaired Armed Services, had taken a liking to Cannon from his first days in the Senate. He had certainly been impressed by Cannon's quick uptake on defense issues, his hard work, and his growing expertise on the U.S. fighter-jet program. Cannon stood out in the Senate by his insistence on personally flying all the new jet fighters developed by the three service branches. He also continued his rise through the Air Force Reserve, winning his second star as a major general in February 1966.

Stennis rewarded Cannon's work in the field by naming him chairman of a special Tactical Air Power Subcommittee of Armed Services in 1969. Although not a formal—or standing—subcommittee, the Tac Air group gave Cannon sway over the increasingly important, high-profile fighter-jet portion of the U.S. defense arsenal. Through this subcommittee, Cannon would control authorizations for all tactical fighter programs, and manage the tactical air portion of the massive military authorization bills passed by Congress every year. As criticism of the U.S. military escalated while the war in Vietnam deteriorated, Cannon would find himself defending the F-111s, F-14s, and F-15s against a rising chorus of opponents. Combined with his vice chairmanship (soon to be a full chairmanship) of the Aviation Subcommittee, Cannon had an unprecedented position as gatekeeper on aviation development in the United States.

Cannon also used his second term to shore up his position with the Nevada gambling establishment, following on the successful effort by the Nevada congressional delegation to reduce the cabaret tax from 20 percent to 10 percent in 1960. The mid-1960s were crucial years for Las Vegas, as the investigations launched by Attorney General Robert Kennedy in 1962 began to reverberate throughout the outposts of organized crime. The most telling blow to Nevada's claim that it scrupulously regulated gambling operations was delivered in a Denver courtroom in June 1966, where Ruby Kolod, part-owner of the Desert Inn and a reputed blackmailer and killer, was appealing an extortion conviction. Las Vegas–based FBI agents testified that they had bugged the executive offices of the Desert Inn in 1962–1963. "We had information coming to our attention that there was a vast sum of money being taken off the top by the ownership of the Desert Inn," one agent testified. Subsequent investigatory pieces in U.S. newspapers put the amount of money allegedly skimmed from six Las Vegas casinos at up to one million dollars a month. Bringing the matter home to Nevadans was a letter to *Sun* publisher Greenspun from FBI director J. Edgar Hoover stating plainly, "The gambling industry of your state occupies a position of major importance in the scheme of organized crime and racketeering. Funds illegally skimmed from certain Nevada casinos have been used for a multitude of nefarious purposes."

The fallout from these revelations was so severe that Governor Sawyer ordered an investigation by the Nevada Gaming Commission. Cannon kept a low profile during these flare-ups, keenly sensitive to the difficulty of winning favorable tax treatment in the Senate for a gambling industry characterized as rife with corruption. He also had reason to be concerned as the various investigations touched on some of his biggest campaign contributors, although the lax reporting standards in place at the time—the same standards that were at the heart of the campaign-finance reforms he was responsible for—kept that information from the public. The Fremont's Levinson, who also turned up in the Bobby Baker probe, was a generous contributor ($10,650 in 1958 and '64), as was Desert Inn part-owner Morris (Moe) Dalitz ($15,000 in '64), who was under indictment on income tax–evasion charges in 1966.

Cannon had another reason to be sensitive to the needs of the casino industry during the 1960s: He had joined its ranks through an association with Frank Scott and other founders of the Union Plaza hotel-casino in downtown Las Vegas. In recognition of his efforts as a private attorney to negotiate a lease for the Union Plaza from the Union Pacific Railroad, and because he and Scott were friends from Cannon's earliest days in Las Vegas, Cannon was included among the seven original stockholders of the Scott Corporation in 1962. The casino opened on July 2, 1971, and the hotel followed a month later. By 1978 Cannon valued his holdings in the Scott Corporation at between $100,000 and $250,000.

Cannon's involvement in the Union Plaza was indicative of his shrewd but cautious approach to investing and his standing within the old-guard business community of Las Vegas. Frank Scott was as upstanding a citizen as Las Vegas ever produced, and although he was not a native, his roots in the town reflected the city's own heritage. He came to Las Vegas in 1936 as the sixteen-year-old son of the storekeeper for the Union Pacific, and lived in a small home behind the railroad storehouse. He scraped together enough money to purchase Roberts Roof and Floor Covering in 1949, following infantry service in World War II. Being in the construction business in Las Vegas following the war was lucrative, and Scott prospered enough to head the Business Men for Cannon Committee that raised money for Cannon's Senate campaign in 1958. The two men and their families remained close friends until each succumbed to Alzheimer's disease in their final years.

Scott's vision of a towering hotel-casino on the site of his childhood home at the historic heart of Las Vegas had a Horatio Alger ring to it. He had begun importuning Union Pacific officials for permission to build a parking garage beneath the railroad depot years before the Scott Corporation was formed, believing that parking would be a prosperous adjunct to the booming Glitter Gulch gambling area along Fremont and adjoining streets in downtown Las Vegas. It was a Union Pacific official who gave Scott the idea of building a hotel on the site of the depot, and he formed the Scott Corporation with that goal in mind. That he would choose Cannon, the newly elected senator from Las Vegas, as a founding investor was not surprising considering the close friendship between the men and Cannon's services when he was in private practice. When his dream of building a hotel-casino neared reality in 1969, Scott reorganized the corporation to bring in experienced gambling professionals. These men, too, represented the legitimate side of the casino industry in contrast to the shady operators who were being identified by the FBI in various court proceedings.

Scott remained chairman and chief executive officer, but Sam Boyd, who owned the El Dorado Club in Henderson, Nevada, was named president, and J. K. Houssels Jr., son of one of the original 1931 Nevada gambling licensees, was named executive vice president. Houssels was a West Point and Stanford Law School graduate who, together with his wife, Jeanne, formed perhaps the only husband-and-wife law firm in Las Vegas in the 1950s. Like Scott and Cannon, Houssels was active in Democratic politics, winning a seat in the Nevada Assembly in 1950. He acquired his expertise as a casino executive with positions at the Tropicana and Showboat hotels before joining the Union Plaza. John D. "Jackie" Gaughan, who came to Las Vegas in 1951 from Omaha, Nebraska, and invested in hotel-casinos including the Flamingo and the El Cortez, was named vice president.

Greenspun referred to the Union Plaza management team as "almost a Blue Book of Las Vegas and its principal industry" when it went before the Nevada Gaming Commission for licensing. "This was one application that went through smoothly and quickly with nary a frown from the commissioners, who just got through raking another group of possibly more affluence but not eminence in the gaming business," he wrote. Cannon had resigned as a member of the board of directors of the Scott Corporation at its reorganization meeting in 1969, sparing him the publicity of a licensing hearing and, properly, removing him from active involvement in the company's affairs.

With his knowledge of the industry, Cannon was receptive to a plan devised in 1965 by Assemblyman William Swackhamer from the tiny northern Nevada town of Battle Mountain to attack one of several nettlesome federal taxes affecting gambling. Although the Kefauver hearings on organized crime in the 1950s were considered more a publicity vehicle for Kefauver's presidential ambitions than a thorough examination of Mob activities, they did produce some concrete results. One of these was a $250 annual federal tax on every slot machine in the United States, devised as a regulatory measure to control the spread of illegal slot machines. The tax was a bust as a means of controlling illegal gambling, as the illegal operators ignored it, but the licensed Nevada casinos had to pay it. Swackhamer's ingenious idea was to keep the tax in effect, thus allowing the federal government to keep "regulating" slot machines, but to rebate $200 of the $250 to Nevada every year. As proposed, the slot-machine rebate would be a painless way to generate an estimated $5 million (based on the number of slot machines in Nevada at that time) for the treasury. Thus, it would go a long way to reduce pressure for increased casino taxes, an idea abhorred by the casino industry that would pay them and members of the state legislature who didn't want to face intense lobbying from the industry against a tax increase.

Cannon and Bible devised an amendment to an excise tax–reduction bill under consideration by the Senate in June 1965 that was almost identical to Swackhamer's original proposal. Cannon had consulted Senator Long, chairman of the Senate Finance Committee, before introducing the amendment and was confident of his support, which was forthcoming. A few other senators opposed it, however, and in the ensuing voice vote it was determined that a majority of the Senate opposed it. For Cannon, however, it was just a temporary setback. He began looking for another opportunity to enact the slot-tax rebate, an effort that would finally prove successful in 1971.

The measure under consideration then was a tax cut bill offered by President Nixon. Because of its sweeping nature, cutting personal income taxes and providing several tax incentives for business, the Nixon bill was subjected to extensive debate in the Senate. Some ninety-four amendments were offered, with forty-four of them winning approval. Showing a deft ability to read his colleagues' mood, Cannon waited until nearly the end of debate on the measure, when the long list of amendments was wearing the patience of fellow senators. He struck on November 15, 1971, proposing basically the same amendment that had been defeated in 1965, and this time it was accepted by voice vote. Although many of the Senate amendments were dropped in conference committee with the House, Cannon prevailed upon Senator Long to hold firm on the Nevada measure, and it survived the conference committee and became law with Nixon's signature in December 1971.

Although conceived as a quick response to tax-increase pressures, the slot-tax rebate went on to attain significant stature in Nevada. Calculated to bring in only $5 million on the twenty-five thousand or so slot machines operating in 1965, the tax rebate grew by leaps and bounds as the Nevada gambling industry continued to expand and the number of slot machines proliferated. When Cannon, working with a different senatorial partner—former foe Paul Laxalt—was successful in 1978 in expanding the rebate to 95 percent of the $250 tax in 1980 and to 100 percent in 1981, the impact on the state budget was estimated at more than $21 million a year, with a cumulative total of nearly $140 million. As a means of overcoming opposition from some senators to "lowering taxes on gambling," Cannon added a provision requiring that the rebate be earmarked for education. The shiny new eighteen thousand–seat Thomas and Mack Center at UNLV—a showcase for the national champion Runnin' Rebel basketball teams of the 1980s and '90s— was one of the principal beneficiaries of this "educational" requirement, as was the twelve thousand–seat Lawlor Special Events Center at UNR, both of which augmented bonds and other revenue sources with proceeds from the slot-tax rebate.

Cannon also became deeply involved in the tangled legal affairs of Benny Binion as his second term began, responding to the pointed reminder from Harry Claiborne that he would see Cannon early in 1965 to discuss Binion's pardon application. Binion, a notorious, colorful, fearsome, and long-lasting symbol of freewheeling, high-stakes Nevada gambling was, like Cannon, a 1946 émigré to Las Vegas. He came not from a European war zone, however, but from a different, if no less dangerous, war zone in Texas.

Leery of a gang-war atmosphere that surrounded illegal gambling in Dallas in the '30s and '40s, Binion "packed his wife and five kids and his cash into a Cadillac and took a 'vacation' to the Southern Nevada desert." He left behind a hardscrabble life as a horse trader, bootlegger, and craps organizer that had led him to kill two men by the age of thirty-two, serving time for one and winning acquittal for the other on the basis of self-defense.

On the surface, the legal situation that was brought to Cannon via Claiborne was straightforward: Binion had served nearly three and a half years beginning in 1953 on income tax–evasion charges brought in Texas, had proved himself to be a solid citizen in Las Vegas since that time, and sought a pardon to clear his name and enable him to vote in federal elections (a right denied to convicted felons). But Claiborne, Cannon, other Binion lawyers in later years, and several prominent Las Vegas citizens underestimated the federal establishment's animus against the rough-hewn former illegal gambler. This was one of those clear differences of perspective on what constituted a rehabilitated citizen that illustrated the different standards Nevadans judged people than others did.

To federal prosecutors, Binion was a two-time murderer, gambler, thief, Prohibition violator, illegal-weapon-carrying income-tax cheat who, in their minds, probably got off easy with the tax conviction. He evoked no sympathy from a succession of attorneys general, presidents, federal judges, parole boards, and others whom Cannon and others petitioned for redress over the years. To the Las Vegas establishment, however, Binion was no different from dozens of other wayward souls who drifted their way following legalization of gambling. Those who became law-abiding citizens while in Nevada, helped build successful gambling and resort operations, donated to charity, and participated in community affairs won the respect and acceptance that other cities accorded residents with more conventional backgrounds. That Binion had a colorful persona and an innovative approach to gambling—basically eschewing betting limits—added to his stature in Las Vegas. The annual World Series of Poker that he launched in 1970 has become a mainstream televised event that brings thousands of visitors to Las Vegas. He is an icon of the city's development.

Cannon bought into the "Binion as persecuted citizen" movement, demonstrating unusual zeal in attempting to win him the pardon he so ardently desired. He pulled all the strings he had, initially as a relatively obscure one-term senator, and later as he grew in seniority and stature, to win favorable treatment for Binion, but to no avail. The initial efforts in 1965 had to do with determining Binion's official prison-release date, which was essential because practice at the time dictated that a person wait five years following release before applying for a pardon. Although Binion had been freed from Leavenworth Prison in 1957, subsequent review of the case determined he had an additional fifty-six days to serve. Binion fiercely resisted going back to prison eight years after he had been freed, but federal officials were just as adamant. Binion reluctantly gave in to the inevitable and began serving his fifty-six days in November 1965. Cannon's actions in 1965 were confined to determining the best course of action following resolution of the official release-date issue. Even in that, however, he demonstrated he was willing to exert maximum influence. As counsel on the best way to proceed in the Binion matter, he turned to renowned Washington attorney Abe Fortas, about to be nominated by LBJ as a Supreme Court justice. Fortas, in turn, consulted Assistant Attorney General Ramsey Clark "to see what he can do and let you know." Conferences and exchanges of letters with Clark followed in 1966.

The first indication that winning pardon for Binion would not be easy came early in 1966, and Cannon was miffed. The federal pardon attorney in the attorney general's office turned down a petition to waive the five-year waiting period, stating in a March 24 letter, "Those in the Department [of Justice] who are in charge of the responsibility of handling clemency matters do not feel that there is any urgent or exceptional reason for granting such a waiver in the case of Mr. Binion."

Cannon's office called on White House congressional liaison chief Mike Manatos, a holdover from the Kennedy White House with whom Cannon had warm relations (Manatos had attended the 1963 Cannon appreciation dinner and read a tribute from Kennedy). Manatos responded that he had talked to Attorney General Nicholas deB. Katzenbach, who was "surprised" at the letter from his subordinate denying a waiver of the five-year waiting period. A later communication from Manatos stated that "Nick [Katzenbach] is still considering the pardon & to disregard the letter."

A handwritten note from Cannon to Conlon revealed the lengths Cannon was willing to travel to win favorable treatment of Binion. "Joe—Call Manatos—I asked them for a return of the favor on this," the note said. In parentheses was an explanation that is hard to decipher: "(. . . my ret. fr. P.R. bringing 2 more votes.)." What had Cannon done to bring two more votes? The words "ret. fr. P.R." are cryptic, and Sobsey, the only living link to

Cannon's staff at the time, could only hazard a guess thirty-five years later: that Cannon interrupted a trip to Puerto Rico to return to Washington and, perhaps accompanied by another senator, cast two votes on an issue Johnson was concerned about. None of it was to any avail, however, as the same pardon attorney wrote Cannon on April 15 reaffirming the Justice Department's decision against waiving the waiting period.

Cannon made another effort in the following year, addressing a letter to Johnson himself, urging "your favorable consideration of his application for a full pardon." Notwithstanding their political ties, Johnson bucked the matter to the Justice Department where Ramsey Clark, with whom Cannon had earlier discussed the Binion case, was then attorney general. The result was the same: "I find no basis for recommending that the President approve the requested waiver," Clark wrote tersely.

Cannon's efforts continued through his remaining three terms in the Senate, but Binion died without receiving a pardon. From the consistent tone of nonsupport coming from both Democratic and Republican administrations, it would appear there never was any sympathy for Binion's case. Why, then, did Cannon, a realist above all else, pursue it so vigorously? Sobsey feels the key had to be Cannon's commitment to Binion's lawyer, Harry Claiborne. "There was no special connection between Binion and Cannon," Sobsey said. "Nothing like the relationship Cannon had with Frank Scott and Jackie Gaughan. And Binion wasn't a big [campaign contribution] giver. But Binion was especially close to Claiborne—you never mentioned Claiborne without mentioning Binion." That Cannon would feel obligated to Claiborne traced to the unusual dynamics of the 1964 election, Sobsey said, where Claiborne first campaigned against Cannon in the primary, then turned into a strong supporter in the general and during the subsequent recount. Sobsey said Claiborne's service in heading up the team of lawyers to represent Cannon during the recount, then heading the legal team to oppose Laxalt's effort to overturn the election through the Nevada Supreme Court, resonated very strongly with Cannon.

Indeed, the Cannon-Claiborne relationship endured for the remainder of Cannon's Senate service, including Cannon's drafting of Claiborne to advise him when the Rules Committee began an investigation into Nelson Rockefeller's fitness to be vice president. Cannon revealed his loyalty to Claiborne by nominating him for a federal judgeship in 1978, which Claiborne received and later had to abandon after a conviction on income-tax charges. Cannon, by then out of the Senate, accompanied Claiborne during his hurried—and losing—impeachment trial in the Senate, a sad return to the chamber where Cannon recorded so many legislative victories.

Although he continued to rise in stature and accomplishment during his second term, Cannon also experienced some severe personal setbacks. Some were only irksome, as when Defense Secretary Robert McNamara ended the practice of allowing members of Congress to participate in the Active Reserve, or when he severed his relationship with the Hawkins and Cannon (it had been renamed shortly after Cannon joined it as Lewis and Hawkins) law firm in 1967 because of allegations that it constituted a conflict of interest. A third blow was not so easy for Cannon to overcome. On Sunday, October 6, 1968, Conlon, the hard-drinking, indispensable pillar of Cannon's political life, died of heart failure in his Schott's Alley apartment in Washington. Only fifty-seven years old, Conlon had suffered a series of heart attacks the year before and spent six months beginning in late 1967 recuperating. He had returned to limited duties in Cannon's office in April. Cannon was in Las Vegas when he received word from Conlon's then wife, Alberta, or "Bunny" as she was known, and left immediately to return to Washington to assist in the funeral arrangements. Cannon issued a statement calling Conlon's death "one of the most tragic personal losses I have ever experienced," and those who had witnessed the remarkable bond between them considered it an understatement. Cannon, who guarded his private life jealously and allowed few persons to penetrate its inner circles, had no friend like Conlon before or after his death.

Not the least of the problems facing Cannon after Conlon died was the question of succession. Sobsey was the loyal second in command, dating his service, like Conlon's, from Cannon's first day in office. But another bright political star had joined the Cannon staff, and he made his own case for consideration as administrative assistant. Jim Joyce, eleven years Sobsey's junior at thirty-one, was a Las Vegas native who, like Conlon, attended UNR and thus had northern Nevada connections and status as a Nevada native. Sobsey had come to Nevada to pursue a news career and, although he, too, lived in northern Nevada for a while, did not attend UNR. Joyce was a bespectacled, pleasant-looking young man with a shy demeanor and a subtle sense of humor. Of the two, Joyce seemed slightly more polished than the larger, burlier, and surlier Sobsey. Who would Cannon choose?

The question seemingly perplexed the senator, who was not one to take an active role in personnel matters within his office. He was perfectly happy to leave those duties to Conlon, but now faced a difficult decision with his good friend's death. He did not rush to judgment, leaving Sobsey and Joyce to twist in the wind for several months. Joyce was not on the scene, having been dispatched to Las Vegas in 1967 to head the senator's office there. Joyce died in 1993, so is not around to comment on the situation, but Sobsey remembers it well. "I really wanted it," he recalled thirty-five years after the event. "So I said 'I'm going to have a campaign.' I got Bible to lean on him, [Clark County Sheriff] Ralph Lamb, Al Bramlet. But he wouldn't make up his mind. I had hired Joyce and I don't know what he had going for him," Sobsey added unflatteringly, reflecting his still-held belief that Joyce at that time was far less experienced politically than he and, moreover, presumptuous to aspire to be Cannon's top aide.

Joyce's political background and service to Cannon did not equal Sobsey's, but he later created one of the state's most successful advertising, public relations, and political consulting firms and won acclaim as the king of lobbyists in Nevada. By the time of his death Joyce had become a revered figure among politicians and political activists, and was included in an *R-J* historical perspective as one of "The First 100 Persons Who Shaped Southern Nevada."

The precipitating event in Cannon's decision making, Sobsey said, was the imminent publication of a new *Congressional Staff Directory* for the Congress that was to convene in 1969. "Cannon hadn't made up his mind, but I could feel in the air, 'Don't bring it up,'" Sobsey continued. "So I told him, 'I just had a call, they're printing a new Congressional Directory and need to know who should be listed as AA.'" According to Sobsey, Cannon replied, "Both of you can be AA," but Sobsey pressed him, saying only one could be listed. At that point, Cannon replied, "Okay, if you want to be it, you can. I couldn't care less."

Whether this is an accurate account of Cannon's decision making or not, only the deceased Cannon or Joyce could verify. But it does fit in with a belief Sobsey developed over the next fourteen years of service to Cannon: that no one ever replaced Conlon in Cannon's esteem. The obligatory announcement was finally made in February 1969, with smiling photos of Sobsey and

Joyce above a headline stating, "Cannon's Press Aides Get Major Promotions." The public did not know of Cannon's paralyzing indecision, and the picture painted in the media was comforting to his supporters. Joyce would join Denver Dickerson, son of former Nevada attorney general Harvey Dickerson and grandson of a former Nevada governor, as one of Cannon's two "field representatives" in Nevada. In practice, Dickerson headed Cannon's Reno office and Joyce the Las Vegas office, appointments that made sense for them and Cannon.

Cannon's reelection campaign in 1970 proved a welcome respite from the 1964 race. For one thing, his two rivals for political supremacy in Nevada, Sawyer and Laxalt, removed themselves from elective politics. Sawyer, who had been defeated by Laxalt in a run for a third term as Nevada governor in 1966, was elected Democratic National Committeeman from Nevada in 1968, a move that "virtually opened his candidacy for Sen. Howard Cannon's post in 1970," according to pundits. But Sawyer declined to mount a comeback against Cannon in what would have been a contentious primary. More surprising was the announcement by Laxalt, who had capped his personal crusade to build the Republican Party in Nevada by winning the governorship from Sawyer, that he, too, was leaving politics after a single term in the Nevada statehouse. That left one other political force for Cannon to contend with as he sought a third term, and it was a formidable one: Richard Nixon, the embattled former vice president and unsuccessful 1960 presidential candidate, who had achieved a remarkable comeback of his own by winning the 1968 presidential election over Hubert Humphrey and a Vietnam War–ravaged Democratic Party.

Nixon made no mistake about his intention to win Cannon's seat for Republicans as part of a drive to overcome a seven-seat Democratic majority in the U.S. Senate. If the goal of a Republican Senate were not incentive enough, Cannon had given Nixon more ammunition by opposing both his controversial Supreme Court nominees, Clement Haynesworth in November 1969 and G. Harrold Carswell in April 1970. Nixon reacted angrily to both of these setbacks.

Nixon put considerable pressure on Laxalt to postpone his announced retirement and run against Cannon, but Laxalt said no. That left William Raggio, the reluctant Washoe County district attorney whom Laxalt had failed to recruit against Cannon in 1964, to carry on Nixon's crusade.

Raggio had all the surface characteristics of a strong candidate against Cannon: A sometimes-crusading district attorney, he fit in with the strong "law and order" climate fostered by the Nixon administration; he was handsome and well liked in the Washoe County environs where Cannon had always struggled to find support; and he would be strongly supported by the Nixon administration. But Raggio proved to be a lackluster candidate, lacking the warmth and political instincts of Laxalt. And after five successive difficult election campaigns beginning with his outsider bid to wrest the House nomination from Walter Baring in 1956, Cannon caught some political breaks.

The first and most important was the absence of a strong primary opponent. A Sawyer-Cannon battle in 1970 would have been a donnybrook of Cannon-Laxalt proportions, but Sawyer—soured on running for office after three campaigns for governor and happily practicing law and operating behind the scenes politically as Democratic National Committeeman—never considered it.

So Cannon was spared the difficult primary battles he faced in 1958 and '64 and was able to meet Raggio with no nagging assaults from within his own party. He won rather easily over Raggio by 24,349 votes out of 147,768 cast in the election. He proved that a moderately liberal senator could succeed in Nevada politics, and won himself some breathing room for the future. By refusing to change course after the narrow victory over Laxalt, Cannon had shown that he would follow his own instincts in the Senate, hewing to the right on national defense and foreign policy issues and slightly to the left on domestic and social issues.

As he began his third term, Cannon continued to wield the influence over air transportation issues that would earn him the nickname of "Mr. Aviation" on Capitol Hill. The ink had barely dried on the Airport and Airway Development Act of 1970 when Congress, under Cannon's leadership, began feuding with the Nixon White House over its provisions. Nixon, fighting a losing battle over federal spending and possessed of an elevated opinion of the scope of executive privilege, escalated a previously sporadically used concept of "impounding" federal funds. After Congress appropriated a certain amount of money for specific federal activities, Nixon would have the federal agencies designated to spend those funds cut back on the congressionally required levels. In this way, the Nixon administration held back significant amounts of congressionally authorized spending, causing wails of anguish from many quarters on Capitol Hill.

The aviation community was among the loudest complainers. It had thought itself immune from White House meddling in congressional spending plans because of the unique funding mechanism of the airport and airways legislation—a trust fund fueled by taxes on passenger tickets. How could the Nixon administration consider airport expenditures inflationary when they came from a separate fund, not the U.S. Treasury, asked aviation supporters? Federal spending was federal spending, replied the Nixon White House, and however you did it, cutting it was better for controlling inflation and lessening pressures for tax increases. Cannon fought Nixon head-on over this issue throughout the 1970s, calling for heavier and heavier spending on aviation improvements and attempting through legislative language to force the president to spend those amounts and not to use trust-fund revenue to pay for other federal activities such as administrative functions of the Federal Aviation Administration.

One example shows Cannon's doggedness on behalf of significant federal support of aviation and his strength vis-à-vis the White House. After two of his airport funding bills were killed by Nixon in 1972, Cannon came back in 1973 with a measure calling for significant increases both in annual airport development grants and in the federal share of airport construction costs, from 50 to 75 percent. Sensing growing congressional resentment over Nixon's restraints on aviation spending, Cannon challenged Nixon to veto the bill, proclaiming that he was confident there were sufficient votes to override a veto. Nixon signed it.

In February 1973, Congress began its investigation of the Watergate scandal, and then evidence came to light that Vice President Spiro Agnew, as Maryland governor, had accepted kickbacks from contractors. The misdeeds of the Nixon administration set in motion a series of unprecedented activities that would lift Cannon from the ranks of unknown senators, solidify his reputation as a consummate Senate man, and even involve him peripherally in the impeachment of Nixon.

Agnew accepted a plea-bargaining arrangement in October 1973 that allowed him to resign to escape prosecution. President Nixon had to consider a replacement for Agnew while contemplating his own chances of surviving the Watergate scandal. In typical Nixonian fashion, he decided that Agnew's successor had to be easily confirmable by Congress and not be a candidate for president in 1976. The latter was important because Nixon had determined that John Connally, LBJ's former friend and adviser who had switched parties after serving as the Democratic governor of Texas, was the man to seek the Republican presidential nomination in 1976. A realist, Nixon had determined that the odds of his serving out a second term in the face of Watergate were only around fifty-fifty, so he knew the man he nominated for vice president might replace him. He did not want that man seeking the Republican nomination in 1976 in opposition to Connally.

As for simply nominating Connally to succeed Agnew, that course carried a major risk. Although he ranked high on almost all lists of most qualified candidates, the turncoat Connally would have a hard time winning confirmation from the Democratic-controlled Congress. Gerald Ford, a broadly popular House minority leader with no significant congressional enemies, was considered almost a shoo-in on that score. Tipping the scales in Ford's favor was his absolute guarantee to Nixon that he would not be a candidate against Connally in 1976.

Thus, Nixon sent Ford's nomination to Congress on October 13, and the House and Senate began considering how to confirm him as vice president. Although the Constitution was silent on the issue, in an act that now seems almost prescient, the activist Eighty-ninth Congress had passed a constitutional amendment dealing in part with just this issue, and the amendment had been ratified as part of the U.S. Constitution less than seven years previous. The Twenty-fifth Amendment settled what had been a constitutional question mark since the eighteenth century, dictating that whenever there was a vacancy in the office of vice president, the president would nominate a vice president and Congress would confirm that nomination.

President Nixon had already fulfilled his role in the process by nominating Ford, but the confirmation process was not spelled out in the amendment. The Senate, upon which rested the duty to "advise and consent" in presidential appointments, was well schooled in such matters. It was long established that the Senate Judiciary Committee considered judicial appointments and the Foreign Relations Committee vetted future ambassadors, for instance. But the vice presidential confirmation was a different animal, and Congress was divided on how to handle it.

The House quickly decided to trust its Judiciary Committee with the confirmation process, but there was less certainty in the Senate. Some members wanted to create a special committee to consider Ford's nomination, while others argued that the job should go to the Rules Committee, of which Cannon had become chairman earlier that year. Eventually, Senate Republicans agreed to concur with the desire of the Democratic leadership and have the Rules Committee conduct the nomination hearings.

It was a shame that the Howard Cannon television viewers saw on the morning of November 1, 1973, as the Ford confirmation hearings opened, was not the dashing war hero of two decades earlier. The trim figure and handsome face, set off with penetrating blue eyes, had sagged considerably through the years. But Cannon's mind was sharp, and his instincts were the same as the tenacious city attorney who had grilled countless utility executives and airline officials in his Las Vegas days. Moreover, Cannon was convinced his committee had a historic role to play in implementing the Twenty-fifth Amendment, and he was impervious to political pressures coming from the House to disrupt the constitutional process.

A group of House Democrats was determined to delay Ford's confirmation in their zeal to bring down Nixon and his administration. The Judiciary Committee had already begun a preliminary investigation into Nixon's impeachment, and several committee members objected to confirming Ford while determining whether to impeach the man who appointed him. Cannon had no sympathy for this effort, however, and made that clear with his opening statement. Some Democrats had proposed that the nomination of Ford "be made hostage to the domestic political warfare currently under way," Cannon said. But, he told the national television audience, "We see no merit –but only danger—in such an approach." Thus, the no-nonsense tone of the Ford hearings was established from the start. As was his wont, Cannon would consider all relevant testimony concerning Ford's fitness for office, but would brook no political shenanigans. The confirmation proceeded quickly, with the committee holding three days of public hearings and nine closed sessions, during which it considered "the most thorough investigation in US history of any candidate for any office in the nation's history." But there was simply nothing there to disqualify Ford as vice president.

The Rules Committee voted 9-0 in favor of Ford's confirmation on November 20, and the full Senate concurred by a vote of 92-3 a week later.

Even the House moved expeditiously, despite misgivings by some Democrats over anything connected to Nixon, voting 387-5 in favor of confirmation on December 6. Because the Ford nomination proved so noncontroversial, it generated little in national publicity for Cannon. He was seen briefly as chairman of the Rules Committee when the hearings opened, quoted on a few topics that came up during the hearings, and then returned to his generally anonymous role in the Senate. But more turmoil, in which Cannon's actions would come under deeper scrutiny, lay ahead.

On May 9, 1974, less than six months after the Senate Rules Committee wound up its investigation of Ford, the House Judiciary Committee opened formal impeachment hearings against Nixon. This set into motion a process in the Senate that had major implications for Cannon and the Rules Committee, which was vested with responsibility for examining the procedures for conducting an impeachment trial of a president. Once impeached by the House, Nixon would be tried on the impeachment charges in the Senate, and the Rules Committee, with Cannon as chair, would consider the charges before presenting them to the full Senate for trial. Since the process had last been tested in 1868 with the impeachment of President Andrew Johnson, the committee had to consider whether changes were necessary for a possible Nixon trial.

The House Judiciary Committee concluded its historic impeachment hearings in late July and voted to impeach Nixon on counts of obstructing justice, abusing power, and contempt of Congress. The full House had not yet considered the impeachment issue when, facing damning evidence and the certainty of an impeachment trial, Nixon resigned effective August 9, short-circuiting the preparations of the Rules Committee. Only a month after Ford assumed the presidency, he issued the controversial pardon that spared Nixon the ordeal of possible prosecution in civil courts following his departure from the White House.

Even though Nixon's resignation denied Cannon the opportunity to be seen on national television directing one phase of the Senate impeachment activities, the Rules Committee still had a historic role to play in the drama created by Nixon's Watergate activities: confirmation of another vice president, this time to fill the vacancy created by Ford's assumption of the presidency. The staff had barely put aside its history books on impeachment when it began its second vice presidential inquiry in a little more than a year.

Instead of the bland, broadly popular Gerald Ford, however, it would judge the qualifications of one of the most well-known figures of American business and political life, Nelson Rockefeller. Ford had selected the former New York governor, presidential candidate, and multimillionaire heir to one of America's great fortunes on August 20, less than two weeks after he assumed the presidency. It would take another four months to get Rockefeller confirmed, however, owing to the differing reactions his nomination received.

In his stewardship of the Rockefeller nomination, Cannon took a middle-of-the-road approach to the issue of Rockefeller's wealth. He never exaggerated its importance, but he did insist on a full accounting of all of Rockefeller's assets, and he allowed a full discussion of their possible impact on his role as vice president. One set of hearings in late September was followed by a break for the 1974 congressional elections, and the committee reconvened on the Rockefeller nomination on November 13. A week later, the Rules Committee voted 9-0 in favor of Rockefeller's nomination and sent it to the full Senate early in December. The Senate approved the nomination by a 90-7 vote on December 10, and the House concurred ten days later, making Rockefeller the nation's forty-first vice president.

Cannon had conducted the Senate hearings with a firm but fair hand, and reaped a fair measure of national attention in so doing. He appeared on CBS's *Face the Nation* program at the start of the hearings and on ABC's *Issues and Answers* toward the end, both firsts for him, and in countless news photographs huddling with Rockefeller or his Rules Committee colleagues. By the end of 1974, therefore, Cannon had gone a long way toward restoring his reputation in Washington, which had taken some hits from the Bobby Baker scandal and the disagreement with President Johnson over campaign-finance reform in 1966. He did it through performance, not public relations, as Cannon never made a conscious effort to win over media critics. His attitude toward the media remained consistent throughout his career: It was usually a negative force in his life and was better off left alone.

One of the more dramatic turnarounds in opinion concerning Cannon occurred through his stewardship of campaign-reform legislation in the latter half of his third term. Cannon had carried the ball for the LBJ-inspired overhaul of the federal Corrupt Practices Act from 1967 to 1971, an effort capped by Nixon's signature of the federal Election Campaign Act of 1971. Principally because of the reporting requirements in this bill—requiring names and addresses of anyone making a contribution of more than one hundred dollars—intrepid reporters were able to reveal the excesses of the Committee for the Re-election of the President (CRP, or CREEP, to critics) in Nixon's 1972 presidential campaign. Buoyed by that success, reformers pushed for even more controls in 1973.

Public financing of all federal elections also had become increasingly popular after the sordid fund-raising tactics of CRP had been exposed through the Watergate scandal. The mind-set of reformers, led by Senator Ted Kennedy, was that no restrictions could keep all tainted money out of political campaigns, so the only alternative was to have the government pay for campaigns for federal office.

These ideas competed with the more traditional reform themes of ceilings on expenditures and contributions, plus establishment of a new entity, the Federal Elections Commission (FEC), to enforce the law. The bill that emerged from Cannon's Rules Committee in July 1973 clamped down on contributions and expenditures, established the FEC, and abolished the equal-time provision. It was a comprehensive attack on campaign ethical violations that had shocked the nation, and Cannon took it to the floor for five days of debate and voting on some fifty amendments in the last week of July. Every major reform component except public financing survived the Senate debate, but, as had happened virtually since Cannon's first days in office, the House balked at the substantive reforms of the Senate bill, and no further action was taken in 1973.

As 1974 dawned, the public shocks from Agnew's forced resignation, additional Watergate revelations, and hints of impeachment made it clear that campaign reform could not long be avoided. The Rules Committee took up a comprehensive reform bill in early January and reported it on February 21. It moved to the Senate floor at the end of March, where Cannon guided it through thirteen contentious days of debate, including two cloture votes to shut off a filibuster against public financing provisions.

The bill that emerged from extensive congressional wrangling—signed by newly elevated president Gerald Ford on October 15—was a truly comprehensive campaign-reform measure. Cannon, whose first stab at campaign reform was the meek bill he led to passage in 1961—and who then balked at any limits on campaign contributions—found himself a prime mover of legislation that overhauled the entire apparatus of campaign fund-raising and reporting. The *Washington Post,* which had become the oracle of political reform with its aggressive pursuit of the Watergate story, called Cannon "instrumental in working out final compromise provisions." Common Cause, the Citizens Lobby that was also firmly in support of election reform, praised Cannon through its Nevada chapter for "the fine way [he] . . . steered the public finance bill through the Rules Committee."

As Cannon was campaigning for a fourth term in September 1976, two actions on the Senate floor illustrated how his primacy in aviation development resonated throughout both the political and the business worlds. A bill Cannon would have supported, permitting reduced airfares for the elderly and handicapped, passed the House on September 21. What caught Cannon's attention was an amendment to the bill inserted by Representative Glenn Anderson (D-CA), Cannon's counterpart as chairman of the House Aviation Subcommittee. To help a small California company called Pacific American Airlines, Anderson proposed allowing the Defense Department to award transportation contracts to unregulated airlines if there were not at least two regulated airlines willing to serve a route.

The amendment struck two hot buttons of Cannon's: airline regulation—about which he had mixed feelings—and the use of nonmilitary aircraft to support Department of Defense operations. Cannon had changed his mind about the latter concept, which as a freshman senator he strongly opposed. In fact, he had become a major force for allowing private commercial carriers to shoulder a greater portion of military air-cargo business. But it was a complicated subject, forcing Cannon to balance his concern for the economic health of commercial airlines—particularly troubled Pan American World Airways—with the prerogatives of the Defense Department. Defense had its own fleet of cargo planes consisting of the behemoth C-5As and C-41s, and Cannon didn't want to see those planes sitting idle at the expense of private carriers.

Thus, it was no surprise that Cannon moved to strike Anderson's amendment when he called up the reduced-fare bill a few days after it passed the House. His reasoning was straightforward and, from his perspective, perfectly logical: The military cargo issue had not been adequately considered by committees in either the House or the Senate, so it should not be accepted. As chairman of the Senate Aviation subcommittee, as "Mr. Aviation," and as a respected floor manager of dozens of airline and military bills, Cannon's opposition was sufficient to doom the Anderson amendment, and it was deleted by voice vote on the Senate floor. Anderson was livid over this slap at a home-state company he was trying to help.

Concerning special-interest amendments proposed by his Senate colleagues, Cannon was more conciliatory. The most dramatic of these was championed by Tennessee Republican Howard Baker, who was becoming one of the Senate's most powerful members following his principled conduct as a member of the Senate Watergate Committee. Senator Baker offered an amendment to assist an innovative air-cargo company that had begun operating a few years earlier in Memphis. The name of the company was Federal Express.

FedEx's founder, Fred Smith, had been able to launch his package-delivery business by exploiting a CAB regulatory exemption for planes with a payload capacity of seventy-five hundred pounds or less. When the business proved unexpectedly successful, Smith sought authority to apply that exemption to larger planes. FedEx was flying two small jets wing-to-wing to some of its busiest markets to meet demand for its service. True to its hidebound nature, however, the CAB refused to accommodate the FedEx request to use larger aircraft, forcing Smith to resort to political remedies. The Baker amendment would not only have solved Smith's immediate problem but also have completely deregulated the air-cargo industry. It proposed simply exempting all-cargo airlines from the regulations of the Civil Aeronautics Board.

The nexus of Cannon and Smith, brought together on an amendment offered by one of the Senate's most respected members, was one of those rare moments in U.S. business and political affairs when all the stars are aligned for a historic change. Smith's background and persona resonated particularly well with Cannon: A son of privilege who attended Yale University as an undergraduate, Smith was also an avid private pilot who had an early job as a crop duster. He joined the U.S. Marines at the height of the Vietnam War and flew more than two hundred missions as a supply pilot, a latter-day re-creation of Cannon's role as a troop-carrier pilot in World War II.

So, the FedEx amendment, offered on behalf of an appealing thirty-two-year-old entrepreneur by a respected colleague, received Cannon's approval. It was quietly inserted into the reduced-fare bill, and the amended measure was sent back to the House for final action. This was a stunning exercise in political power, as with but a few words of support for Baker's amendment,

Cannon undid decades of regulatory procedures controlling cargo airlines. With that simple agreement by the Senate's most powerful aviation expert, the cargo industry would be completely free to operate as it saw fit.

Anderson's pique over the failure of his own special-interest amendment, however, doomed the cargo deregulation provision at that time. Anderson refused to accept the reduced-fare bill without his pet provision, and the measure—along with FedEx's hopes—died at the end of the session. But the momentum created by Senate passage of a major aviation deregulation measure was unstoppable. Early in 1977, Cannon would not only revive the FedEx provision but also begin a tenacious assault on the entire structure of U.S. airline regulation.

Cannon also struck another major blow on behalf of Nevada's legal gambling industry in his third term. Following up on his successful 1971 amendment of a Nixon administration tax bill to rebate 80 percent of the federal slot-machine tax to Nevada, Cannon zeroed in on another nettlesome result of the Kefauver assault on organized crime and gambling: an occupational tax on sports-betting operators and a 10 percent tax on their gross proceeds. Like the slot-machine tax, this levy struck Nevada's gamblers as discriminatory. As they knew from personal experience, it also caused serious disruptions in their day-to-day conduct of business.

Since the margins on sports betting were thin—business was, after all, based on the predictably unpredictable world of athletic contests— operators could not simply absorb the 10 percent federal wagering tax, as it was known. As with all taxes, it was passed on to the sports-betting customers, not always in a straightforward way. Here's how one veteran of the Las Vegas sports-betting world described practices in the industry: "For example, if you were a regular customer and went to the window to bet $1,100 to win $1,000 on a football game, the guy might write the ticket for $11 to win $10. It was between you and him, you see, and that way the tax was on only $11, not $1,100. The eleven bucks was all that went through the machine." Even a mainstream publication such as *Sports Illustrated* recognized the illogic of this situation, commenting in a 1961 article, "It is estimated that 95% of all wagering on sports in Las Vegas is done sub rosa, or man to man, to avoid the tax, and that if the government were more tolerant and reasonable business at the sports books would be up 1000%."

Already struggling with this difficulty, sports-betting operators in Nevada were shocked when the federal government proposed in 1969 to not only extend the 10 percent wagering tax to wagers not covered by the initial law but also to increase the occupational tax on sports-betting employees from fifty dollars to one thousand dollars a year, a 1,900 percent increase. "If this bill passes, it will bankrupt the legal books in Nevada," one of the northern Nevada operators wired Cannon.

As they had on the cabaret and slot-machine taxes, Cannon and Bible teamed up to derail the 1969 bill. They authored separate amendments to not only get around the occupational tax increase but to eliminate the 10 percent wagering tax altogether. As was the case with the other taxes, it took a while before the Bible-Cannon assault achieved its goal. A tariff measure passed by the House in late 1973 to suspend or end import duties on a variety of products provided the opening they needed. When the bill made its way to the Senate floor in August 1974, Cannon worked his magic once again. After securing the requisite support from Finance Committee chairman Russell Long, Cannon offered an amendment to exempt the legal sports-betting houses in Nevada from the 10 percent tax. It was accepted by voice vote.

In the inevitable compromise with the House, which historically berated the "Christmas tree" tax provisions added to their simple revenue measures by the Senate (the Constitution states that all revenue measures must initiate in the House), the Cannon amendment was changed somewhat: Instead of exempting Nevada sports books from the wagering tax, it lowered the tax from 10 percent to 2 percent and increased the occupational tax from fifty dollars per employee per year to five hundred dollars. It was a deal the sports books could easily accept, especially considering there were only eleven of them in operation in 1969 and the employee base was small. "Even at 2% it was feasible for a well-run sports book to make money without having to engage in creative bookkeeping," one account noted, and history bears him out. By 1999, the number of sports books in Nevada had increased from eleven under the 10 percent tax regimen to seventy-five, with a total of $2.75 billion wagered. Instead of the seedy "turf clubs" of the 1950s and '60s, today's sports-betting establishments are lavish monuments to America's love of gambling on everything from horse races to college and professional team sports.

Cannon's position in the Senate toward the end of his third term was impressive, and it undoubtedly played a large role in his relatively easy 1976 reelection. Laxalt had been elected to succeed Bible in the Senate by a razor-thin margin over popular Nevada lieutenant governor Harry Reid in 1974, making Nevada the only state in which Republicans won a Senate seat following Watergate, and Nevada Republicans faced a talent shortage in opposing Cannon. Their candidate was a one-term congressman named David Towell, who had been defeated for reelection to the House in 1974 by one of Nevada's rising Democratic stars, Jim Santini. A former real estate broker from the small northern Nevada town of Minden, Towell was not considered a major threat to Cannon. He was elected only after Democrats defeated Representative Baring in a bitter primary battle, and thus benefited from the intraparty rivalry. Aside from the humorous aspects of a "Cannon-Towell" race, the election created little drama, and Cannon cruised to victory.

Sun columnist Alan Jarlson summed up Cannon's rising stature in early 1975, noting that Cannon had carved a place for himself in history as "the man who made a president, a vice president and now a fellow US senator." Jarlson was referring to Cannon's role in the nominations of Ford and Rockefeller and his hand in deciding a disputed New Hampshire Senate race between Republican Louis Wyman and Democrat John Durkin. After Wyman and Durkin virtually deadlocked in 1974 (only two votes separated them), Cannon tested his theory espoused during the 1964 battle with Laxalt that the Senate had the power of deciding its own membership in cases of contested elections. It was not a pleasant exercise, and after months of indecisive hearings, Senate floor debates, and a Republican-led filibuster, the Senate in 1975 declared the seat vacant, and another election was held. Democrat Durkin prevailed in that second contest.

Notwithstanding the rather murky outcome of the Wyman-Durkin contest, Jarlson's analysis was that Cannon had joined the "giants who have ventured forth from [Nevada's] desert climes" to "cast long shadows over the affairs of our nation." This mentioning of Cannon in the same breath as Pat McCarran and Key Pittman was interesting not only because it was the first time such a comparison was made in print but also because it occurred through Cannon's performance on the relatively insignificant Senate Rules Committee. A closer analysis of Cannon's efforts on the Armed Services Committee to maintain the nation's supremacy in tactical airpower, or of his efforts to develop the commercial aviation infrastructure through his role as chairman of the Senate Aviation Subcommittee, might have revealed some of his more substantive accomplishments. But the public's perception of what makes an elected official valuable is often colored by unexpected events that capture its fleeting attention. If it took stewardship of the Ford and Rockefeller nominations to elevate Cannon in Nevada's opinion, he would not argue.

The fact was that as 1976 drew to a close, Cannon had received his second consecutive overwhelming victory, was well respected among his colleagues, and could look forward to having a Democrat in the White House for the first time since 1968 following the election of President Jimmy Carter. Elevated to the status of "Senior Senator" by Bible's resignation, a healthy, energetic Cannon headed back to Washington for the Ninety-fifth Congress with optimism and ranking fifteenth among the one hundred senators in seniority.

CHAPTER 7

The Barriers Fall

"The dynamic of deregulation had an awful lot of points where if you'd pulled a certain person out or put a different attitude in, it probably would have taken much longer and wouldn't have been nearly as dramatic as it was," recalled Charles M. "Chip" Barclay, one of the closest observers of the march to deregulation of the U.S. airline industry. "But one of those key points, that if you pulled out, would have been Cannon's decision [to support it]," Barclay added. "It would have been decades before deregulation had happened" without that decision.

Barclay's recollection is an excellent prism through which to view the airline deregulation story, because he was both a close adviser to Cannon and something of an outsider. A former small-communities expert at the Civil Aeronautics Board, Barclay was brought to the staff of Cannon's Senate Aviation Subcommittee in mid-1977 to help out with the politics of deregulation. One of the key obstacles to winning congressional support for any loosening of airline regulation would be mollifying representatives of small communities, who believed these areas would not be served unless government required airlines to do so. It would be Barclay's job to assure these representatives that regulatory reform or deregulation did not necessarily mean abandonment of small communities.

As a relative latecomer to airline politics in the Senate, Barclay regarded Cannon as many in the nation's capital did: as someone who might acquiesce to a lessening of regulation, but not much more. "People thought Cannon might do a little bit of tweaking, but he was known as an ally of the industry," Barclay said, representing the conventional wisdom surrounding the issue.

Cannon would prove conventional wisdom wrong, as he waged an uphill fight against most major airlines, their unions, the trade associations representing various factions of the aviation industry, and a cautious House of Representatives to forge a landmark airline-deregulation act. What Barclay and others who did not know Cannon well failed to realize was Cannon's personal disillusionment with the CAB and his ability to change an entrenched position as conditions required. That the CAB was a hidebound, unimaginative body was not news to Cannon, who could recall its arcane reasoning from his early days as Las Vegas city attorney trying to win the body's approval for competitive service between Las Vegas and Los Angeles. The CAB's requirement that two other airlines flying that route besides Western Air Lines not pick up or drop off passengers when landing in Las Vegas—to protect Western's monopoly service between the cities—was one of his earliest introductions to the rigidity of federal bureaucrats.

In addition, he had butted heads with the CAB countless times as Las Vegas, Reno, and other Nevada cities petitioned for additional carriers, lower fares, or other improvements in airline service. The ten-year effort to convince the CAB to permit service between Texas and Las Vegas epitomized Cannon's frustrating run-ins with the agency. After all that time and countless petitions, hearings, and personal lobbying, the board agreed to allow one carrier to serve the route.

But Cannon was slow to accept the idea of radically changing the rules of airline regulation, and his close association with the industry was undoubtedly one of the reasons. Despite the success of upstarts such as Pacific Southwest Airlines in California and Southwest Airlines in Texas, which had vast markets to exploit without incurring CAB regulation by crossing state lines, the regulated carriers abhorred the idea of eliminating regulation. This was no surprise, as the CAB's rationale for determining fare prices was providing the carriers a 12 percent rate of return. Along with that came almost certain protection against new competitors—the CAB had not allowed a new "trunk" carrier since it was established as the Civil Aeronautics Authority in 1938. Indeed, when charter operator World Airways applied in 1967 to offer scheduled low-cost service between New York and Los Angeles, the CAB studied the request for six and a half years, then dismissed it because the application was "stale."

Thus, the airline executives who lobbied Cannon constantly on various issues would unanimously caution him against tinkering with the existing system, even though they themselves were often driven crazy by the rules. Many a time, for instance, TWA or United or American would like to add a potentially lucrative route to their systems or abandon ones that were not making money. But the CAB's rigidity extended to these requests as well, as Cannon's experience in winning increased service to Las Vegas taught him. It would be a fair assessment to say that the heads of the major carriers would have liked the regulatory environment to soften regarding adding or dropping routes but to remain inflexible concerning additional competitors on their turf or lowering fare prices. Their concerns, like the CAB's, were completely inward-looking, with little thought to what the traveling public might like.

A situation so rife with inequities cried out for remedy, and Congress was the likely forum for concocting one. If Cannon were too cautious to act boldly, however, there was little chance that someone else in the Senate would. He was, after all, "Mr. Aviation," chairman of the Aviation Subcommittee, and chairman of the Rules Committee. The latter position insulated Cannon from challenge, as through it he controlled not only the routine allocations of office space and other building perks but also the budgets of all Senate committees. If a revolt against the CAB were going to be launched by another committee, for instance, that committee would have to petition the Rules Committee for funds to launch an investigation.

Given this situation, it took a senator with an outsized personality and a large ego to assault the airline regulation fortress. There was such a person in the Senate, and it was Cannon's ally in the election-reform fight, Senator Ted Kennedy. Kennedy, the handsome, charismatic bearer of the Kennedy political legacy, sniffed out the issue of airline deregulation as a potentially popular issue in 1974. Kennedy had multiple reasons to champion a popular cause, not the least of which was his need to remain viable as a presidential candidate and, hand in hand with that goal, solidify his place in the Senate. Chagrined by Senator Robert Byrd's victory over him as majority whip in 1971, embarrassed by news accounts of his playboy conduct, and haunted by the specter of Chappaquiddick, Kennedy in the mid-1970s was searching for gravitas and hungry for public acclaim. Although the cancer that struck his son Teddy at the end of 1973 caused Kennedy to turn down overtures to seek the 1976 Democratic presidential nomination, the White House was never far from his mind. With these currents surrounding him and the resolutely clueless CAB creating a target of opportunity, Kennedy was poised to take on the aviation bureaucracy.

For someone of Kennedy's ambition and temperament, the normal constraints of Senate decorum would not present an obstacle to pursuing a course for which he had neither experience nor proper legislative jurisdiction. Lacking either a major committee chairmanship or membership on the Senate Commerce Committee, Kennedy turned to the one legislative outpost from which he could conceivably launch his assault—the Subcommittee on Administrative Practice and Procedure of the Senate Judiciary Committee. This subcommittee's rather amorphous provenance had allowed Kennedy to hold hearings on high-profile issues ranging from the draft to Watergate, and his aides on the committee saw the actions of the CAB as clearly falling within the scope of "administrative practice and procedure."

To tighten the focus on regulation, Kennedy in mid-1974 called on a Harvard Law School professor teaching administrative law to join him for dinner at his McLean, Virginia, home to discuss the situation. True to Kennedy's reputation for attracting the best and brightest minds to assist him in legislative endeavors, the professor was Stephen G. Breyer, currently an associate justice of the U.S. Supreme Court. At the time, Breyer had only a sterling résumé and some Senate experience to recommend him. A San Francisco native, he possessed Stanford and Oxford undergraduate degrees, a Harvard law degree, a Supreme Court clerkship, and Justice Department and Senate Watergate Committee experience. Kennedy hired him in August 1974, and Breyer turned his considerable intellect on the CAB.

As Barclay's comment about the many threads of the deregulation tapestry indicates, Kennedy was not a lone voice decrying CAB policies. The agency's nominal boss, President Ford himself, had been a longtime believer in minimal federal regulation. In a sense, activities by these two parties in 1974 and '75 constituted a race to claim the high ground, with Cannon reduced to bystander. Breyer decided to concentrate on the charter-airline segment of aviation initially, not surprising since it was the latest example of the CAB's blindness about low-cost flying.

Although the CAB had flirted with discounted rates in the 1960s—the youth standby fare was the most notable example—charter airlines were a lone bastion of economical air travel in the mid-1970s. One of the most popular of their offerings was "affinity charters," in which groups such as schoolteachers or firemen could get lower rates by flying as a group. These were accounting for 40 percent of domestic traffic, 54 percent of international travel, and 80 percent of the business of supplemental (nonscheduled) airlines. Out of concern for one of its cherished trunk airlines, struggling Pan Am, the CAB proposed in September 1974 that transatlantic charter carriers *raise* their fares to eliminate a competitive threat to the trunks. This would undoubtedly help Pan Am, while passengers and the charter airlines, the CAB apparently thought, could fend for themselves. The CAB followed up its recommendations the next month by announcing that it would force charter rates up and, as if that were not enough, make it harder for the charter airlines to offer affinity-group charters. Breyer must have thought the agency was conspiring to offer Kennedy an opening, so the Administrative Practice and Procedure Subcommittee opened hearings on the charter situation on November 7, 1974.

The most concrete result of these initial hearings was testimony by a Justice Department official that the CAB had violated the law by setting minimum charter rates, and that the Ford administration now opposed them. With that victory in hand, Breyer and Kennedy wrapped up the charter hearings and promptly announced they would hold further hearings on the broader issue of airline regulation early in 1975. In doing so, Kennedy observed the letter if not the spirit of the "law" of committee jurisdiction. Speaking of his committee's intention on the Senate floor in December 1974, Kennedy spoke repeatedly of his subcommittee's authority to examine CAB procedures. According to Kennedy biographer Adam Clymer, Kennedy used the word *procedures* thirteen times in less than fifteen minutes.

There is much Washington lore about Cannon's alleged displeasure with Kennedy because of Kennedy's bold steps in examining the CAB's regulatory procedures, but Breyer plays it down. Admittedly, Breyer operated from a more remote intellectual plane than the politically attuned Senate staffers, but he offers one piece of evidence to disprove the idea of anti-Kennedy animus on Cannon's part. It had to do with the mundane matter of funding for "ADPRAC's" proposed hearings, using Breyer's verbal shorthand for the Administrative Practice and Procedure panel. "We wanted $30,000 to pay for the hearings," Breyer recalled nearly thirty years later from his seat on the Supreme Court. "Cannon [as chairman of the Rules Committee] approved it. He wouldn't do that if he opposed the hearings, would he?" Breyer asked.

It was not as if Cannon were asleep during these early stirrings of regulatory reform, as he had particular reason to chafe over the CAB's dismantling of charter programs. One of the prime destinations of foreign charter flights was glamorous Las Vegas, and tourism officials there welcomed these visitors eagerly. Cannon was a well-known champion of such innovations as affinity charters, and he was not blind to the CAB's inattention to consumer concerns either. In a December 1974 speech of his own, Cannon told his Senate colleagues, "Never in my memory have we had a Civil Aeronautics Board so callous to the needs of the public."

The issue simmered but did not reach a boil in either 1975 or 1976. The Ford administration issued a position paper in October 1975 calling for major reforms, but legislation from sources including the president, Kennedy, and even the CAB did not reach the hearing stage until April 1976. Cannon conducted those hearings within his Aviation Subcommittee, but two major obstacles prevented progress. One was the Democrats' reluctance to help out President Ford with legislation in an election year in which he was considered vulnerable. And another was a fact that many who berate Cannon for acting too slowly on airline deregulation fail to appreciate: The chairman of the full Commerce Committee, Senator Warren Magnuson of Washington, was adamantly opposed to deregulation—partly out of fear that disruption in the aviation business would adversely affect Boeing Aerospace, located near Seattle. Not having his chairman on board would have made it difficult for Cannon to act aggressively in 1976 even if other factors did not do so.

Cannon had his own reelection campaign to contend with in 1976, and even though David Towell did not inspire great fear, Cannon never took an election for granted. That meant he spent as much time in Nevada as possible, and he would have neither time nor inclination to focus on an issue that took as much attention as airline deregulation. His action on the cargo deregulation amendment in September 1976 showed he was anything but an outright opponent of sweeping change, however, and presaged his aggressive pursuit of the broader issue in 1977. It was then that the considerable Cannon strengths as a legislator showed themselves and the tide began to turn in favor of a new day for aviation in the United States.

As Cannon returned to Washington for the Ninety-fifth Congress in 1977, the major change in the deregulation dynamic was the replacement of Gerald Ford by Jimmy Carter in the White House. This was no small matter, as Carter proved not only as committed to airline deregulation on paper as Ford but willing to risk political capital to achieve it. Moreover, the Democratic staffers on the Commerce Committee were more disposed to aid a Democratic president achieve legislative success than a Republican one.

But there was still a major obstacle to action on significant aviation regulatory reform—Magnuson's considerable negative presence as committee chairman. As long as Magnuson remained opposed to significant reform, Cannon would face an uphill battle in getting legislation to the Senate floor. Cannon was strongly in command of his Aviation Subcommittee, but even an overwhelming endorsement by that panel did not translate into success on the committee level if the chairman—particularly one as formidable as Magnuson—remained opposed. "Maggie," as he was known, was a Senate "whale," as the term for entrenched, powerful members was understood. He had served in Congress since 1944, making him the third-ranking senator in terms of seniority in 1977. He was also second in seniority on the powerful Appropriations Committee and chaired its subcommittee that approved funding for labor, health, education, and welfare programs. Senators with an interest in appropriations for these programs—staples of Democratic domestic policy—would not cross him lightly.

Given the conventional wisdom that Cannon was an ally of the airlines, Magnuson's position as chairman of Commerce gave the established carriers comfort that the flawed but profitable regulatory regime would stay in place. Even the considerable ferment that Kennedy had created through his hearings did not count for much in the political calculations that mattered in the Senate—jurisdiction, seniority, and clout. This was the status quo as Barclay came on the scene in 1977, and he described the insiders' appraisal of a possible showdown between Cannon and Kennedy this way: "Everybody thought Cannon was just going to crush him" because of his chairmanship of the Aviation Subcommittee and his legislative success and acclaim as chairman of the Rules Committee.

As it turned out, Cannon did not want to crush Kennedy. Whether perturbed by Kennedy's encroachment on his turf or not, he did not harbor a grudge that would doom further progress on aviation reform. Cannon was, at bottom, a remarkably practical man, largely unaffected by the extremes of passionate feeling. Overcoming whatever rancor Kennedy's tactics had incurred was his realization that Kennedy had helped move the public toward a more receptive attitude concerning regulatory reform, plus given nascent reformers within the CAB bureaucracy itself hope for a better day. Moving the Senate in that direction—particularly the members of the Commerce Committee—was Cannon's job. It was a job that Kennedy, for all his charisma and publicity-garnering ability, was unsuited for. He did not serve on Commerce and had no allies on that middle-of-the-road body who could act as surrogates for him.

Cannon's strategy, if mostly instinctual behavior can be called strategy, was to move slowly on the issue, allowing the logic of regulatory reform to prevail over the considerable fears of his fellow committee members. Cannon was shrewd enough to realize that the obstinacy of the CAB made the best case for relieving the body of its authority over a major segment of the U.S. economy, so he allowed that side of the agency to be highlighted in hearings opened in March 1977. As an added bonus, Cannon had on the committee a perfect foil for the hopeful surge of reform that Kennedy's efforts had unleashed: the unyielding Maggie, who planted himself squarely in the way of significant progress. As witness after witness made the compelling case for taking airline matters out of the hands of a body that had managed to guarantee that most flights in the United States would be about half-full, and then set fares high enough to allow the airlines their 12 percent rate of return, Maggie remained unmoved. There is nothing like sharp contrast to illuminate what could have been a murky public-policy issue, and the contrast between reformers and the gruff, rotund, unyielding Magnuson was as sharp as anyone could ask.

Lack of support for reform from Cannon's fellow committee members necessitated an extraordinary number of hearings, followed by an even longer series of "markups," where bills are usually given final tweaking before moving on to the full Senate. The initial stage comprised fourteen days of hearings during March and April, where the unfamiliar language of regulatory reform was drummed into the heads of those members who bothered to attend: automatic market entry, which would replace CAB prohibition of expansion with specified procedures for allowing existing airlines to add new routes to their systems; a "zone of reasonableness" for fares to rise above or fall below existing fares without CAB approval; and a new CAB policy geared toward granting permission for new airlines to begin service. As Cannon's committee pointed out, the CAB had received seventy-nine applications for new service between 1950 and 1974 and granted none.

With a compelling record in favor of overhauling the CAB compiled during those initial fourteen days of hearings, Cannon and his staff took a time-out to draft a new compromise measure. The new bill was designed to address many of the concerns expressed by committee members, particularly concerning small-community service and protection of employees who might be fired as a result of new competitive pressures. Despite all the economic evidence that regulatory reform would revolutionize air travel in the United States, most Commerce Committee members remained focused on these mundane political concerns. This new draft was unveiled in June 1977, and Cannon pushed for markups to reconcile remaining concerns and get the bill on the Senate floor. What transpired was probably unparalleled in Senate legislative annals: No fewer than twenty markup sessions were required before the committee finally voted 11-2 in favor of Cannon's revised bill on October 27, 1977.

The entire hearing process was remarkable for the lack of enthusiasm for the bill under consideration, but the markups brought the conflict between Cannon and the rest of the committee, particularly Magnuson, into full view of the Washington establishment. *Congressional Quarterly,* providing thorough, unbiased coverage of the process, noted the emerging dynamic in its understated manner. "Senate Aviation Subcommittee Chairman Howard W. Cannon (D-Nev.), the only clear champion of the deregulation movement on the Commerce Committee, was forced to compromise repeatedly during the markups," the publication noted. "One of the most reluctant members was Magnuson, who frequently questioned provisions in the bill, as well as Cannon's contention that it would lead to lower fares. As chairman,

Magnuson controlled the markups and resisted Cannon's attempts to speed up the process."

What had moved Cannon from a perceived position as "an ally of the industry" to "the only clear champion of the deregulation movement"? One answer was that Cannon's public persona masked his true intentions, a fact that was true throughout his political career. Cannon made no effort to influence what outsiders thought about his state of mind. He was the ultimate poker player on public-policy issues, hoarding his own cards and giving away nothing concerning his leanings and intentions. Central to this ability was his lack of concern over what others thought of him. Cannon was an odd combination of prickliness over perceived slights by the media, colleagues, or others who did not know him well and stubbornness in refusing to bend his actions to popular will. If, in his own mind, he was doing the right thing on a particular issue, he didn't see the need to explain his actions to anyone else. At the same time, he would become greatly irritated when someone misjudged him or excoriated him based on a false impression of what he believed. It was an interesting combination of characteristics.

Concerning airline deregulation, the opinion of so-called Washington insiders that Cannon was co-opted by the airline industry was an example of this misperception. Cannon was certainly close to many in the aviation community, and listened with respect to their fears about unbridled competition. But many made the cynical judgment that because Cannon was close to airline executives, he was also in their pocket. On this, they were clearly wrong.

Another misconception about Cannon, perhaps held by no one else besides Magnuson, was that he would be cowed or discouraged by stubborn behavior. Magnuson's strategy in delaying the markups on airline regulatory reform was a combination of attrition and intimidation. He apparently believed that if he strung out the hearings long enough, Cannon would give up and move on to something else. But one attribute Cannon had shown since his early days sitting through interminable sessions of the Las Vegas City Commission was what might be called "iron butt." He could listen to mind-deadening testimony until the last person was standing, seldom displaying impatience or fatigue. If Magnuson was trying to outlast Cannon, he was using the wrong tactic.

Nor was Cannon intimidated by Magnuson's formidable reputation. Leaving the Aviation Subcommittee hearing room day after day following another seemingly unending markup, he was the picture of a busy, engaged senator. I would sometimes accompany him on his walk from the hearing room several corridors removed from his private office in suite 259, using the time to pass along messages or get his approval for various projects. I had to hustle to keep up with his brisk pace as he rushed through the venerable halls of the Russell Building, which contained most of Cannon's official life: the hearing room for the Aviation Subcommittee and the Armed Services Committee offices, both on the second floor, and, on the third floor, the Rules Committee offices. Cannon hummed an unfamiliar tune as he quickstepped along the corridors, perhaps one of those 1930s-era numbers played by the Lumberjack Collegians, but he would respond quickly to my questions. If he was harboring any fear about what Senator Magnuson's opposition might portend for his career, he was keeping it a secret.

One Aviation Subcommittee staff member who worked closely with Cannon on the deregulation bill averred that Cannon had an epiphany sometime during the 1977 hearings. Robert Ginther was a former Seattle television newsman who came to Washington to work for Magnuson and ended up in charge of the subcommittee staff, reporting to Cannon. Ginther was a valuable ally of Cannon's in the deregulation effort because, although personally loyal to Magnuson, he was a proponent of deregulation. He served, therefore, as a bridge between the two powerful personalities who came to symbolize the opposing poles in the deregulation debate.

Barclay, Ginther's fellow staffer brought aboard to massage the small-communities issue, recalls Ginther telling him of Cannon's conversion to deregulation advocate. "After the [first round of] hearings, I remember Ginther saying that the boss, Cannon, is going off to play golf and think about the whole thing," Barclay recalled. "And, lo and behold, Cannon comes back after a weekend of golf in Vegas and says, 'We're going to do this.'" Explaining Cannon's renewed dedication, Barclay could only make a supposition because, true to his nature, Cannon didn't share his thinking with the staff. "I think that Cannon had the same kind of catharsis that most people go through if you really sit down and think about it," Barclay surmised. "Maybe there was a reason to regulate airlines in the earliest days, but once they were mature, you've got this totally mobile resource that can be moved instantly where the marketplace wants it. So why do we have five people in Washington deciding the prices and service for seventy thousand domestic markets?"

If Cannon was convinced after his Las Vegas golfing hiatus, the same could not be said for his colleagues on the Commerce Committee. The marathon series of markups was a trial of Cannon's patience and his deal-making prowess, and also a perfect illustration of how great a leap he had made in embracing the deregulation rationale. Barclay called the new bill fashioned by Cannon and his staff after the initial round of hearings a "radical" proposal, and anyone who witnessed the timorousness and apprehension of Cannon's fellow senators would have to agree.

Perhaps the best example was the automatic-entry provision that was intended to end the CAB's practice of denying existing carriers the opportunity to serve new markets. Cannon grasped from the outset of the hearings that automatic entry was the key to allowing the airlines some flexibility to raise or lower fares. He patiently explained that a company with a monopoly on a certain route could raise fares without justification if it didn't face the threat of another airline competing with it. Instead of recognizing the logic of this position, many committee members claimed automatic entry would cause chaos, reflecting the line handed down by the protected airlines themselves. So Cannon began casting about for a compromise that would allow all airlines some automatic entry but provide some advantages to small carriers least able to withstand competition.

Whereas that approach might appease some members, it concerned others, particularly Republican senator John Danforth of Missouri, home of TWA. Danforth was under more pressure from antideregulation forces than perhaps any other member of the committee. But he was also a thoughtful, principled man who consistently sought solutions to deregulation hurdles rather than additional roadblocks. To appease TWA, Danforth wanted automatic entry and route protection equal for all airlines, with no special concessions for smaller carriers. Cannon gulped and then swallowed Danforth's proposal, presenting it to the committee on August 4. He optimistically hoped for a vote on the issue before Congress adjourned for its August recess and members would scatter to their home states where antideregulation lobbyists could harangue them outside the Washington deal-making atmosphere.

His hopes were dashed as the Cannon-Danforth compromise stirred up even more apprehension. Perhaps the most bizarre suggestion came from Democrat John Melcher of Montana and Republican Ted Stevens of Alaska, who argued that the CAB, of all entities, should draft the automatic-entry provision. Wrangles over this and other suggestions caused the committee to adjourn for the August recess without the crucial automatic-entry provision settled.

It was late September before Cannon, still suffering under Magnuson's foot-dragging, could corral the recalcitrant Commerce members for another hearing. Just as his instincts told him, the delay proved injurious to the deregulation cause, as a devastating suggestion from a powerful Senate source awaited them. Democratic senator Daniel Inouye of Hawaii, who was gaining prestige as a potential future Senate majority leader, proposed to drop all automatic-entry provisions from the bill. For the first time, Cannon lost his temper, angrily denounced Inouye's proposal, and urged the committee to finish marking up the bill. "This bill has pretty nearly been studied and debated to death," he said. Dropping his diplomatic demeanor, Cannon said the Inouye proposal would "gut" the bill and lambasted arguments against automatic entry as "pure nonsense." Perhaps seeing Cannon aroused in defense of a key deregulatory principle emboldened undecided committee members, because on a showdown over the Inouye proposal, they turned it down by a vote of 13-5. That cleared the way for a similarly one-sided vote in approval of the Cannon-Danforth compromise on automatic entry.

Defeating the most damaging of the antideregulation measures was undoubtedly a turning point in the Commerce Committee's consideration of airline deregulation, but there were still major hurdles ahead. On one of these dealing with applications for new routes, Cannon revealed one of his key legislative philosophies: Keep the bill moving forward no matter what. Melcher was again the protagonist, objecting to a policy clause in the bill that stated the CAB need only decide that a proposed new service was "consistent" with public service and necessity. Seemingly innocuous, this was actually a dramatic reversal of one of the principles the CAB had used to block new applicants in the past. That principle was that a potential new carrier had to show that its service was "required" for public convenience and necessity. In addition, Cannon's bill shifted the burden of responsibility for proving a case for or against a new route application from the applicant to an airline opposing the application. This was, indeed, a radically procompetitive idea, and Melcher, admittedly influenced by airline lobbyists, objected to it.

Although Cannon's effort to free cargo carriers from regulation had failed due to the intransigence of Representative Anderson, Cannon had not forgotten the story of FedEx. In appealing to his colleagues to accept the principles of automatic entry and fare flexibility, Cannon could readily recall the example of this principle that FedEx represented.

But the same could not be said for his colleagues on the Commerce Committee. Although his amendment to keep the burden of proof on new applicants was defeated on an 8-8 tie vote, Melcher, a temperamental first-term senator who could be as stubborn as the Montana cattlemen he represented, vowed to fight on. Cannon, at the end of his considerable patience after six months of hearings, responded that he was "not interested in engaging in a filibuster on this bill." He agreed to accept Melcher's amendment, and the committee went along, paving the way for a final vote to report the Cannon bill to the Senate floor. Melcher and Inouye cast the only two votes against it.

His frustration in not winning more support from the Commerce Committee found a release in a renewed push for cargo deregulation. Working its way through Congress during the same period that the airline regulatory reform bill was before the Commerce Committee was an innocuous bill dealing with an aviation insurance program. Approved by the House in May, it was amended by Cannon to include the provision freeing cargo airlines from CAB regulation. This time the House approved the concept, and the amended bill was cleared for the president's signature by early November. FedEx received its lifeline to expand on November 9, 1977, and the rest, as the saying goes, is history.

Exasperation was certainly part of Cannon's motivation for accepting Melcher's weakening amendment, but what also induced him to concede was his vast experience in steering bills to passage on the Senate floor. Cannon had learned that bringing a bill to Senate passage and eventually to the president for signature was a series of bargaining sessions and deal-making. Committee consideration was one stage for compromise, the Senate floor was another, and the conference committee was still another. Unlike Melcher, Danforth, Stevens, and other deregulation fainthearts, Cannon was a veteran of these pit stops and was confident of his ability to navigate them successfully. He may not have known at the precise moment that he accepted Melcher's amendment that he could strengthen the bill along the way to enactment, but, as events proved out, he had the desire and legislative skill to do it.

By the time the committee-passed bill, s2493, the Air Transportation Regulatory Reform Act of 1978, reached the Senate floor in April 1978—slightly more than a year after the initial hearings began—Cannon had received one additional boost in his ability to deliver it to President Carter's eager pen: chairmanship of the full Commerce Committee. The inexorable processes of death and the Senate seniority system were responsible, as elderly Arkansas Democrat John McClellan died on November 27, 1977, leaving the chairmanship of the all-powerful Appropriations Committee open. Magnuson was next in line for the post, and he eventually succumbed to the lure of controlling the federal purse strings. Senate rules prevented Maggie from holding both the Appropriations Committee chairmanship and that of the Commerce Committee, so Cannon assumed the Commerce chairmanship in early 1978. It was a masterful feat of diplomacy for Cannon to maneuver around Magnuson and win Commerce Committee support for the airline bill, but he would not face any such challenges in managing it in the Senate. The charge to Senate passage would be led by "Chairman Cannon."

Although it was somewhat overshadowed by the attention paid to airline deregulation, Cannon's rise to the chairmanship of the Commerce Committee was a significant milestone. Commerce is one of the Senate's major committees, those such as Appropriations, Judiciary, and Armed Services that control legislation touching broad segments of American life. Under Commerce's purview came not only transportation issues such as regulation but also the broadcast industry, consumer issues, and telecommunications. Because Commerce passed on nominees for positions on the Federal Communications Commission, the Interstate Commerce Commission (ICC), the Federal Trade Commission, and others, it was a vital force in many segments of U.S. business. Although Cannon would give up his role as chairman of the Rules Committee in exchange for the Commerce post, it was an exchange he was glad to make. Cannon had achieved some major successes on the Rules Committee, but it had also been a sore point because of the constant wrangles over election-reform legislation and the touchy issue of financial disclosure.

Cannon's handling of the airline deregulation measure was the clearest example of his legislative prowess. He left nothing to chance, carefully considering the concerns of any senator who had qualms about the bill and finding a solution if possible. He also demanded a comprehensive hearing process, which produced a record no one could assail for incompleteness. All arguments for and against particular provisions had been well vented in the

Commerce Committee, so no surprises were waiting when the bill moved to the floor. And he demonstrated—as he had on any number of earlier occasions—an uncanny feel for his colleagues' mood. By the time Cannon went to the Senate floor to seek a vote, he felt confident he would succeed.

Because of these facts, the Air Transportation Regulatory Reform Act had easy going in the Senate, contrary to its rocky journey through the Commerce Committee. On the major compromise Cannon had accepted in committee, weakening of the automatic-entry provision, Cannon had a weapon far more powerful than Melcher. Senator Kennedy offered an amendment to revert to the more procompetitive position of requiring opponents of new airline service to prove that the service was not in the public interest, and Cannon gave his full support. This was a compelling combination for the vast majority of senators who knew little about the specifics of the airline bill: Kennedy's image as a liberal reformer was tempered by support from the more conservative Cannon. It had worked before as Cannon managed the election-reform bill with its bold proposal for public financing of federal elections—a Kennedy idea—to Senate passage, and it worked on the airline bill. Kennedy's amendment, restoring the bill to the state that Cannon favored, passed easily, 69-23, and the full bill was passed shortly after by an even larger margin, 83-9.

Interestingly enough, Cannon never referred to the measure as an "airline deregulation bill," but chose to use the softer term of "regulatory reform." This was politically wise, as *deregulation* had become a buzzword, and, by eschewing it, Cannon assumed the stance as an objective outsider detached from the fashionable reform crowd. He knew that success in winning Senate approval of his bill depended on support from the large percentage of conservative-to-moderate members of the Senate, and tossing around the scary term *deregulation* would hurt that goal.

It was also factually correct, because, for all its far-reaching reforms, there was one element of the bill as it passed the Senate that kept it from being a true deregulation measure: It kept the CAB in place and depended on new policy language and numerous specific directives to drag that agency into a procompetitive mind-set. There was every reason to believe this would happen, particularly since President Carter had named the forward-thinking Alfred Kahn to head the CAB. Kahn, a respected economist, had been the leading voice from within the CAB arguing for pricing flexibility and competition. But regulatory reform was not deregulation, and s2493 as it passed the Senate was more accurately the former than the latter. It might have remained that way if not for unwitting actions by deregulation opponents in the House of Representatives.

At first blush, House consideration of the airline reform bill was disastrous. If nothing else, it provided ample evidence for Barclay's assertion that without Cannon, deregulation would have been delayed for a long time. The key moment when a mild reform measure came undone was in March 1978, when Representative Elliott Levitas (D-GA) offered a substitute bill to the one the House Aviation Subcommittee had been marking up. As *Congressional Quarterly* reported, "The Levitas proposal lacked almost all deregulation provisions," and its approval "stunned" subcommittee chairman Glenn Anderson, who had opposed Cannon on the air-cargo deregulation measure but was working effectively to achieve some measure of reform.

Levitas, who hailed from the home state of Delta Airlines, was known among deregulation proponents as a "Deltacrat" for his unwavering allegiance to the carrier. Therefore, his action did not surprise followers of the legislative process. As the Carter administration lamented the Levitas measure, Cannon and his staff picked up on one appealing aspect of it. Levitas was enamored of the then fashionable concept of "sunset legislation," whereby federal agencies were given a set period of time to prove their usefulness before being "sunsetted"—or put out of business. Levitas applied the sunset concept to the CAB, abolishing it as of December 31, 1983. This was a golden opportunity for Cannon to shore up his bill in the only key area where it fell below true deregulation status. Barclay describes the reaction from his wily boss as Levitas ventured down a path he thought would be amenable to the powers at Delta Airlines: "By the time this thing gets into conference, Cannon says, 'Let's use the House's provision against them. Let's say we accept your provision.' So they sunset routes first, then rate protection and then the whole board. I don't think, frankly, that Cannon thought you'd ever get rid of the whole board, but that was eventually what wound up happening," Barclay recounted.

Cannon's strategy relied on his ability to convince House conferees to accept the true reform provisions of his bill rather than their own, and that happened as well. "Both the automatic entry program and the program to ease the granting of new service on routes where there was unused authority had been bitterly fought by the House Public Works Committee, but were strengthened in conference," reported *Congressional Quarterly.* It was a total rout for Cannon, the man who Washington insiders predicted would not dare to shake up the airline regulatory status quo. By the time President Carter signed the bill into law, he had received "all he wanted in a deregulation bill," *CQ* said.

Continuing his record of leading passage of significant legislation under every president he served, Cannon shone at the White House ceremony to honor the bill signing. Carter singled him out for praise, along with Senator Kennedy and other bit players, but knowledgeable observers knew who deserved credit for airline deregulation becoming law. As Cannon left the bill-signing ceremony, his knack for understatement resonated in Barclay's memory. Surrounded by a handful of aides who had worked alongside him to steer the bill to passage, Cannon issued his highest praise for a successful effort. "That went well," he commented, as he moved hurriedly on to the day's next appointment.

Rumination, backslapping, or other self-congratulatory conduct was simply not in Cannon's character, and those who served with him had to live with that reality. As a senator, Cannon retained the persona of the calf roping cowboy he had been in his youth. The calf roper strikes quickly before his prey can get up a full head of steam, aiming his lariat expertly soon after cowboy and calf burst from the chute. When the calf is upended, the roper adroitly dismounts his horse and completes the action with a quick rope tie around the calf's legs. That done, he unostentatiously exits the ring, while the calf is untied and, looking dazed, retreats to safety. No pause for applause, no dramatic bows to the crowd for the calf roper. He does his job and moves on to the next challenge.

In the years since deregulation was enacted, it has been subject to countless analyses from economists, business interests, and airline passengers. Although many have noted that the bill did not protect airlines from the normal challenges of the marketplace—from rising fuel prices to labor disputes to recession—it would be hard to find anyone in America willing to go back to the pre-1978 regulatory model. As Americans search the Internet for budget fares, and carriers such as Southwest, JetBlue, and others take advantage of free entry, unregulated air travel has become part of the fabric of American life. Perhaps the most telling example of what the legislation meant to the industry was revealed as the clock wound down to enactment. "Four days before the deregulation bill was to become law, a line began to form outside the Washington offices of the CAB," noted one account. "Soon, about 30 airline company representatives were standing in the line, patiently waiting for Carter to sign the bill so they could begin filing for new routes under the liberalized conditions set by PL 95-504."

Cannon's participation in the bill-signing ceremony for airline deregulation was one of many instances of successful cooperation between him and the new Carter administration, even though that administration was generally considered inept in its dealings with Congress. Notwithstanding some examples of cooperation, there was never a bond between the senator and the president that Cannon had enjoyed with Kennedy and Johnson. Johnson and Cannon were particularly like-minded public officials, combining a conservative upbringing with progressive views on the power of government to improve people's lives. They both also understood that politics was not always a pretty undertaking, and were not averse to getting their hands dirty trying to achieve what they considered worthy goals.

Cannon reaped many benefits from the new Democratic administration, however, particularly from a Transportation Department that was eager to please Mr. Aviation. With airline deregulation completed shortly after Carter took office—one of Carter's few legislative victories—the administration had its eyes on similarly liberating legislation for the trucking and railroad industries. The route to both went through Cannon's Commerce Committee.

Thus, good things started happening for Nevada. In August 1978, just as the airline bill was nearing final passage, the U.S. Federal Highway Administration announced it had agreed to designate a much-needed stretch of freeway through Reno as part of the interstate highway system. That action made twenty-five million dollars available immediately and speeded up construction of the link by several years, according to Reno officials.

Shortly after Cannon supported Carter in his controversial decision to cede control of the Panama Canal to Panama, Transportation Secretary Brock Adams tossed another bouquet Cannon's way. Instead of terminating Amtrak passenger train service to Nevada, as had been considered in an earlier reorganization plan, Adams said in February 1979 that Amtrak would actually improve Nevada's service. In addition to preserving Amtrak's route from Chicago to San Francisco, which went through Reno, Adams said the railroad would add a route from Utah through Las Vegas. Thus, Las Vegas, which could trace its birth to the advent of rail travel, would regain passenger train service it had lost in 1968, including service to the teeming population center of Los Angeles, which had been Las Vegas's initial source of visitors in its early days. One of the Reno newspapers, in praising Cannon's "considerable muscle in Washington," noted that the changes "had been made for political reasons."

As if to underline that Cannon was on a roll in his fourth term, the Washoe County Airport Authority voted unexpectedly in July 1979 to change the name of Reno International Airport to Cannon International. It was a stunning accolade, making Cannon the only living senator with an airport named after him. That it came from the northern Nevada city that had never warmed to him following his defeat of Fred Anderson in 1958 and Paul Laxalt in 1964 was even more surprising. As it turned out, the airport name change was too much of a good thing for Cannon's career. Communities, especially small, relatively isolated ones like Reno, identify closely with major public facilities such as airports. To abruptly eliminate the hometown name from their airport, especially in favor of a politician who did not warm many hearts in Reno, struck many citizens as an outrage. Within two years a grassroots movement to change the name again was successful, and a compromise name of Reno Cannon International was approved. A decade or so after he left the Senate, Cannon's name was dropped completely, and the facility is known today as Reno-Tahoe International Airport.

Although Chet Sobsey and other Cannon political allies considered the effort to rename the airport an unwise gesture, its success in 1979 epitomized Cannon's stature in Nevada. That was underlined by a survey conducted in May 1980 by the Associated Press bureaus in Nevada to determine the state's most powerful people. Leading the list was Cannon, the state's senior senator and head of its congressional delegation. It was a heady moment, indicating Cannon had eclipsed even the state's governor, Republican Robert List, and his onetime nemesis, Laxalt, in the estimation of some of the state's most prominent citizens. Twenty-two years after winning his Senate seat from Molly Malone, Cannon had achieved undeniable success in Washington, and was recognized by opinion leaders in his home state as a powerful political force. Cannon wasn't introspective, nor was he wont to bask in the good opinion of others. But he could be forgiven for thinking, sometime in 1979, that his hard work had paid off and that he could look forward to continued success.

Human experience has developed numerous remedies for such lapses of judgment, however, as evidenced by such folksy phrases as "riding for a fall," or the crude but evocative maxim that the higher one climbs up the ladder of success, the more one's backside is revealed. Cannon was about to experience these truisms to a shocking degree, as forces were at work even at his moment of seeming triumph to undermine his hard-fought success.

CHAPTER 8

Mistaken Impressions

Will Ris, like Barclay an ex-CAB employee drafted to Cannon's Aviation Sub-committee, was driving down Wisconsin Avenue in northwest D.C. in his "little Volkswagen Beetle" one evening in February 1980. Ris, an able young lawyer with a sparkling wit and ingratiating manner, had been hired in 1977 to provide assistance in drafting the airline legislation. He had moved on to the next hot issue facing his boss, trucking deregulation, in early 1979, and had been working for several months to fashion a trucking bill that would do for that industry what the airline bill had done for aviation. Ris was shocked, therefore, to hear the news coming over Washington radio station WTOP that February 5 evening. According to news reports, Senator Cannon was under investigation for potential bribery relating to trucking legislation. "I almost had an accident. . . . I literally had to stop the car. . . . I was just dumbfounded," Ris recalled nearly twenty-four years later.

He was not alone among Cannon employees, family members, and friends to be shocked by the leaked highlights of a Department of Justice (DOJ) investigation. Details were murky and subject to differing interpretations by various news organizations, but the upshot of the allegations was clear: Cannon was suspected of making a deal with the Teamsters Union to impede progress on trucking deregulation in return for favorable consideration on land the union's pension fund owned near his home in Las Vegas.

Ris's consternation was greater than most because only four days before news of the investigation broke, Cannon had introduced a tough, comprehensive trucking regulatory reform bill that Ris had drafted. The reaction among the media and other Washington observers to that bill was a mixed bag for Cannon: universal agreement that it was a strong bill balanced with disbelief that Cannon had come up with it. The latter reaction indicated none of these groups had paid much attention to Cannon's performance on airline deregulation just two years earlier. "But to the trucking industry, Teamsters, supporters of decontrol, and the press, it came as a surprise when Cannon . . . introduced a strong reform bill," recounted Dorothy Robyn in her excellent chronicle of the trucking deregulation episode, *Braking the Special Interests.*

The Cannon-Ris bill was rendered almost irrelevant in light of events that followed, events that would leave Cannon without a moment of peace from the day news of the investigation was leaked until he left office three years later. The government's contention that Cannon was trying to derail trucking deregulation instead of working diligently to achieve it was the result of numerous factors. Among them were his hazy image as a deregulator, his association with some seedy elements in Las Vegas, and a Kafkaesque confluence of events. It began with the government's persistent attempt to stop the corrupt connection between the Teamsters Union, organized crime, and Las Vegas casinos.

As part of this effort, the DOJ's Organized Crime Strike Force had been tapping the phones of suspected Teamsters pension-fund manipulator Allen Dorfman in an operation called Pendorf (Penetrate Dorfman). Bored FBI agents holed up in a building near Dorfman's Amalgamated Insurance Agency Service in suburban Chicago picked up something more interesting than the usual semiliterate, expletive-laden conversations sometime in 1979: the name of a prominent U.S. senator, Howard Cannon. Of more interest to the investigators was the connection of Cannon to pending legislation concerning deregulation of the trucking industry. Although it is not surprising that these conversations stirred the crime-force investigators to look into the situation, it was surprising to Cannon supporters that they pursued their investigation to such extraordinary lengths as to fatally damage Cannon's reputation, threaten him with imprisonment, and eventually end his political career.

The heart of the DOJ investigation into Dorfman and Cannon was the interest of Cannon's Las Vegas neighbors, and the senator himself, in a 5.8-acre parcel of land located just across the street from Cannon's residence within a gated golf-course community called the Las Vegas Country Club. Like countless other home owners in similar situations, Cannon's neighbors reacted negatively to announced plans to develop the 5.8-acre parcel for high-rise condominiums. They enlisted their senator's help in heading off the planned development because of fears the hundreds of new residents in the proposed condominiums would flood the country club's streets with more cars than they were designed to handle, as well as drive down overall property values by adding hundreds of new homes to the existing supply. A flyer sent to all residents in November 1978 stated the plans were to build three nine-story towers, a total of 303 units, on the less-than-six-acre parcel. That amounted to a density of more than 50 units per acre, in contrast with approximately 4 patio-style townhomes per acre on Cannon's side of the street. In a show of community resolve, they prevailed upon Cannon to appear personally before the Clark County Planning Commission during a Senate recess that November. Fresh from his White House appearance with President Carter for signing of the airline deregulation bill, citizen Cannon appeared in opposition to the condominium project on November 21.

The home owners' group was successful. The planning commission recommended rejecting the request for a use permit, and the county commission followed its recommendation. But the condominium project was not dead. New developers requested a permit to construct a smaller project consisting of 102 units, with a maximum height of two stories. At that point, Cannon's neighbors decided to take matters into their own hands by purchasing the land outright and downsizing it to the single-family configuration of the rest of the country club. In late December 1978, after Senator and Mrs. Cannon had returned from an extensive visit to China, the home owners met with Cannon in his district office located in the Federal Building in downtown Las Vegas. At that point several different strains of Cannon's life came together to produce the most fateful decision of his career.

One of these strains concerned family matters, which were extremely important to Cannon. His daughter, Nancy, who had chafed under the restrictions of being a senator's daughter during the turbulent 1960s—for one thing she couldn't understand her father's support for the Vietnam War—had moved to Las Vegas immediately following graduation from high school in 1970. An A student at the well-regarded Bethesda–Chevy Chase High School in suburban Maryland, Nancy was also headstrong and desirous of leading her own life. One way of establishing her independence was through marriage, and on Valentine's Day 1971 she wed a long-haired rock-and-roll drummer named Robert Bjornsen. Notwithstanding some initial discomfort over this alliance, Senator and Mrs. Cannon accepted Bob and avoided a rupture in relations with their daughter. In fact, Cannon took an active role in helping the young couple get started in Las Vegas, providing moral and financial support for a number of Nancy's business ventures, as well as leads for Bob's real estate career. Bob had settled into a position as vice president of a real estate agency, the DeSure Corporation, following graduation from UNLV.

As soon as Cannon heard of his fellow home owners' desire to purchase the 5.8-acre tract that was causing them so much concern, he thought of Bob and the sizable commission Bob's company could earn from handling the transaction. He enlisted Bob to determine who owned the land should the home owners go forward with their plan. If the land had been owned by a local bank or a private land speculator, Cannon would probably have served an additional one or two terms in the Senate and risen to untold heights as a legislator and power broker for his state's interests. As it turned out, however, the land was owned by the Teamsters pension fund and was managed by an agent, Victor H. Palmieri and Company. This fact loomed enormously in Cannon's future.

Cannon participated in the first of several meetings with the home owners in late December. In his own notes about that meeting, Cannon stated that the group authorized Bob to make an offer of $1.3 million to Palmieri. A series of failed negotiations ensued, with the home owners' initial offer being raised to $1.4 million at Palmieri's insistence. That offer, along with three others on the property, was rejected, allegedly because it failed to meet strenuous conditions imposed by Palmieri. Still another offer was submitted at the $1.4 million price, but Palmieri then responded that it had an offer of $1.6 million and was again rejecting the home owners.

Cannon's notes indicate that the home owners eventually reached the conclusion that they were "being given the runaround" and that some of them dropped out of the bidding process. "It appeared that Palmieri was using our group to jack the price up and our money was returned by the escrow agent and we abandoned our efforts," Cannon wrote. "We thereafter were told that the property had been sold for $1.6 million and the buyer would rezone for single-family lots, so our objective was accomplished." Would that it were that simple.

In the early stage of the home owners' interest in purchasing the property, Cannon's notes state that he was asked by his neighbors "if I knew anyone in the Teamsters to find out who we should deal with and what type of purchase could be worked out." Turns out he did, and that knowledge proved to be a very dangerous thing, indeed. Cannon's choice as go-between was the notorious Dorfman, who to an outsider's eyes would be the last person a U.S. senator should be talking to about any subject, particularly a land purchase in which he had a personal stake.

Dorfman was the stepson of Paul "Red" Dorfman, an associate of Al Capone's who allegedly helped Jimmy Hoffa win the support of Chicago mobsters in Hoffa's climb up the Teamsters ladder. Allen's reward for his stepfather's services was the Teamsters' insurance and claims-processing business, Amalgamated Insurance. So high was he in Hoffa's esteem that when Hoffa went to jail in 1967, he designated Dorfman as his stand-in on matters relating to the pension fund. "Allen speaks for me on all pension fund questions," Hoffa allegedly proclaimed.

To Cannon, however, Dorfman was the Teamsters' man in Las Vegas, the one who had the "juice" to get things done. This was a peculiarly Las Vegas perspective, dealing with a shady character on a legitimate matter. But to Cannon and other city residents who had observed the absorption into accepted society of characters such as Gus Greenbaum, Cannon's friend Ben Goffstein, Moe Dalitz, and Benny Binion, it caused no trepidation. Besides, it happened that Dorfman was trying to reach Cannon.

The deregulation fervor that had blossomed through enactment of the airline deregulation bill had spread to trucking, with an early flash point being regulatory actions of the Interstate Commerce Commission, the surface transportation counterpart to aviation's CAB. Under the leadership of activist chairman Dan O'Neal, the ICC had been acting suspiciously like a deregulator instead of a regulator, raising hackles within the ranks of the Teamsters Union and the trucking industry. In a particularly bold move, the ICC in November 1978 had pared back a request for an increase in freight rates by the Southern Motor Carriers Rate Conference, saying that truckers would have to settle for rate increases that generated no more than a 14 percent rate of return. Because it was a dramatic reversal from the ICC's historic role as a rubber stamp for rate increases approved by rate bureaus, the action caused trucking stocks to fall, and caused general consternation throughout the industry. The ICC's action threatened the cozy relationship between high freight rates and the lucrative contracts routinely negotiated by the Teamsters for its three hundred thousand freight haulers. If the guaranteed 12 percent rate of return maintained by the CAB had raised eyebrows, it was nothing compared to the 20 percent returns that were normal in trucking before the ICC's 1978 action.

The concern spread all the way to the top of the Teamsters Union, where President Frank E. Fitzsimmons became involved. He called on Roy Williams, then vice president of a Teamsters unit in Kansas City and soon to become Fitzsimmons's successor. Fitzsimmons's message to Williams was direct: He was to contact Dorfman and set up a meeting with Cannon to complain about the ICC's startling moves. Dorfman called Cannon's Las Vegas office just before Christmas 1978, when Cannon and his wife were in China, so Cannon had a reason to call Dorfman back when the home owners' group was becoming interested in the Teamsters-owned land that concerned them. He did so, was unable to reach him, and turned the matter over to Lee Alverson, one of his employees in the Las Vegas office. Alverson eventually contacted Dorfman and set up a meeting for January 10 to discuss "Nevada Teamsters problems."

It was this meeting that caused Cannon myriad problems and eventually cost him his Senate seat. On the surface, the meeting was routine. Although Dorfman and Williams were present, the main speaker at the meeting was Edward K. Wheeler, a well-connected Teamsters attorney from Washington. The accounts of Wheeler, who was never implicated in the ensuing investigation, and Cannon concur: The discussion centered on the ICC's actions and their potentially harmful effects on Teamsters members everywhere, including Nevada. Cannon, long accustomed to hearing complaints about government policies, listened politely but was noncommittal. When the discussion ended, Cannon escorted Wheeler, Dorfman, and Williams to a waiting room outside his private office.

There, in the singularly most misguided moment of his more than thirty years of public life, Cannon introduced the visitors to Bjornsen, who was conveniently visiting the office at the same time as the Teamsters contingent. "My best recollection is that I told Mr. Dorfman when I introduced him to my son-in-law in the reception room that our group made an offer on subject land to the Palmieri company," Cannon recounted in notes on the meeting. To Cannon, this may have been merely an opportunity to impress someone high up in the Teamsters that he was part of a group that wanted to buy the 5.8-acre parcel. Given the fact that other groups were also bidding on the property, Cannon evidently felt it wouldn't hurt to establish that an important U.S. senator was one of the contenders.

It is impossible to know exactly what was in Cannon's mind in making this point with Dorfman. To government prosecutors overhearing the subsequent efforts by Dorfman and others to make sure Cannon's group got the land, it was proof of a corrupt bargain: delay or obstruction on the trucking deregulation bill in exchange for help with the land purchase. A fuller examination of Cannon's activities on behalf of trucking deregulation belies the allegation that either before or after meeting with Dorfman he obstructed it in any way. Indeed, absent the cloud hanging over his actions as a result of the investigation, Cannon could be seen as the unsung hero of the deregulation fight, just as he had been concerning airline regulation. But if his intention in mentioning his interest in the land was not corruption, what did he have in mind that day?

Certainly, he wanted to help Bob's career by involving him in a high-dollar property sale. He also wanted to show the influential members of the home owners' group that he had the clout to sway the Teamsters. But those motives do not fully explain why Cannon went down such a disastrous path that January day in 1979. A normally shrewd man who showed no proclivity to venality during his time in the Senate, it is hard to classify the action as simply a serious misjudgment. Was Cannon naive about Dorfman's character and willingness to try to influence him? His daughter, Nancy, believes that was a large part of the problem. "He just didn't realize how evil they were," Nancy recalls. "I don't think he knew how the organized-crime mind works." Adding to the problem, Nancy says, was Cannon's sense of himself as outside the normal realm of human experience. "He had survived so much, the war and everything, they [Dorfman et al.] didn't scare him. It was egocentric on his part, a miscalculation based on the belief that 'you can't touch me.'" Nancy had reason to know better.

Early in her return to Las Vegas from Washington, Nancy landed a job at the Stardust Hotel on the Strip, parlaying some experience as a bank teller with her dad's connections. Working as a casino cashier at the Stardust, she was introduced one day to infamous Las Vegas figure Frank "Lefty" Rosenthal, who had assumed control of the property even though he was not licensed to do so because of a checkered past. The story of how Rosenthal ran the Stardust without obtaining a license is told, colorfully if not completely accurately, in the book *Casino: Love and Honor in Las Vegas* by Nicholas Pileggi and the movie *Casino,* with Robert De Niro playing the character based on Rosenthal. "Lefty liked my miniskirt," said Nancy, who was slim and pretty, with flowing brown hair. As a result, he promoted her to a position as his "secretary," although she could neither take shorthand nor type very well at the time. She recalled her job as following Rosenthal around the casino and writing in a notepad as he barked orders to various subordinates. The idea was to make the employees think that everything Rosenthal told them to do was being chronicled by his secretary. He also trusted her with making hotel reservations for Kansas City and Chicago mobsters under false names, and she arranged complimentary dinners and shows for them all over town. Rosenthal boasted to Nancy of his standing within the mobsters' "organization," and often gloated because he employed the daughter of Nevada's powerful U.S. senator. He thought the Cannon connection might in some way prove helpful in his dealings with state gaming officials over his elusive gaming license.

Nancy's position close to Rosenthal gave her a front-row seat at one of the classic Mob shakedowns of a Las Vegas casino. The Stardust eventually lost its license because Nevada Gaming Control Board agents discovered some seven million dollars' worth of skim from the slot machines over a period of three or four years. As she observed the various machinations leading to the Stardust's downfall, Nancy became aware of the name Allen Dorfman, and felt he was keeping a close watch on all skimming operations involving Teamsters-connected properties. She also knew that when someone fell out of favor with the hidden Mob elements, they sometimes turned up either missing or buried in the desert. Although she left the Stardust in 1977, she kept track of the property's problems through press accounts and continued to consider Dorfman and other shady characters as people to be avoided at all costs. She was appalled, therefore, to find Dorfman's name and Chicago telephone number listed among her father's appointments for January 10 when she picked him up at the airport the day before. "Why would you need to call Allen Dorfman?" she asked that evening. "He's a nobody," Cannon replied with a shrug, implying that he was much more powerful than someone like Dorfman. He added that there was nothing to worry about, that he had the situation totally under control. Reflecting on the situation twenty-five years later, Nancy said, "He seemed like he was treating me more like a naive little girl at that point, not thinking that I had any level of understanding on these kind of matters, or any real need to know more about them. To him it was just a matter for the boys to deal with." On this point, at least, "the boys" should have taken counsel from the "naive daughter," who had more inside knowledge of the Las Vegas underworld than her father and his friends.

Whatever his motivation, Cannon fell unknowingly into a prosecutorial trap by mentioning his group's interest in the 5.8-acre parcel to Dorfman and Williams. Although there was no proof of it—and Cannon denied it vehemently—the FBI concluded that Cannon and the Teamsters had closed a deal sometime during that January 10 meeting, a deal to stymie trucking deregulation in exchange for the land. As FBI agents continued their surveillance in the coming months, they uncovered occasional snippets of conversation that seemed to support their contention. In one, on April 26, 1979, Williams told a confidant, "I got whistled in by the senator. He did everything he said he would. He got that legislation away from Kennedy and put it on the back burner." On May 21, Dorfman called Cannon and attempted to set up a meeting in Las Vegas over the weekend of June 1–3. "You will be there?" Dorfman asks, receiving a curt grunt of acknowledgment from Cannon. "I'd like to see you. I will call you on the first." A few days later, Dorfman was taped saying, "The senator is too good a friend of mine. I'm not putting up my bucks and I'm not going to let him put up any of his. I've known him too long, and we're too good friends." These conversations were overheard during a period of considerable activity by Dorfman, Williams, and other Teamsters associates to attempt to steer the land acquisition to Cannon and his fellow home owners. Although evidence indicates that Cannon himself lost interest in the matter in February when his deposit money was returned to him, investigators had reason to pay more than casual interest to ongoing Teamster efforts concerning the land because Cannon's son-in-law, Bob, was right in the middle of them.

Bob proved a willing, if naive, tool in the hands of Dorfman and his confederates. He never gave up on putting a deal together, no matter how many times the Palmieri Company thwarted him. And Bob was not alone in trying to keep a deal alive, as some of Cannon's closest associates—and Las Vegas's most influential residents—were also involved. One group was led by R. G. "Zack" Taylor, a retired general who had played a major role in the development of Nellis Air Force Base—hand in hand with the Senate's most ardent champion of tactical airpower, Howard Cannon. Taylor had moved from the U.S. Air Force to the chairmanship of First Western Savings in Las Vegas, where he considered a proposal to purchase and develop the 5.8-acre tract. One of his fellow businessmen who looked at the deal was Frank Scott, Cannon's close friend and founder of the Union Plaza hotel-casino. To these sharp-eyed businessmen, however, the deal was simply not viable economically, so they backed off.

Another party's interest in the land, however, was not so easily explained. Early in the submission process with Palmieri a seemingly unchallengeable offer of $1.6 million came from the Stardust's nominal owner, Allen Glick, another resident of the Las Vegas Country Club. Glick is one of those emblematic Las Vegas characters: a seemingly honest real estate speculator who had made a lot of money in the San Diego area and wanted to indulge his fascination with Nevada casino life by owning one of his own. Financed by a suspicious loan from the Teamsters pension fund—suspicious because of the small amount of his own money he invested to receive a $62.7 million loan—Glick was able to purchase the Stardust and the venerable Fremont in downtown Las Vegas. On paper—a license from Nevada gaming authorities—Glick ran the Stardust. In fact, Rosenthal, connected to Chicago Mob bosses, was in charge.

Since Glick was little more than a cat's-paw for the Mob, it would be no problem for Mob-Teamster elements to cool Glick's interest in the land across the street from Cannon's home. And that, in the eyes of the DOJ, is just what they did. Following entreaties by Dorfman and others, Glick withdrew his prohibitively high offer for the land, leaving the way clear for Cannon's group, represented by son-in-law Bob, to have a shot at it. It was during this episode that Bob's inexperience in dealing with characters such as the Teamster associates was made most clear.

The news of Glick's withdrawal was relayed to Bob by William Webbe, one of the key players in the conspiracy to win Cannon's group the desired land. Webbe, an employee of Dorfman's Amalgamated Insurance, was in Cannon's outer office during the January 10 meeting between Cannon and the Dorfman-Williams-Wheeler triumvirate. There, sitting next to each other in the reception area, Webbe and Bob discussed real estate opportunities in Las Vegas, including the fateful 5.8-acre tract. From that moment on, Webbe was the chief Teamster lieutenant in dealing with Bob.

Webbe was understandably excited when he told Bob that Dorfman had succeeded in convincing Glick to withdraw. All but painting Bob a picture of what was happening, Webbe suggested that Bob get back in touch with a Palmieri representative "and tell him your offer is still good in case the other is withdrawn." Instead of leaping at the opportunity to move his father-in-law's interest into the opening, Bob seemed confused about what Webbe was telling him. "Ah, yes, I guess I should [recontact Palmieri]," Bob replied, but he never did. When quizzed about this wiretapped conversation before a grand jury in Chicago, Bob said he simply didn't know what Webbe was referring to. The prosecutors related more of Webbe's conversation to him, including a statement that "your offer is the only one." Bob replied that the conversation sounded familiar, but, taken out of context, he didn't know what it referred to. The prosecutor bore down: "Well isn't Burke [the Palmieri representative] with the Palmieri company and wasn't this the only transaction you had with them?" he asked. Bob replied that he didn't know "what specific action [Webbe] was referring to." He added: "He called me up and told me something and I responded to him, but that doesn't mean I knew what he was talking about. . . . I didn't know what he was doing."

Dorfman himself also called Bob to get him to resubmit an offer after Glick was out of the picture, but was no more successful than Webbe. "That kid's not too smart," Dorfman commented after the conversation. To which Webbe replied, "But he's really a nice guy."

Bob was simply too naive to recognize a strong-arm tactic to favor his group's bid when one was described to him. He just didn't get it. His being "not too smart" in Dorfman's eyes meant only that he was too honest to recognize the Teamsters' tactics. His notes on the various stages of the DOJ investigation that involved him were insightful, coherent, and well written, indicating anything but a lack of intelligence. But he was a nice guy, as well as woefully unprepared to be negotiating with the likes of Webbe, Dorfman, et al. His naïveté was best exemplified by his actions when subpoenaed to testify before the Chicago grand jury. He took a red-eye from Las Vegas, to save money on the airfare, and arrived in Chicago bleary-eyed and, most amazingly, without a lawyer. Bob was shocked to realize the seriousness of the DOJ investigation and, particularly, the gravity of possible charges against him. He did not understand how negotiating the sale of land for some of Las Vegas's most prominent citizens could land him in jail as part of a bribery conspiracy.

In addition to the damaging comments from Williams and Dorfman, which would be shown to be only braggadocio, DOJ investigators had other seemingly suspicious events to consider during 1979. Shortly after the January 10 meeting in Cannon's office, Senator Kennedy—who had leaped out in front of the trucking deregulation issue as he had with airline deregulation—held a much-publicized press conference in Washington to proclaim his intention to seek full deregulation of the trucking industry. This was followed by Cannon's formal moves to forestall Kennedy's plan to have deregulation legislation referred to the Judiciary Committee. Cannon made it clear he would oppose Kennedy, even to the point of seeking a ruling from the Senate parliamentarian on which committee was the proper home for a trucking bill. By showing his willingness to submit the question to the parliamentarian, Cannon also indicated he thought the full Senate would support him, as a ruling in favor of the Commerce Committee would be subject to a Senate vote. Cannon's message to Kennedy was clear: I'll seek a parliamentarian's ruling on referral, and I'll prevail if you seek a Senate vote. Whether Kennedy was merely bluffing or thought he might actually prevail on the referral issue, he caved in to Cannon and agreed to refer the bill to the Commerce Committee, with a face-saving sequential referral to Judiciary after Commerce was through with it. Although this was one of the strongest indications of Cannon's strength and reputation in the Senate, to the DOJ it fitted perfectly with what they conceived was the corrupt bargain agreed to on January 10: Cannon would derail trucking deregulation.

Another innocent action by Cannon that year added further fuel to the DOJ's prosecutorial fire.

In speaking to an ICC-sponsored workshop in suburban Virginia on October 22, Cannon rebuked the ICC for its most recent attempts at deregulation by executive action. Stating his opposition to independent regulatory agencies ignoring Congress, Cannon said, "We're mad as hell and we aren't going to take it anymore," borrowing a catchphrase from a popular movie. Deregulation, if it were to happen, must be accomplished through the legislative process, Cannon said. Although perfectly reasonable and defensible, to a suspicious DOJ it was another blocking move by Cannon.

The internal workings of the Organized Crime Strike Force in Chicago were and are unknown to outsiders. Attempts to discuss them for this book with the head of the Chicago group, a prosecutor named Douglas Roller who is now a St. Louis criminal defense attorney, were unsuccessful. So one is left to infer strategy and decisions by the group in light of events at the time. Interpreting those events, one could surmise that Roller and his team was enthusiastic about what they had uncovered through their wiretaps during 1979. Whether they felt the plot they uncovered was sufficient for indictments of Cannon and others by year's end, no one but they can say. But it is fair to speculate that the Chicago prosecutors were caught by surprise by Cannon's introduction of the Ris-drafted deregulation bill on February 1, 1980. Everything they had surmised about Cannon's intentions and actions was contradicted by that action, especially given the cries of anguish coming from the Teamsters Union and various trucking interests in Washington.

Teamsters president Fitzsimmons, for instance, telegrammed Cannon that the bill was "completely unacceptable," and that the union would exert maximum efforts to have it changed. Coming as it did almost a year after Cannon had allegedly entered into a corrupt bargain with Fitzsimmons's appointed lieutenant, Roy Williams, to derail or delay trucking deregulation, the bill presented a problem for Roller. Was it a coincidence that Roller or others involved in the investigation leaked news of their investigation of Cannon just four days after the bill was introduced? Again, Roller declined to comment on that, just as he declined to comment on the general practice of leaking details of the investigation throughout 1980. Was the initial leak in February, and numerous others during succeeding months, a tactic by prosecutors to sway opinion in Washington about the strength of the government's case? One book on the subject offers an insight into this possibility, explaining that Roller was concerned about winning continuing approval for his wiretaps of Dorfman under the investigation code-named Pendorf. The initial results of the wiretaps were not producing anything of interest, and the possibility that a federal judge would not continue approving the wire-taps loomed large. "There was always the specter of the ax falling on [Pendorf]," Roller told the author. "It disappeared when we got Cannon." That admission implies a vested interest in keeping Cannon publicly portrayed as an accomplice in a bribery conspiracy, and the actions of Roller or others associated with the case throughout 1980 lend credence to such an interest.

The leak attack against Cannon was comprehensive and inestimably destructive to his reputation and future Senate career. It began with a report on the ABC *Nightly News* by Capitol Hill correspondent Brit Hume on February 5. Crediting FBI sources, Hume gave a succinct account of the investigation: "The FBI suspects that Allen Dorfman, a Teamster crony with orga-nized crime connections, found a way to reward Sen. Cannon for steering the legislation into his Commerce Committee, where it has since died." The factual errors of Hume's account, and of the many others that followed, were significant. For instance, Dorfman never "found a way to reward Cannon," as he could not budge Palmieri from its desire to award the deal to someone else. As disturbing as the inaccuracies and contradictions of the media were, one aspect stood out: the degree to which media accounts reflected the gov-ernment theory about the case, no matter how much that theory was con-tradicted by facts. Hume's assertion that trucking legislation was steered to Cannon's committee, "where it has since died," was a misstatement of reality. It was matched by the *Washington Post* story on February 6, which quoted sources saying the investigation involves trucking deregulation legislation "that has been languishing in Cannon's committee since its introduction last year." On the home front, the *R-J*'s Washington correspondent echoed the common verdict, declaring, "Cannon won [the jurisdictional dispute] and the bill has since for all intents and purposes died in his committee."

It is obviously no credit to Hume, George Lardner Jr. of the *Post,* or the *R-J* reporter that these statements were demonstrably incorrect. But it is even more telling about the government's apparent conviction that it was neces-sary to turn public opinion in the direction of Cannon's supposed inatten-tion to deregulation legislation. This was, after all, the sole predicate for its case, a predicate that was seriously endangered by the fact that Cannon had introduced a strong deregulation bill just days before the investigation story emerged. Cannon's supposed reluctance to act on trucking deregulation—contrasted by Kennedy's perceived leadership on the issue—became the accepted reality in Washington. It was also portrayed that way throughout Nevada, where the news media was far removed from goings-on in Washington and its members lacked the opportunities of journalists like Hume and Lardner to examine the government's assertions.

In fact, Cannon was far down the path of steering trucking deregulation to passage before he learned of the Teamsters investigation on February 5, 1980. True to his track record on airline deregulation and countless other measures, he was going about it slowly and meticulously, but leaving little doubt—to those who bothered to pay attention—that he intended to take significant action on the matter. The most remarkable thing about Cannon's speech to the ICC workshop in Reston the previous October was not the "We're mad as hell" statement—which was merely a colorful way of telling O'Neal and his fellow commissioners not to get too far ahead of themselves—but a bold promise Cannon made. "It is my personal goal to see that legislation expressing the will of the Congress is on the desk of the President of the United States no later than June 1, 1980," he told the group. Why was Cannon confident enough to make such a prediction, which was certainly not typical of his performance on other controversial issues, and seemed dubious given the entrenched opposition by the Teamsters and other powerful interests? The answer was that he had spent much of 1979 slogging through the various minefields presented by trucking regulatory reform, listening to both proponents and opponents, gauging the support he would have from the Carter administration, and consulting with his more cautious counterparts on the House Public Works Committee. He did it quietly, without the fanfare Kennedy generated by his less substantive actions on the issue, but thoroughly and with purpose.

Once Cannon had settled the issue of proper jurisdiction for trucking reform in early 1979, he moved quickly to not only accommodate Kennedy but also to get a bill on the Senate floor. "From that point on [establishing Commerce Committee jurisdiction] . . . I never got anything but complete support from Sen. Cannon to just move the issue expeditiously and with the notion that we were in favor of deregulation," recounted Ris, who was

Cannon's chief staff resource on the issue. When Kennedy introduced a bill on March 21, 1979, dealing solely with the issue of antitrust immunity for the rate bureaus that had consistently approved higher freight rates, Cannon held an oversight hearing on the subject a week later. Kennedy was the leadoff witness, followed by strong opposition by a Teamsters representative. One part of the Teamsters' testimony was a list of regulatory actions by the ICC that its witness claimed were harmful to the Teamsters. When Cannon introduced his own reform legislation the following year, he affirmed every one of those actions.

Cannon held two other hearings in early 1979 on different aspects of the trucking issue—freight-transportation regulation and the household-goods transportation industry. When President Carter finally worked out a squabble within his own administration about how to proceed on the trucking issue in midyear, Cannon appeared with him and Kennedy at a White House ceremony to announce an administration-sponsored bill. Kennedy introduced that bill on June 25, and Cannon began hearings in the Commerce Committee the next day. Again, Kennedy was leadoff witness, and again a Teamsters representative spoke in strong opposition. This witness made ten specific legislative proposals to mildly change the regulatory structure, but Cannon did not incorporate a single one of them in his eventual bill.

A series of six more hearings ensued, covering issues such as the effect of regulatory reform on fuel consumption and on small communities, a concern similar to that expressed over airline deregulation. In October, Cannon huddled with the House Public Works Committee on the increasingly volatile issue of the ICC's deregulatory moves. He reached agreement with his House counterparts on a timetable for producing a trucking-reform bill, a move that was intended to avoid the uncoordinated action by the House Aviation Subcommittee on the airline bill. In other words, Cannon was ensuring that trucking regulatory reform would go more smoothly and be approved more quickly. Having achieved that level of cooperation, he made his prediction of having a bill on the president's desk by the following June.

Cannon was by now becoming more confident that forces were aligned to ensure legislative success, but he did not stop. He held four more hearings around the country, including two in Nevada and a joint hearing with the House Public Works Committee in Chicago. As the committee neared the end of this series of hearings, Ris sent Cannon a memo making recommendations for a comprehensive trucking-reform bill and asking for his instructions. At a follow-up meeting in early December, Cannon instructed the staff to begin drafting a bill. An outline of Cannon's position was shared with the House Public Works Committee to continue the spirit of cooperation between the panels, and staff held additional meetings with interested parties on all sides of the issue. One of those interested parties was the Teamsters, who presented six specific items to make the legislation more acceptable. Cannon rejected all of them and instructed staff not to include them in his bill. So concerned were the Teamsters over the bill that, on the eve of its introduction, Fitzsimmons sent the aforementioned telegram to all senators on the Commerce Committee stating that the Cannon bill was "completely unacceptable" and urging them to help change it in markup.

This was the preparation Cannon undertook before introducing his bill on February 1, 1980, preparation that was rendered invisible by the DOJ leakers and their willing foils in the news media. Information that Cannon had actually acted forcefully and intelligently in pursuing trucking regulatory reform would obviously undercut one of the DOJ's key charges against Cannon: that he had agreed to derail, or slow down, the legislation. The other key part of its brief was that Cannon agreed during the meeting with Dorfman and Williams in January 1979 to take the bill out of Kennedy's hands to "bury" it in the Commerce Committee. Notwithstanding the sworn testimony of Cannon and the corroborating statement of Teamsters attorney Wheeler that the issue of jurisdiction wasn't even broached at that meeting, this scenario was as far-fetched as the idea that Cannon had acted to impede the bill.

Kennedy had held hearings before his Antitrust and Monopoly Subcommittee on the antitrust implications of rate bureaus back in 1977. Cannon was too busy shepherding the airline bill to passage at that time to do anything about trucking, but he realized what Kennedy was up to. After he became chairman of the full committee in 1978, Cannon had his staff director, Aubrey Sarvis, begin a series of consultations with the Antitrust Subcommittee staff director, David Boies, on the issue of jurisdiction. Boies, who moved on to become one of the nation's premier attorneys, representing the government in its antitrust suit against Microsoft and Al Gore in his legal wrangling over the 2000 election results, among other high-profile cases, gave a deposition on the matter after word of the Cannon investigation leaked. In his sworn statement, Boies made it clear that Sarvis had argued consistently during 1978 that the Commerce Committee claimed full jurisdiction over the matter. This was months before Cannon met with Dorfman and Williams, which bears directly on the government's case.

By leaking information about the January 10, 1979, meeting in Cannon's office, the government underscored the correlation between it and Kennedy's January 12, 1979, press conference announcing his sweeping deregulation proposal and subsequent actions by Cannon to guarantee that Kennedy's and all other bills on the subject be sent to his committee. "See how quickly Cannon leaped into action to uphold his part of the bargain with the Teamsters," the leakers implied. In reality, Cannon's actions in 1979 were merely the follow-up to negotiations between Sarvis and Boies in the previous year. Cannon was committed to fight Kennedy over the jurisdiction issue well before he held the meeting with Dorfman and Williams. To maintain his credibility as a strong committee chairman, he had no choice. This was a Capitol Hill version of "mano a mano" combat, where Cannon would have looked weak if he conceded jurisdiction to Kennedy.

Cannon maintained his composure during the several days of hectic, contradictory, and damaging news coverage that followed the initial leak on February 5. Since he was caught completely off guard by the news, his first instinct was to verify that what the media was reporting had some basis in fact. To determine this, he went right to the top, contacting FBI director William Webster. Webster was anything but forthcoming, telling Cannon only that there was no current investigation under way against him. To Cannon, this meant that the media reports were erroneous, and he cautiously indicated that during the day on February 6. As it turns out, Webster's comment was only a semantic smoke screen, as he apparently meant that the investigation that had raised suspicion about Cannon was aimed at Dorfman.

By the time Cannon held the first hearing on his trucking-reform bill two weeks later, he was his usual unruffled self. Utilizing the wry humor of Ris, Cannon opened the hearing on February 21 with what was for him almost a comic monologue. He welcomed the overflowing crowd to "the only place in town where it is possible to watch legislation languish before your very eyes," poking fun at the *Washington Post* account of the DOJ investigation. Indicating how much the *Post*'s ill-informed reporting had stung him, Cannon offered to buy Lardner, the *Post* reporter, a year's subscription to the paper's own business section, where the previous year's hearings and progress had been substantially covered.

Using humor to deflate a potentially uncomfortable situation was a good tactic, and it presented Cannon as above the Teamsters furor. He followed that hearing with two others, then held markup sessions on March 6 and 11, after which the bill was reported by the Commerce Committee by a 13-4 vote. It moved to the Senate floor on April 15 and was approved by a vote of 70-20. Reflecting the conscientious coordination Cannon had undertaken with his House counterparts, that body eventually decided to approve a somewhat milder version of Cannon's bill and even give its measure the title and number of Cannon's, S2245. This tactic meant that if the Senate accepted the House changes, the bill could go to the president without a House-Senate conference committee.

The House passed it by an overwhelming margin on June 19, and the Senate accepted the minor House amendments and cleared the bill for Carter's signature the next day, missing Cannon's prediction the previous October by only nineteen days. Carter signed it into law on July 1, with Rose Garden ceremonies reflecting Carter's renewed pleasure over having another of his major domestic initiatives completed. "These are my heroes back here and I'm very grateful for what they've done for the country," Carter said of the assembled House and Senate members. The first to be singled out was Cannon, whom Carter praised for his "yeoman work in preparing a basis for a better understanding not only of the consumers and the shippers of our country, but the trucking industry itself and the American public." Kennedy, who was sharing a stage with a man whose office he was officially seeking by that time, also commended Cannon first, describing him as "the leader [on trucking deregulation] in the United States Senate." It was a gracious acknowledgment by Kennedy of Cannon's true worth on the trucking bill and could, at least for a moment, assuage Cannon's concern over the ongoing wreckage of his reputation caused by the DOJ investigation.

Notwithstanding the Rose Garden glow, Cannon faced an onslaught of negative news as 1980 wore on. The initial leak in February was followed by additional leaks in early March to Nevada news outlets concerning subpoenas issued by the Chicago grand jury for records of the infamous land sale. "But the *Times* learned that subpoenas were issued for the records of DeSure Corp., with which Cannon's son-in-law Robert Bjornsen was associated," read one account. Although it was perfectly normal for subpoenas to be issued in an investigation, the controlled release of information orchestrated by federal prosecutors ensured that each detail, no matter how insignificant, was reported aggressively by whatever organ the leakers favored at the time.

Prosecutors had a willing ally in the *North Las Vegas Valley Times* and its pugnacious associate editor, Ned Day. The always-struggling newspaper emerged in the 1970s to provide an alternative view of Las Vegas life from that of Greenspun's *Sun* and Reynolds's *R-J,* and it was quite successful on its limited terms. Its editor was Robert Brown, the former *R-J* editor who had resigned during the 1964 Cannon-Laxalt race and gone to work for Laxalt, a fact that made Cannon and his staff perpetually suspicious about the newspaper's coverage. Day became a cult hero in Las Vegas because of his wise-guy demeanor and sometimes revelatory stories, carried alternatively in the paper's news section or Day's bylined column. Whatever his accomplishments as an investigative reporter, however, Day was just another willing recipient of leaks on the Cannon investigation.

As bad as the Teamsters stories were, Cannon had still another bombshell awaiting him in 1980. On April 20, a Sunday, the *New York Times* carried a damaging story across three columns at the bottom part of its front page that took up most of an inside page as well. It alleged that over the previous five years Cannon had used his official position to influence government actions that enhanced the value of his personal holdings. Coming from the august *Times,* appearing on a Sunday when it would have the widest readership among Washington-area subscribers relaxing over their breakfasts, and picked up by numerous other news organizations—including virtually all outlets in Nevada—the story was devastating to Cannon. It initiated an immediate investigation by the Senate Ethics Committee. Full of revelations about Cannon's business association with Frank Scott and other prominent Las Vegas business interests, larded with financial details and hints of inside information about national defense plans, it was written in a style suggestive of a major exposé. In truth, the story contained no information that Cannon himself had not previously made public and relied on a large dose of speculation to rise to a level of major concern. Even though the *Times* charges would be found to be groundless by the Ethics Committee by the end of July after a thorough investigation, the negative publicity they engendered added more baggage to Cannon's sagging reputation.

A few months after the Ethics Committee cleared Cannon of any wrong-doing in the matters covered by the *Times,* a much greater threat to his life and career also ended: The Justice Department announced on December 18 that it was not seeking an indictment against him in the Teamsters matter. The *Times,* citing "sources close to the inquiry," reported that the decision was a "close call," a contention that still rankled with Cannon's attorney, John Dowd, twenty-four years later. "When all is said and done, there was absolutely no case at all," Dowd said.

Dowd acknowledged that Roller's Chicago Organized Crime Strike Force office, the U.S. attorney for Illinois, and the Organized Crime Section of the Justice Department initially agreed to seek an indictment, but that was before Dowd had his day in court. Reviewing the evidence against Cannon, Dowd concluded that the government's case rested almost entirely on uncorroborated hearsay among the Teamsters and their cronies. "In nineteen months of tapes, all they had was [Cannon] saying 'Uh huh' when Dorfman called him and said, 'Are you gonna be in Vegas this weekend?' [the May 21 phone call]. And that's all in nineteen months of wiretapping," Dowd recounted. "Among themselves, the wiseguys were all bragging to one another, but what I had was the public record," Dowd added, referring to Cannon's stewardship of the trucking bill.

Dowd carried Cannon's record on trucking and thorough knowledge of what was on the government's tape recordings into a showdown meeting with Justice Department officials in Washington in September 1980. He told them, "You have nothing. . . . [Y]ou don't even have a meeting that weekend [between Cannon and Dorfman]." Based on his own experience with the high bar of evidence the Justice Department requires for major prosecutions, Dowd couldn't believe the government would go to court with uncorroborated statements from "liars, frauds, and cheats, all puffing each other up."

Recalling his conversation with Irvin Nathan, then a deputy assistant attorney general, Dowd said, "You can't introduce the testimony of Tony the Tuna from Chicago talking to Dorfman and Dorfman telling him, 'Yeah, how he and Howard are hanging out.' You can't do that without corroboration." Dowd's "Tony the Tuna" reference was to an actual conspirator in the attempt to bribe Cannon, Joey "the Clown" Lombardo.

In his handling of this confrontation with the awesome forces of the U.S. Department of Justice, Dowd demonstrated how smart a choice Cannon had made in picking him from legions of high-powered D.C. attorneys. Although relatively unknown in these circles, Dowd had recently left the Organized Crime and Racketeering Section of the Justice Department and was intimately familiar with its procedures. Dowd is today known as "the man who got Pete Rose" because he handled the investigation for Major League Baseball into Rose's gambling activities. That investigation demonstrated clearly that Rose had, indeed, bet on baseball games while managing the Cincinnati Reds, and led to Rose's banishment from the game. Although Rose steadfastly denied the charges for more than a decade and demonized Dowd along the way, he eventually conceded what most impartial observers had long ago concluded: The charges were true. At the time Cannon hired him, however, Dowd's chief recommendation was his experience with the Organized Crime and Racketeering Section.

At the showdown meeting, Nathan presented Dowd with forty-eight questions he and his fellow Justice Department officials had devised based on Roller's investigation. To Dowd, the questions represented "the easiest assignment we ever had" because all questions and accusations against Cannon were easily refuted. "So we did this sort of delicious job of responding," Dowd remembered. "We didn't have any problem at all. And they went back, and they reversed [the earlier decision to seek an indictment]," Dowd said simply.

The *Times* story quoting an unidentified source terming the decision a "close call" does not jibe with Dowd's account, nor do after-the-fact interviews with unidentified persons involved in the case in which they claimed the decision to reverse Roller's recommendation was politically inspired. Contacted about the matter, Nathan, still a Justice Department official in Washington, pleaded lack of memory about specifics of the case. Indicating the "political" charges were still in his mind more than twenty years after the fact, however, he did make one point: "[The decision not to indict] was made solely on the merits. There were no political considerations at all."

Dowd, a balding six-foot-plus, packing some heft on his frame, has the demeanor of a tough beat cop. He bonded with Cannon just as similarly rough-hewn men such as Ben Goffstein, Jack Conlon, and Frank Krebs had done over the years. With his pugnacious attitude toward the prosecutors, Dowd had an ally in the quietly determined Cannon. "The senator was tough as nails," Dowd said.

If Dowd had reason to celebrate after the indictment was dropped, however, the people who were charged with protecting Cannon's reputation and reelection knew there was trouble ahead. They and Cannon would herald the decision not to indict as vindication, just as they had heralded the earlier clean bill of health from the Ethics Committee. But they realized what a terrific beating Cannon had taken in the media by the two investigations, and that further fallout could be expected. Dowd would have extreme difficulty negotiating with the Ethics Committee over the Teamsters matter, never succeeding in getting the body to drop its investigation of Cannon, which had the effect of keeping the story alive throughout the following two years. There would follow indictments of Dorfman, Williams, and others in a conspiracy to bribe Cannon, plus their trial, and additional damaging news reports concerning Cannon's establishment of a defense fund to defray his legal expenses.

Cannon had undergone a drastic reversal in perception by Nevada voters during 1980, and it would be a monumental challenge to overcome before his reelection less than two years later. The man who had earned his constituents' respect and votes by effective work in the state's and nation's behalf was suddenly suspect, his integrity challenged. Innocent business dealings with respected Las Vegas citizens were cast into suspicion, suspicion that could not be eliminated by favorable rulings from the Ethics Committee or the Justice Department. Cannon would have to win over Nevada voters once again, starting almost from scratch, just as he had done in winning his seat in 1958. He was sixty-eight years old, soon to be sixty-nine, and a new Republican president had caught the nation's fancy and brought control of the Senate into Republican hands for the first time since 1955. The next two years would be more challenging than anything Cannon had experienced since his c-47 collided with another over Holland in 1944.

CHAPTER 9

The Heartbreaking Fall

To an outsider it might have seemed that as Cannon approached his twenty-third year in office in 1981 it was time that he stepped aside. He was nearing seventy years of age and had served for four terms, milestones that may have influenced other men to call it quits. But such a concept never entered Cannon's mind. His mastery over the airline and trucking deregulation bills and his rise to the upper echelon of Senate seniority (he ranked ninth in 1981) told him he could still be a powerful broker of Nevada interests in a fifth term. And although to many Nevadans it might have seemed that he was ancient and had served forever, Cannon was not old in Senate terms. Moreover, he was healthy, vigorous, and totally comfortable in the culture and tradition of the Senate. It was a club whose membership he still cherished.

Much had changed in Nevada since Cannon's 1958 victory over Molly Malone, however, most notably its population, which had increased from less than 300,000 to 800,508 in 1980. Moreover, a new generation of political leaders was becoming known to Nevada voters, including Republicans such as Robert List, elected governor in 1978, and Democrats Jim Santini, first elected to the House in 1974, former lieutenant governor Harry Reid, who narrowly lost to Laxalt in the 1974 Senate race, and Attorney General Richard Bryan, elected in 1978. Most of the new-breed Democrats were content to develop their careers under Cannon's shadow, which, as the 1980 Associated Press survey made clear, was the largest of any politician in the state.

But one was not, and the feeling that 1980 had marked a national change in the electorate, combined with Cannon's devastating personal setbacks, was too tempting for him to resist. Jim Santini was ready to take on the king.

Since winning election to Nevada's single House seat in 1974, Santini had compiled consistently large winning percentages in '76 (77 percent), '78 (70 percent) and '80 (68 percent). In his 1980 victory, he received nearly 40,000 more votes (165,107) than Cannon had received in 1976 (127,295), a reflection of the rapidly growing population. Moreover, he was born and raised in Reno, where his father was a prominent banker, and his grandfather had been president of the University of Nevada. He launched his political career in Las Vegas, winning election as justice of the peace in 1970 and moving to a district court judgeship in 1972. Thus, he could claim footholds in both ends of the state.

A generation younger than Cannon at forty-three, Santini in 1980 exhibited youthful energy despite prematurely gray hair. A natural campaigner and verbose speaker, he struck people variously as pleasantly exuberant or as a "typical Washington windbag." He was once described as "the only hyperactive adult I've seen."

He had entered the House with Cannon's support, both in his campaigns and in his committee assignments. Cannon had lent staff members including Sara Denton, head of his Las Vegas office, and John Brodeur, a young special assistant in Washington, to help in various campaigns, and Brodeur eventually joined Santini's staff as administrative assistant. When Santini first arrived in Washington, Cannon called on Representative Harley O. Staggers of West Virginia, chairman of the powerful—and, to newly elected congressmen, desirable—House Committee on Interstate and Foreign Commerce to help Santini obtain a choice seat on the panel.

Santini's political lineage was traditional mainstream Democratic in his early days, and he served as Nevada chairman of the presidential campaigns of both liberal Jerry Brown, the former California governor, and moderate Jimmy Carter in 1976. In seeking reelection to his second term, he latched onto timeworn Nevada causes such as the Southern Nevada Water Project and other topics Cannon had long championed—bringing Amtrak service to Las Vegas, obtaining funds for a massive railroad track relocation project in Elko, and working to improve air service between Reno and Las Vegas. Cannon may have raised his eyebrows at Santini's assertion of influence on turf he had cultivated for so long, but he did not rebuke the brash young politician. Cannon's staff was more quickly suspicious of Santini's grasp for credit on many issues, as it was under Jack Conlon's leadership concerning Grant Sawyer. A 1978 profile of Santini by a Reno newspaper caught the tension. "He'll take an easy headline, he can't pass up the opportunity," an unnamed Cannon staffer was quoted as saying. "Santini knows no shame. There's nothing he won't try to get credit for."

That was an opinion I shared as Cannon's press secretary during his last term. Since Cannon's stature as the author of transportation deregulation measures, an acknowledged military and civilian aviation expert, and a successful advocate for federal funds for Nevada was widely accepted in Nevada and Washington, I wondered why Santini showed so little respect. Cannon received more deference from his former bitter political enemy Paul Laxalt, who readily acknowledged Cannon's role as senior senator and head of the Nevada congressional delegation, than he did from Santini.

Thus, as the Cannon-Santini race became bitterer over the coming months and years, Cannon's staff joined him in the perception that it was more personal than political. If Cannon perceived Santini as primarily a turncoat, his staff was convinced that Santini was disrespectful and ungrateful for favors Cannon had granted. But, with all his ambition and impatience, Santini needed something else to push him to the fateful decision to oppose Cannon within the Democratic Party. The Justice Department and the *New York Times* story of April 20 supplied it. Sig Rogich, a Las Vegas advertising executive and political consultant who managed Santini's campaign against Cannon, described the situation in the middle of 1980. "After [Cannon] had his problems with the Teamsters and received an enormous amount of bad publicity, his job approval rating fell to what I think was the lowest of any incumbent U.S. senator running for reelection at that time. And we knew at that point that he was not going to be reelected. Almost anyone could have won against him with an approval rating as low as his. He was getting relentless bad press," Rogich recalled.

As 1981 dawned, Santini's ambition was evident to the Nevada news media, who wrote numerous stories about the possibility of a Cannon-Santini contest in 1982. Santini was not coy about the prospect, admitting as early as February that he was giving the race "very serious consideration." Cannon was uncharacteristically open about the situation himself. Asked whether he could beat Santini, Cannon replied, "I think I could. I'm a good campaigner and I would look forward to a challenge from anyone. I've done a good job for the people and I think I could beat anyone."

One observer looked beneath the surface of Cannon's reply and recognized a little of what motivated him. "Some sources close to the senator say he is furious at Santini for making it clear to a number of people that he will run against him. These sources claim that Santini, on more than one occasion, told Cannon that he would not run against him, PERIOD," wrote columnist Don Digilio.

To the hard-edged Rogich and other professional politicians, the Cannon-Santini race was simply about numbers and opportunity: Cannon's abysmal approval rating following his media pummeling during 1980 and Santini's chance to move up to the Senate. From that view, Cannon's position was hopeless. He simply could not overcome the baggage from the previous year, especially against an attractive, youthful candidate who was quick to adopt the Reagan message of reduced federal spending and taxes.

Santini's and Rogich's analysis of Cannon's vulnerability seemed justified by a stunning poll revealed in early May 1981. When asked, "Who would you like to see as the Democratic candidate for US Senate in next year's election—present Sen. Howard W. Cannon or present Congressman Jim Santini?"—respondents overwhelmingly favored Santini, 53 percent to 27 percent. The numbers were shocking to a man who had been in office for twenty-two years and who had achieved both statewide and national acclaim.

Cannon was not in a position to counter this bad news. Preoccupied with his legal and reputation struggles throughout 1980, he had lost touch with much of his Nevada constituency. Sara Denton, who had taken control of Cannon's Las Vegas office in the 1970s, saw the erosion of Cannon's support among longtime backers, but was helpless to stop it. Time and time again, she recalled, Cannon would rebuff her efforts to have him meet and greet key constituencies when he was home from Senate business. He preferred to meet with family members or close friends such as Frank Scott and Zack

Taylor, Denton recalled, receiving solace in their formidable financial and social prominence.

Sometime during the trying days of 1980–1981, however, Cannon broke out of his funk and found the spark to wage a rousing comeback. Standing up to Santini's challenge became a matter of honor and pride. Santini's desire to run against him stuck in his craw and violated the personal sense of political morality he had lived by for more than twenty-five years: One should not challenge an incumbent of one's own party. That Santini played by a different set of rules was something he could not forgive, and the race he waged to defeat him was an indication of how deeply he felt about this principle. Denton's appointment schedule would not be ignored during 1981, as Cannon seemingly was determined to meet any group or individual who might support him. Flying back and forth from Washington constantly, he put the issue of his age to rest by dint of personal effort, "matching Mr. Santini mile for mile and chicken dinner for chicken dinner."

Compelling national events overshadowed Santini-Cannon campaign tactics in 1981, but those events provided a handy script for the political roles of the combatants. Reagan's election the previous November had galvanized the nation, as the amiable former actor and California governor offered a stark contrast to what was described as "the politics of the past." Striking a decidedly anti-Washington chord, Reagan espoused on a national scale what Laxalt and his supporters had been championing in Nevada since the 1960s. More alert to changing trends than Cannon, and seemingly less committed to bedrock principles, Santini eagerly embraced the new Reagan doctrine.

Even though the House had remained Democratic during the Reagan sweep of 1980 that turned over the Senate to Republican control, Santini did not rally to the Democratic cause. Instead, he joined a group of conservative southern Democrats called the "Boll Weevils" who supported changes in traditional Democratic policies. When Reagan made his bold bid for political fame with a huge tax- and spending-cut package early in 1981, Santini announced himself in the president's corner. He backed up his verbal support with several votes indicating a departure from Democratic orthodoxy, including two crucial votes on the House floor that helped the Republican spending plan win approval.

For his part, Cannon was more reluctant to support Reagan. Nevertheless, he had to consider Reagan's unquestioned popularity in Nevada and Santini's positioning as an acolyte of the president. As the various parts of Reagan's budget and taxation plan were considered in the Senate, they were subject to numerous amendments to water them down, and Cannon voted for several of them, consistently stating that he was trying to insert more fairness into Reagan's policies or soften potentially devastating blows to the nation's tax base. As events unfolded in the coming year, it became clear that what Cannon sacrificed in ideological purity he made up for in political points among Nevada Democratic groups affected by the Reagan budget.

What Santini and his advisers may have overlooked in their zeal to become Reaganites was the fact that Santini had to win a Democratic primary before he could take on a Republican opponent in the 1982 general election. There may have been truth to the Santini camp's belief that Santini would be the strongest candidate in the general election, but they perhaps underestimated Cannon's ability to fight a rearguard campaign within his own party. Rogich's contention that anyone could beat Cannon after his 1980 pummeling may have indicated overconfidence by Santini and his supporters, overconfidence that Cannon would capitalize on in waging a dogged war to win over key Democratic constituencies such as the elderly, teachers, and union members.

Early polling results and Santini's popular flirtation with Reagan's policies weren't the only problems facing Cannon in 1981. The Justice Department had not given up its pursuit of Dorfman and other Teamster figures because of the decision not to indict Cannon. On May 22, the DOJ issued an indictment naming Williams, Dorfman, and three others in a conspiracy to bribe Cannon to forestall trucking deregulation. The bribe, Justice alleged, was "an exclusive right to purchase" the 5.8-acre tract in Cannon's neighborhood.

On its face, the indictment should not have caused Cannon any major concern, as the crimes allegedly committed by the conspirators could have been undertaken completely without his knowledge. In practical terms, however, the indictment was the worst news Cannon could have received. Coming just five months after his deliverance from DOJ investigators, it put the whole sordid mess back in the papers and on the airwaves just as Santini was presenting himself as a bright new challenger to Cannon. Roller, head of the Chicago Organized Crime Strike Force, announced he planned to send all evidence in the case to the Senate Ethics Committee. The committee, which had launched a preliminary investigation of Cannon way back in February 1980, had been basically frozen out of the process while the Justice Department was conducting its investigation. All of a sudden, they were given a prominent role, a development someone on the committee evidently relished.

The CBS *Evening News* on June 3, 1981, reported a startling comment from an unnamed member of the Ethics Committee. "It's a tough case. We have no idea if this could lead to the expulsion of Senator Cannon," the anonymous senator reportedly said. He went on, promising that the Ethics Committee "would do the job that the Carter Justice Department did not do when it originally investigated the matter," according to news anchor Dan Rather. It was as if the nightmare of 1980 was being replayed, that the charges against Cannon were to be considered anew despite a nineteen-month investigation by the Justice Department that had cleared him.

Bringing in the Ethics Committee proved a new way to remind Nevada voters of Cannon's 1980 woes, as the five defendants in the conspiracy indictment objected stridently to the committee cranking up its investigation of Cannon. Showing a rational concern about elected officials' predilection to leak juicy charges, they argued that their right to a fair trial would be jeopardized if the government's case was turned over to the Ethics Committee. Cannon, who wanted the matter decided by the Ethics Committee as soon as possible, was caught in the middle of the legal skirmishing. An initial judicial decision not to allow the case to go to Ethics was quickly overturned by a higher court, touching off a new wave of stories about what the Justice Department's tapes might reveal. No matter that those tapes didn't have anything on them to warrant an indictment against Cannon in the first place, the matter was treated in the media as if startling developments could come at any moment.

Cannon's reelection chances probably reached their nadir in late summer 1981. The devastating May poll showing Cannon behind Santini by nearly thirty points was replicated by a second more comprehensive poll in July that showed almost the same result. Cannon, however, was not daunted by the seemingly unending cascade of bad news. He simply did not believe the May poll showing him so far behind—his handwritten notation said, simply, "BS." He felt that Santini, coming off a successful campaign in November 1980, would naturally fare better in early polling, and realized that he would pay a heavy price from the Teamsters investigation. But he also realized that in July 1981, the election was more than a year away, and he would have ample time to make up lost ground. His strategy for doing so was simple and vintage Cannon: work harder than his opponent, emphasize seniority and what it meant for Nevada, and continue to produce tangible results that overshadowed ideological differences. As a result of his attention to home-state needs, his positioning as a less-than-enthusiastic supporter of Reaganomics, and general rebuilding of his reputation, Cannon was able to stem the erosion of public support that had fueled Santini's early success. Thus, the polls began to have a more hopeful tint as 1981 ended, and the spirits of Cannon's staff began to rise.

The first indication that Santini's May and July polling strength was eroding came in October, when a poll reportedly commissioned by the Republican Senatorial Campaign Committee showed Cannon running neck and neck with Santini. Then in December, a poll commissioned by the campaign of Mary Gojack, a Democratic candidate for Congress, showed Santini ahead of Cannon by only 42 to 41 percent, with 17 percent undecided, prompting headlines proclaiming "Cannon, Santini Race Gets Closer."

As 1982 dawned, the polls and political commentators agreed that Cannon had leveled the playing field with Santini, reversing the seemingly catastrophic difference in support indicated by polls in May and July of the previous year. But the race was far from over, as Santini's popularity among younger, more conservative elements of the Nevada Democratic Party, his youth, and his aggressiveness made him a formidable opponent. One area where Santini's continued strength was evident was in fund-raising, and the year-end 1981 reports shook Cannon's staff. Santini had raised nearly $800,000 during the year compared with $541,000 for Cannon, bringing Santini's campaign war chest (including $183,000 left over from his last House campaign) to just under $1 million.

Along with his fund-raising advantage, Santini also had working for him the residual baggage Cannon carried from the April 1980 *New York Times* story and the Teamsters investigation. News reports in late 1981 and early 1982 indicated that Santini was pondering how to use those against Cannon. In November 1981 Ned Day wrote that Santini's forces "have been digging up old newspaper clippings, talking to old Capitol Hill cronies, touching base with those shadowy Washington figures who know all the old war stories, who know where the bodies are buried."

Santini's challenge was to find a way to impugn Cannon's character without appearing to try to reap benefit from the senator's troubles. He decided on making an issue of financial disclosure, challenging Cannon to match him in a full accounting of debts and liabilities, along with public disclosure of income tax records. "It is time for public officials to be held accountable not only for their performance and their abilities, but for their ethics as well," Santini said at a February 16 press conference. Santini denied he was attempting to resurrect Cannon's past business dealings, but added it was "impossible to tell" if Cannon improperly profited from such dealings unless he made a full financial disclosure.

There is no account of how Cannon regarded Santini's ploy, but one can speculate he was perplexed—and angered—on several accounts. For one thing, no one had labored more diligently on the issue of clean election laws than Cannon, who was one of the two or three people most responsible for every piece of election reform then governing candidates for federal office. For another, the biggest obstacle to reform efforts throughout his career had been the House of Representatives, which Santini had inhabited for eight years without raising a peep about campaign reform, much less advancing the cause. And as for disclosure, Cannon had supported the Senate-initiated Public Officials Integrity Act in 1977, which, when passed a year later, established strict disclosure requirements.

Through two campaigns before the disclosure law was enacted, in 1970 and 1976, Cannon had voluntarily disclosed personal assets, liabilities, and net worth. He had, in fact, done everything that Santini was demanding in 1982 years before the congressman issued his challenge. If Cannon enjoyed irony, he could reflect that his personal holdings had been given more scrutiny than those of any elected official in Nevada history. How, Cannon might have wondered, could anyone fall for Santini's transparent attempt to bring up doubts about his integrity couched in the guise of a call for full disclosure?

In his February news conference, Santini had only announced plans to reveal his income tax returns. He waited until April 7 to actually do so, calling another press conference in Reno to pass out returns from the past seven years. Although the returns were of little interest to newspeople, Santini used the forum to claim that integrity would be a major theme of his campaign, and that it would be a major point of difference between him and Cannon. Releasing his income tax returns, Santini said, would reveal how Cannon became a millionaire during his term in the Senate. "He suggested Cannon may be trying to 'hide something,'" one account noted.

This was all political trumpery on Santini's part, using one of the oldest ploys in politics to cause resentment of Cannon—that he was richer than the average Joe. Cannon's May 15, 1982, disclosure form would show a net worth in excess of $1 million. Since Cannon's first voluntary financial disclosure in 1970 had shown a net worth of slightly less than $200,000, how had his fortunes improved so much? The answer was that as a longtime Las Vegan, Cannon had the opportunity to make investments that grew as the city did. Most of Cannon's wealth derived from real estate investments and his stock in the Scott Corporation, both of which had escalated in value over the years. But Santini was less interested in the facts behind Cannon's wealth than in planting doubts about the senator's integrity.

Santini may have realized, like Laxalt in 1964, that impugning Cannon's integrity was crucial to his chances, because not much else was going his way in 1982. The Nevada State Education Association provided the first concrete evidence that Cannon's strategy of concentrating on traditional Democratic blocs was proving successful. After comparing the voting records of Cannon and Santini, the association's leadership recommended to its six thousand members that they support Cannon in the primary.

Another blow to Santini's hopes was delivered by the Nevada AFL-CIO in early May, as that group endorsed Cannon at its state political convention, and its executive secretary, Claude "Blackie" Evans, called Santini a "traitor to the labor cause." The labor organization had fifty thousand members statewide, and they were determined to defeat pro-Reagan, antilabor forces. Their work in turning out voters proved crucial to Cannon's campaign in the closing weeks of the primary.

As Cannon continued to shore up his standing within Democratic ranks, Santini attempted to backtrack from the Reagan policies he had embraced in 1981. "Don't look now, but Rep. Jim Santini seems to be putting more distance between himself and President Reagan," wrote Reno political reporter Martin Griffith in March. Citing Santini criticism of specific Reagan budget cuts and opposition to the president's spending in the Caribbean basin, Griffith noted, "What's particularly surprising to some political analysts is that this is the same Jim Santini who bolted from his party last year to wholeheartedly embrace Reagan's tax and budget cuts. So why the about-face?" Cannon had his own answer to that question, and it filled his speeches to partisan or Democratic-leaning groups throughout 1982: unemployment near 10 percent nationwide, high interest rates, and increasing federal deficits that threatened to rise to $100 billion or more, an unprecedented figure at the time.

Santini's camp escalated its anti-Reagan rhetoric as the year went on, and Santini cast a vote that helped defeat the Reagan-endorsed budget plan. But Santini's earlier support of Reaganomics had been cemented in Democrats' minds, and he only succeeded in looking more like a political opportunist.

Thus, with polls showing his support eroding, with Cannon making headway among strong Democratic constituencies, and having lost confidence in identification with Reagan as a popularity booster, Santini was left with only the "integrity issue" as a possibly persuasive weapon. When he formally filed to oppose Cannon in early July, Santini renewed his call for Cannon to reveal his income tax returns and borrowed a line from the *New York Times* by indicating that Cannon had used his office for personal gain. Referring to the growth of Cannon's wealth between 1970 and 1982, Santini said, "There's a tremendous legislative rags-to-riches story there I believe the people of Nevada are entitled to learn about."

In contrast to Santini's one-note announcement, Cannon was full of ammunition against his opponent when he filed his own reelection papers on July 20. He repeated earlier-announced support for a constitutional amendment requiring a balanced federal budget, called for cuts in defense spending, and reiterated his claim that his seniority would be of benefit to Nevada in years to come. He also attempted to put Santini on the defensive because of his harping on Cannon's alleged lack of integrity, contrasting his "high-road" campaign with Santini's "gutter-brand mudslinging attack." Showing more confidence in his position than earlier in the campaign, he said Santini's strategy "has all but lost him any chance he had to convince Nevada voters he could handle the job."

This was a turning point in Cannon's race against Santini, the vrst time he publicly displayed belief that he was ahead and would prevail. Referring to another recent poll, he said Santini's tactics had taken him from a position of leading by twenty-four points to a point where "according to both Democratic and Republican polls, I now hold a six to 15 point lead and I am still gaining." The pugnacious attitude mirrored Cannon's stance on another hot-button issue emerging in the summer of 1982—the National Conservative Political Action Committee, or NCPAC.

The group was an unintended consequence of the most recent wave of campaign-reform legislation Cannon had steered through the Senate and into law. To accommodate a Supreme Court challenge to the strict campaign-spending limitations of Cannon's 1974 reforms, Congress passed a modified package of reform in 1976 that allowed unlimited "independent expenditures" on campaign issues. These expenditures could be directed toward issues or party-building activities, but could not be associated with a specific candidate.

NCPAC was one of the first organizations to take advantage of the independent-expenditure concept, raising some $1.2 million to spend on races involving six Democratic senators in the 1980 elections. Four of those Democrats—Frank Church in Idaho, George McGovern in South Dakota, Birch Bayh in Indiana, and John Culver in Iowa—were defeated, thanks in part to NCPAC's stridently negative television advertisements against them. The group's founder, Terry Dolan, was quoted as saying, "A group like ours can lie through its teeth and the candidate it helps stays clean." Flush from its success in 1980, NCPAC announced it would vastly up the ante in the 1982 election cycle, promising to raise $10 to $12 million to use against an array of "liberal" senators, Cannon among them.

The group announced that it would spend $113,000 against Cannon through polling and negative television advertising. For all the fear NCPAC inspired by its ability to spend large sums on negative television ads, however, the group was heavy-handed and poorly prepared in its Nevada efforts. For one thing, the criticisms of Cannon were less than convincing, claiming that Cannon was against school prayer, soft on national defense, proabortion, and anti–senior citizen. Cannon had a solid record to contradict NCPAC on all those issues. Partly because of this sloppy research and partly because of an inbred antipathy to eastern groups telling it how to think (NCPAC was headquartered in the Washington suburb of Arlington, Virginia), the Nevada media was hostile to NCPAC. Editorialists echoed Cannon's expressions of horror that such venom-spewing zealots would interfere in a Nevada election and were united in their belief that the group should take its attack ads elsewhere.

Cannon did not stop with a vigorous anti-NCPAC stance, however. He went one step further in linking the group closely with Santini, and it was a linkage Santini spent the rest of the campaign trying to undo. The crux of

Cannon's case against Santini was the one issue highlighted by NCPAC that gained some traction—congressional pay raises. NCPAC claimed that Cannon had voted to increase his own pay five times, and Santini quickly took up the charge, combining it with his message that Cannon was part of a big-spending, taxpayers-be-damned clique that should be retired. His rhetoric about Cannon "becoming a millionaire while in office" also went along nicely with the pay-raise charges. Cannon had consistently voted against pay raises for members of Congress, but NCPAC, with its less-than-compelling regard for truth and its ability to dramatize individual Senate votes, paid no heed to that fact.

As the scorching Nevada summer wound down, Cannon and Santini were locked in seeming stalemate. The idea of debating each other on television, first advocated by Santini in the early days of his challenge and occasionally resurrected as the campaign wore on, began to resonate. Cannon had initially taken the traditional incumbent's position that debates served mainly to give challengers a forum to attack, so he sidestepped the issue. But as it became apparent that Santini could claim as much right to the voters' support as Cannon, the senator gave in. A schedule of three debates was approved by both sides: the first in Las Vegas on August 14, the second in Elko on August 23, and the last in Reno on August 27. The debates provided a fitting climax to a nearly two-year personal battle between the aging, wounded Cannon and the ambitious, aggressive Santini.

The debates dominated media coverage during their two-week run, prompting reams of copy about who fared better, comparisons of their voting records, and endless surmising about what effect they would have on the election's outcome. No clear consensus emerged on any of these issues, as most commentators said the situation at the end of August was pretty much the same as it had been for some time. "Debates Don't Alter Senate Race" headlined a Reno paper over a story by political editor Griffith.

Cannon believed he had achieved one objective through the debates—dispelling any doubts voters may have had about his energy or ability to mix it up with a younger challenger. Whether Santini thought he won the debates or not, he evidently realized as September dawned that he had not clinched the election that was two weeks away. His hammering away on the "integrity issue" during the debates indicated he thought that was his most potent weapon, but he faced a crucial strategic decision at the end of August.

It was then that Rogich revealed the results of his research into negative Cannon publicity. His firm had prepared two "powerful but highly negative commercials" to use against Cannon in the final days. In one, nicknamed "Lady Integrity," a little old lady was depicted in a park setting with her dog, pondering her dire financial circumstances. A voice informs her of Cannon's wealth, and repeats the claim that Cannon was the only man to become a millionaire while sitting in the Senate. "The look of disillusionment and disgust on the old lady's face tells the rest of the story," Day noted in a September 1 column.

That was nothing compared to the second proposed ad, called "Long, Long Time," an effort called by one television executive "one of the most powerful political commercials I've seen."

> This advertisement begins with a black and white photo of Cannon (screen left) looking suspiciously like former Chicago mayor "Boss" Richard Daley—arrogant, imperious and jowly. It's accompanied by a soundtrack that features a honky-tonk tenor sax and a female voice singing the tune "It's been a long, long time." . . . Then comes the clincher. In sequence, as the music continues, a series of newspaper headlines begin appearing screen right, opposite Cannon's picture.
>
> The shrewd combination of the three ingredients—the "Boss" Cannon picture, the honky-tonk music and the headlines—makes for a devastating impact.

The import of Day's column, however, was not merely to describe the ads, but to note that the Santini campaign had decided against using them. It was not a sudden attack of conscience, but a political calculation. The *R-J* had just endorsed Santini in the primary over Cannon, and that fact, according to Day, caused the campaign to shelve the ads because of fear of voter backlash and agreement that Santini didn't need them. Santini turned down requests to discuss the Cannon race for this book, so the question of why he backed off from the ads remains unanswered.

The final widely publicized poll the week before the primary showed a race that was statistically too close to call, with Santini ahead by a 45-41 percent margin but 13 percent of the voters listed as undecided. In the end, the most accurate assessment of the race came from the person who had poured his heart and soul into it, and who, it turned out, had a better feeling for the electorate than all the polling companies combined. On the eve of the election, Cannon said he thought he would beat Santini by about five percentage points if the turnout in Clark County was 60 percent or better. Clark County's turnout was right around 60 percent, and he beat Santini by five percentage points, 50 to 45 percent, or 54,162 votes to 48,979.

Nevada's political journalists pondered many issues in finding a reason for Cannon's comeback, citing his support among traditional Democrats, Santini's shifting positions on issues such as Reaganomics, anti-NCPAC sentiment, and Cannon's ability to outcampaign his younger challenger. To Aubrey Sarvis, who had taken a leave of absence from his Commerce Committee post to help out with the campaign in the final weeks, the answer was simple. "The old man did it," Sarvis said, dismissing other factors. Sarvis perceived that the main reason Cannon beat Santini was his indomitable will. The same intense desire to win that compelled him to undertake his solitary 1956 campaign for the congressional nomination overcame all obstacles in the race against Santini—the daunting polls, Santini's attacks on his integrity, his age, the campaign squabbles, and the enduring threat of bad news from Chicago. Cannon wanted to beat Santini because to lose to someone like him—a turncoat, an opportunist, and a dissembler in Cannon's eyes—stoked all the considerable competitive fires that simmered just below his placid surface. Thus, as Santini contemplated the wreckage of a promising career the day after the election, Cannon basked in the warm glow of victory, receiving congratulatory calls from Senate colleagues Ted Kennedy, Robert Byrd, and John Glenn, the Ohio astronaut-turned-senator who shared Cannon's love for the U.S. space program.

Cannon then pondered the Republican Senate primary—conducted almost in secret because of the riveting drama of the Cannon-Santini race—and its surprising result. Cannon's initial calculation of that result would have been optimistic, because of all the formidable opponents Cannon had encountered—Walter Baring, Fred Anderson, Harry Claiborne, Paul Laxalt, Raggio, Santini—Jacob "Chic" Hecht seemed by far the least threatening.

The late Chic Hecht was an easy man to underestimate, and no one ever underestimated him more or paid a heavier price for it than Cannon. Slight of build—he was the only opponent Cannon ever faced who was shorter than he—speaking with a lisp, and possessed of only a modest political record, Hecht did not appear to be a strong candidate. He had entered the

Republican primary at the last moment and conducted a low-key campaign that emphasized a few simple points: He was the only Republican with prior legislative experience (as state senator), he was a longtime Nevada resident (one of his strongest opponents had lived in Las Vegas only a few years), and he was 100 percent supportive of President Reagan and his policies. Hecht had strong political ties with Laxalt and, through him, to the Republican juggernaut led by smiling, popular President Reagan. During the first of his two terms in the Nevada Assembly, Hecht served as senate minority leader under Governor Laxalt, and took an active role in later Laxalt campaigns. He was the southern Nevada chairman of Reagan's unsuccessful 1976 presidential bid and deputy chief of Nevada's "Reagan for President" drive in the winning year of 1980. He shrewdly calculated the overwhelming popularity of Reagan's policies in Nevada and the equal rise in stature of Laxalt within the Reagan administration. Nevadans loved Paul Laxalt, and they loved Ronald Reagan.

Consumed by his race against Santini, Cannon had lost sight of how brightly the "Reagan Revolution" still burned in the consciousness of Nevadans. Even when presented with postprimary polling data that showed Nevada voters still harbored doubts about him, Cannon could not take Hecht seriously. Following one discussion of the polling data, Chet Sobsey recalled Cannon telling him, "I'm more likely to be run over by a Mack truck than to lose to Chic Hecht."

The most telling finding of the poll, conducted immediately after the primary for Summa Corporation, the Howard Hughes organization in Nevada, was that only 49 percent of voters gave Cannon a favorable job rating. "The attrition caused by the campaign against Santini is reflected by Howard Cannon's significantly lower job rating," said pollster Frank M. Goldsmith. "It has now dropped to the break-even point, and few US Senators or Congressmen have ever won reelection with a rating as marginally unsatisfactory as this one."

This was an ominous judgment, and should have told Cannon he was no better off after nearly two years of bitter conflict with Santini than he was in the gloomy days of late 1980. If the Cannon camp had perceived events correctly, it would have adopted a drastically different campaign strategy than it did against Hecht. Instead of assuming that Nevadans would stop thinking bad things about him without Santini constantly railing about his lack of integrity, it would have realized Cannon's image needed a drastic makeover. Instead of dismissing Hecht as an ineffective stand-in for Reagan-Laxalt, it would have forced the inexperienced campaigner to defend the high unemployment, high interest rates, and burgeoning federal budget deficits that were the by-products of Reagan's tax and budget policies.

But there was no sweeping new strategy coming from the Cannon camp. The campaign was exhausted, both financially and intellectually, from the Santini fight. Cannon's team disastrously believed that a low-level campaign against Hecht was its reward for withstanding the primary assault. For his part, Cannon would not shirk his campaign duties, as he continued his exhaustive schedule of coffees, small-group appearances, and mailings to targeted voters that were the staple of the primary fight. But Cannon was wandering in the wilderness of his own misconceptions, never understanding the grave peril the Hecht candidacy represented.

National Republicans were not so misguided, though, and they rallied behind the Hecht campaign. Hecht received advice from such heavy hitters as the late Lyn Nofziger, Reagan's former chief political adviser who had recently opened his own consulting firm. To direct the campaign's media relations and advertising activities, Hecht chose Ken Rietz, a California advertising and production expert whose credits included producing the glitzy 1980 Republican National Convention for television.

Hecht also received crucial backing from President Reagan himself. After he decided to run, Hecht was whisked off to D.C. for a meeting with Reagan and Nofziger, courtesy of Laxalt. The upshot of the meeting was they were "quite anxious" to see Cannon defeated, Hecht recalled. Nofziger told Reagan, "We're going to need you two times in Nevada for Chic," a request that Reagan fulfilled. "They promised me an awfully lot," Hecht said, "and they came through." In addition to Reagan's two trips, Vice President Bush, Senate majority leader Howard Baker, and Treasury Secretary Donald Regan made campaign visits on Hecht's behalf. Nofziger gave Hecht's primary campaign the patina of Reagan support by stopping in Las Vegas late in August and all but anointing Hecht as the White House's favored candidate. "If Reagan people and Laxalt people are going to remain loyal to the best interests of the President and Sen. Laxalt they'll go ahead and vote for Chic Hecht," Nofziger told reporters, who covered his visit as if he were a head of state.

Hecht's brain trust devised a formula for his campaign that was as simple as it was effective: keep the candidate out of reach of the media, eliminate speeches (that lisp), and hoard campaign cash for a late-breaking media blitz that emphasized Reagan's support of Hecht and attacked Cannon on such basic issues as attendance (which had fallen way off career-long norms as a result of the Santini primary challenge). The media barrage would wrap Hecht completely in a Laxalt-Reagan blanket and allow the accumulated effects of Cannon's Teamster and integrity troubles to drag the embattled incumbent to defeat.

Whether as an offshoot of this strategy or out of genuine moral concerns, Hecht took two steps early in his campaign that seemed brilliant in retrospect. Understanding how Cannon had manipulated the NCPAC issue effectively against Santini, he wrote the organization immediately after the primary and asked it not to intrude in the general election. Even though NCPAC stubbornly insisted on spending advertising dollars against Cannon—and, indeed, launched a last-minute flight of negative ads on one Las Vegas television station that caught Cannon by surprise—Hecht was never associated with them.

Hecht also refused to make hay, directly or indirectly, of Cannon's Teamster troubles. "I refused that [raising the integrity issue]," Hecht said. "I would not let them put that in. He had served his country, he was an air force general, and he spent twenty-four years in the Senate. He had served the state very well; it was just that his time had come." This was similar to his stance in the primary election and speaks well of Hecht's innate decency, but it also had a political calculation to it. Hecht felt deeply that the nasty Cannon-Santini race had alienated voters and that by contributing to the negativity he would harm himself.

Discretion on the Teamster issue was made easier by the fact that the endless bad news created by the Justice Department investigation continued throughout 1982 and right up to election day. Uniformly negative stories did the work of destroying what was left of Cannon's reputation without help from the Hecht campaign. Early in the year Cannon discovered that journalistic excesses such as the *New York Times* story and various misstatements of fact about the investigation were not the end of his troubles with the media.

A reporter with the *Chicago Tribune*, Douglas Frantz, who had been covering the Teamsters investigation, began sniffing out a defense fund Cannon had established to help defray his considerable legal expenses. Frantz was pleased to find that many of Nevada's colorful casino interests with shady reputations were among the contributors to Cannon's fund. That fact alone, however, probably wouldn't have raised many eyebrows in Nevada, as the same people—Moe Dalitz, Al Sachs, and so on—also routinely contributed to Santini and Laxalt, among other Nevada politicians. But Frantz somehow concluded that Cannon had effected a change in Senate rules to allow the establishment of such funds. This was, simply, a falsehood—Cannon applied for permission to establish the legal-defense fund months after the Ethics Committee had approved such vehicles and played no role in that approval—but it gave Frantz's story the added spice it needed to create interest among the Nevada media. Among other prominent coverage, the Sunday, May 16, edition of the *R-J* responded with a blaring front-page headline over Frantz's story. Frantz attributed the information about the change in U.S. Senate rules to a spokesperson for the Senate Ethics Committee, who denied saying it. Nevertheless, the damage was done, and Cannon was once again faced with having responsible authorities trail behind erroneous media accounts to correct the record.

The big bonanza for Hecht in terms of negative publicity, however, was one of those serendipitous events that all the clever political consultants in the world couldn't have arranged: On October 21, less than two weeks before the November 2 general election, the Teamster trial opened in Chicago. Roller had been denied his indictment of Cannon, but as he laid out the case against Williams, Dorfman, and the other defendants, it made little difference. He told the jurors, and a large media contingent, that Williams had conspired to offer Cannon the land across from his Las Vegas home. "In return, the prosecutor said, Mr. Cannon, who was then chairman of the Senate Committee on Commerce and Transportation, was to 'control and delay' legislation opposed by Mr. Williams to deregulate the trucking business," reported the *New York Times*. There it was for Nevada voters to see, the damning charge that had hung over Cannon for nearly three years. "So, although Cannon is not accused of any wrongdoing, he seems nonetheless very much on trial," noted the *Los Angeles Times* after a week of testimony. And, indeed, it must have seemed that way to Nevadans following developments through wire-service accounts in their local papers.

The arc of Cannon's campaign seemed to reach its downward limit just about the time the Teamster trial opened. The initial postprimary polls showed Cannon with a significant lead over Hecht, a fact Hecht did not dispute. Hecht had commissioned a name-recognition survey just before he filed in the Republican primary and found he was known by only 3 percent of Nevada voters, "with a 5 percent margin of error," he added with a chuckle. Even after he entered the primary contest he would eventually win, polls matching him against Cannon showed him thirty to forty points down, he recalled. Polls taken just after the primary also showed large leads for Cannon.

Even with his lead in the polls, mounting a respectable campaign required hundreds of thousands of dollars, and Cannon ended the primary battle with just $153,065 in the bank. He had raised a little over a million dollars for the race against Santini, but would face a much harder time raising funds against Hecht, mainly because there were only about seven weeks between the September 14 primary and the November 2 general election. Cannon raised a respectable amount in that time, $549,141, but it paled in comparison to Hecht's $1.1 million. The difference would be reflected in Hecht's elaborate television, radio, and print ads; billboards; and other campaign activities such as more sophisticated polling than Cannon could afford.

Cannon's main campaign weapons would be his energy, reflected in his indefatigable efforts at small-group meetings, and directed mailings that, as an incumbent U.S. senator, were produced and mailed free of charge. However, if the 1982 general election proved anything, it was the superiority of a mass communications medium such as television over directed mailings. Cannon's television and radio ads were never more than adequate, and this weakness was glaringly apparent in 1982. When Sarvis went to Reno in the final weeks of the primary campaign, he was struck by how poor Cannon's television ads were. Cannon himself called his media "pure, unadulterated bullshit" in a postprimary meeting and told Sobsey to "scrap the whole bunch and start over." But, in an afterthought, he decided to retain spots that included endorsements from some of his Senate colleagues, and other endorsement ads by Grant Sawyer and Reno mayor Barbara Bennett.

The mixed bag of ads favored by Cannon highlighted a weakness in his television campaign—lack of a theme or simple, coherent message that would resonate with voters. Particularly considering the blows his reputation had taken from the Teamster investigation and Santini's attacks on his integrity,

Cannon needed media advisers who understood how to present him to voters in a fresh, compelling way. Instead, he got a hodgepodge, whereas Hecht had the advantage of image specialist Rietz.

As invaluable as Jim Joyce had proved to Cannon throughout his years on his staff and as a campaign consultant for two previous campaigns, he must share some of the blame for the lackluster 1982 general election effort. Joyce had been effective in the primary, helping line up the traditional Democratic groups who were alienated by Santini's adoption of Reagan's policies. He took particular pride in Reno mayor Bennett's endorsement of Cannon, a move he heralded as critical in Cannon's victory. But given his background in advertising and political consulting, Joyce should have insisted on a better media effort, and he made one grievous strategic misjudgment.

One way to demonstrate Cannon's superior grasp of issues over Hecht was through a debate, but Joyce refused to consider it, claiming a debate would give Hecht legitimacy that his record didn't warrant. *R-J* managing editor Mary Hausch reminded Cannon of this refusal in the election's aftermath, when Cannon chided the media for not "smoking out" Hecht more on his positions. She cited the *R-J*'s interest in sponsoring a debate and Joyce's refusal to go along as proof that Cannon's own team had turned down the ultimate smoking-out opportunity. "Knowing your superior knowledge of the issues facing our nation, I was continually amazed that you, or your staff, did not want a face-to-face meeting to occur," she wrote. In a sad testament to how Joyce had let him down, Cannon wrote in the margin of Hausch's letter, "Is this true?" The proud senator had not even been informed of perhaps the single most important decision of the campaign.

Both Rietz and Hecht used the same phrase to describe the type of campaign waged against Cannon: "California-style." To Rietz, who had worked on California campaigns for Nixon and unsuccessful lieutenant governor candidate Mike Curb, it was the only style he knew. It stressed a heavy media bombardment keyed to negative impressions of the opponent divined through polling. In a postelection interview, Rietz said he spent two-thirds of Hecht's $1 million–plus campaign budget on media, most concentrated in the final weeks.

What this foretold was the diminution—or outright abandonment—of the person-to-person style of Nevada campaigning. No more would there be committees for candidates in every county, elaborate headquarters operations located in the major cities, or innumerable small-group gatherings throughout the state. With a larger and more distracted audience, the simplistic world of a thirty-second television commercial would constitute the voters' primary knowledge of candidates.

Cannon himself made the Hecht campaign more successful by almost totally ignoring it. In an interview, Rietz said he was surprised that Cannon never took Hecht seriously and noted that "it allowed us to go on with our strategy. We were able to conduct that race the way we wanted, and there was no counteracting to our campaign."

Hecht's campaign started slowly, given a strategy of making no speeches, issuing few news releases, and granting no media interviews. To get him in front of voters in a safe, positive way, it had a wonderfully effective tactic—the presidential visits. The first came on October 8, with Reagan and the full presidential entourage appearing with Hecht before a large, adoring Homecoming Day crowd on the Reno campus of the University of Nevada.

Reagan flew south later that day for a private, $1,000-per-person event at entertainer Wayne Newton's sprawling complex in southeast Las Vegas. An estimated $50,000 of the proceeds went to Hecht's campaign, and Hecht received the added benefit of a Reagan endorsement in front of two hundred of the city's best-heeled residents. Attacking Cannon's most potent campaign weapon, Reagan told the crowd that "seniority is not an issue when you're the minority party" and uttered a phrase that resonated deeply within Hecht's heart: "If you like what I'm doing and you want me to continue, you've got to send me Chic" was the way Hecht remembered it twenty-two years later.

When Reagan returned to Las Vegas on October 28, five days before the election, the Senate race had entered a decisive phase, although Cannon and Hecht perceived things completely differently. The Sunday before Reagan's visit, both the *Gazette* in Reno and the *R-J* in Las Vegas carried front-page stories all but conceding the race to Cannon, based on a poll commissioned jointly by the two publications. Cannon led Hecht 47 to 34 percent, with 18 percent undecided, a margin pollster Hugh Schwartz called apparently insurmountable. "It's very hard to see a scenario where Cannon could lose," Schwartz said. But Hecht had reason to believe otherwise. With access to new day-to-day tracking polls paid for by the Republican Senatorial Campaign Committee, Hecht knew that he was rapidly closing the gap. Cannon, who didn't utilize tracking polls, was oblivious to the disaster lurking for his campaign.

With the newspapers' poll results widely publicized and the added bonus of an endorsement from Reno's *Nevada State Journal* announced just the day before, Cannon was relaxed when Reagan made his second visit. He sprinted to the three network affiliates in Las Vegas to render an opinion on Reagan's speech just as they were reporting it on their evening newscasts. A confident Cannon said he was glad to have the president in Las Vegas, but wished he would come back after the election when the visit wouldn't be for pure political benefit. He criticized Hecht for a comment noted in the Reno paper's endorsement—that Hecht couldn't think of a single thing to disagree with Reagan about. Cannon offered nearly 12 percent unemployment in Clark County and a record federal deficit of $110 billion as things that perhaps should have caused Hecht some concern.

The endorsement of Cannon by the Reno paper, which had supported Santini in the primary, was surprising to the Cannon camp. Praising Cannon as an independent thinker, the paper said, "The same cannot be said for Chic Hecht. He follows President Reagan down the line on almost every issue, revealing few if any thoughts of his own. Such intense me-too politics is much too simplistic for the problems facing the United States. In fact, it is frightening." Here was a powerful Cannon campaign theme, delivered, ironically, from a source that had supported Santini. That the Reno paper turned against Reagan and his champion Laxalt was a remarkable statement about Hecht's shortcomings as a candidate. But Cannon had not made a case against Hecht on this ground or any other. Many a Cannon supporter looked back at the Hecht campaign and wished for a single encounter before hostile reporters that would have contrasted Cannon's experience in government with the simplistic nostrums Hecht used in answer to every question presented him. Even though Cannon's campaign turned the Reno endorsement into an ad in the campaign's final days, it was too little, too late to stem the tide that would carry Hecht to victory.

Hecht's 5,657-vote win over Cannon (120,377 to 114,720) was the result of sound campaign strategy, a well-heeled campaign treasury that paid for the television campaign from mid-October on, Reagan's visits, and a one-two punch of negativity that staggered Cannon one last time: NCPAC opened its media blitz on Cannon's attendance and the pay-raise issue at almost the same time that the Teamsters trial in Chicago raked up its unsavory brew again. On television for the last two weeks of the campaign voters saw endless repetitions of Hecht being embraced by Reagan and other top Republicans. Giant newspaper ads compared Hecht's desire to cut federal spending to Cannon's reputation as a big spender. In the news columns, readers pored over testimony from the Teamsters trial. On television, the NCPAC assault ran continuously on one channel.

It was, finally, enough. Enough currents swept through Nevada in the campaign's final days to wash Cannon away after decades of effort by Laxalt and his fellow Republicans to accomplish that feat. One person with intimate knowledge of the campaign called the Hecht win a "fluke," a once-in-a-lifetime confluence of events that no one could have planned or prevented. But Hecht had a different take on the victory, giving credit to his mentor, Reagan confidant, and symbol of Nevada's rugged independence. "Laxalt, Laxalt, Laxalt!" Hecht said when asked to name the greatest factor in his victory. Laxalt steered him to Nofziger and Rietz, Laxalt provided the support from Reagan, and Laxalt's Senate staff and former aides played major roles in Hecht's campaign. "I had so much support from Laxalt and his family, all his friends up north," Hecht recalled. In a comment indicating that the smoldering resentment from the 1964 Cannon-Laxalt race remained strong in 1982, Hecht remembered one reaction from the Laxalt camp about his victory. "They all said the same thing afterwards: 'We got even.'"

Why was Cannon misjudged so completely by a variety of newspeople, political opponents, investigators, and, eventually, the voters of Nevada, who issued the final verdict on his senatorial conduct? That question lurks most prominently over his career, and provides a key to his personality and his destiny. But there is no single answer, as indicated by comments from several people who knew him intimately.

Chet Sobsey, who was introduced to one side of Cannon's persona in his political campaigns of 1956 and 1958, emphasizes a lack of warmth, equating that with unalloyed political ambition. "He was dedicated to only one thing, the aggrandizement of Howard Cannon," Sobsey said in retrospect about the man he served for twenty-four years, but seemingly never really understood. "I still don't know what makes him tick," Sobsey added.

Many things undercut Sobsey's analysis, including Cannon's long, loving relationship with Dorothy; the love and admiration of his daughter, Nancy, and son, Alan; and his close friendships with people like Frank Scott and others. In addition, Sobsey's professional relationship with Cannon, which weakened rather than grew over the years, was atypical of others who served him for a long time. Frank Krebs, Sara Denton, Aubrey Sarvis, Lee Walker, and others saw more in their boss than Sobsey. All besides Krebs, who is deceased, look back at their years in the Senate with satisfaction and appreciation for the opportunity.

But all those see a kernel of truth in what Sobsey said. "He was a cold fish" was the blunt assessment of Chet Smith, an aide to many Nevada politicians who spoke highly of none of them. Sara Denton, who accompanied Cannon on innumerable visits with interest groups, elderly people, local politicians, and favor seekers, looked beyond the facade. Cannon's most telling personality trait, she said, was shyness. He was not comfortable among strangers, and, instead of dominating a room of people he did not know, would seemingly be dominated by them. That's why he would invariably seek out a friend or relative, if he could find one, when entering a campaign function. He was more at ease asking about a constituent's family, job, or medical condition than glad-handing the masses.

Cannon also did not seem to need many people. This was a by-product of his austere cowboy upbringing, and the inward-looking nature of the Mormon religion. Misunderstood by nonbelievers, reviled and persecuted throughout their history, Mormons turned to family for sustenance and distrusted outsiders. Howard and Dorothy did not socialize widely either in Washington, D.C., or in Las Vegas. They had each other, their families, and close friends, and made do with them.

Cannon was also stubborn and loyal to a fault. He befriended controversial characters such as Ben Goffstein, Jack Conlon, and Harry Claiborne, and stuck with them throughout their lives—and even after. He helped Goffstein's widow, Dottie, and Conlon's widow, Bunny, sort out problems with their husbands' estates while serving in the Senate. If he had outlived Claiborne, who died in 2004, Cannon would probably have been involved in some issues of his tangled personal life. One of the most poignant moments of Cannon's life came in October 1986, when Claiborne was fighting a desperate battle to save the federal judgeship bestowed upon him by Cannon.

Convicted in 1983 of filing false income tax returns, Claiborne was utilizing his full constitutional rights in demanding impeachment and conviction by Congress to remove him from the bench. Federal judgeships are conferred for life, and Claiborne did not intend to let the conviction—which he bitterly contested—end his career. After the House had voted four articles of impeachment in July, the Senate acted to try Claiborne on October 9. Sitting in the well of the Senate chamber were Claiborne, his lead attorney, Oscar B. Goodman—the current mayor of Las Vegas—and Cannon. Cannon, who was a major figure in so many dramatic Senate roll call votes—on the 1964 cloture motion, the Panama Canal treaties, the airline and trucking deregulation bills—dutifully tallied the yeas and nays on the four articles of impeachment. The Senate convicted Claiborne on three of the four articles and, by so doing, removed him from office.

It could not have been a comfortable moment for Cannon, returning to the Senate chamber to represent a client who evoked almost no sympathy from his congressional accusers. It does not take much imagination to speculate that many of those House and Senate members lumped Claiborne and Cannon together as examples of inevitable Nevada corruption. Cannon had endured one of the most humiliating experiences of his life at the hands of federal prosecutors, returning to Chicago following his defeat by Hecht to testify in the Williams trial. As he answered "No" to a series of questions lodged by Williams's attorney—Was a bribe ever offered? Did you discuss derailing the trucking bill?—Cannon became more closely associated with the defendants than ever. Indeed, he was a defense witness for Williams, not because of any sympathy for the Teamsters or their actions but because he could only answer honestly that the nefarious deeds laid at their door were unknown to him. Williams, Dorfman, and the other three defendants were found guilty of conspiring to bribe Cannon. To underscore the lurid aspects of the Teamster case, Dorfman was shot dead in a Chicago parking lot following the conviction lest he be induced to reveal secrets of Teamster involvement in the Las Vegas underworld.

Driven from office because of his own brush with federal prosecutors, Cannon could only reflect on the price of association with Las Vegas as Claiborne suffered the same fate. No one made Cannon return a call to Dorfman to set up a meeting in his office, and certainly no one made him mention the attempted land purchase, but Cannon paid a high price for that decision. Claiborne's alleged sins were of a different nature than Cannon's, but both men were examples of the power of the federal government to investigate, impugn, and prosecute individuals who incur its wrath.

Cannon has not basked in public acclaim since leaving office. Unlike many of his contemporaries, no buildings in Las Vegas or elsewhere in Nevada bear his name. This seems odd considering the effect he had on Nevada and the United States during his Senate career. He was a leading force in shaping the nation's tactical air defenses during a time of explosive growth in the size and importance of Nellis Air Force Base outside Las Vegas, and his influence undoubtedly played a role in that base's success. He worked quietly and effectively to aid Nevada's gambling industry during a period when it was under the greatest scrutiny from federal forces in its history. He played a low-key but nevertheless important role in the ongoing process of keeping the nation's campaign laws congruent with democratic principles and honesty. And he engineered the most comprehensive dismantling of federal control over the vital transportation industry in the twentieth century.

But he was a workhorse, not a show horse, and somehow never projected an image as sweeping as his accomplishments. He was not embittered by lack of adulation and was ever grateful for the wondrous things his life brought him: a military record as stirring as any of his generation, a public career that took him to the forefront of national policy, financial success, and a close, loving family. It wasn't a bad life for a former Utah cowboy.

Cannon remained in Washington for eleven years following his defeat. He had been doing the usual ex-member-of-Congress things, consulting with defense contractors on legislation affecting them, serving on various boards of directors, and delivering the odd speech at political functions. But he faded almost to oblivion, as most ex-members do, and daughter Nancy began expressing concern over her parents' welfare as they reached their eighties. Finally, Nancy convinced them to return to Las Vegas in 1993, where they lived a mostly happy and peaceful retirement.

Cannon received one more painful political jolt in 1994 when the powers in Reno—far removed from memory of Cannon's services to the community—eliminated his name from Reno Cannon International Airport. There is a Howard W. Cannon terminal in Reno-Tahoe International Airport, as the facility is now known, as well as a Howard W. Cannon Aviation Museum amid the vast sprawl of McCarran Airport in Las Vegas. Neither reflects the impact Cannon had on aviation in Nevada and the world.

Chic Hecht fulfilled the limited promise of his Senate career by serving only a single term, giving way to Richard Bryan in 1988. Jim Santini switched parties to become a Republican and run against Harry Reid for Laxalt's seat when Laxalt retired in 1986. But Santini was defeated, and now lives in the D.C. area as a lobbyist. By 1988, therefore, Nevada Democrats had undone the work of Laxalt and his fellow Republicans in helping elect Hecht. Harry Reid and Richard Bryan replaced Alan Bible and Howard Cannon as a Democratic Senate duo until Bryan's retirement in 2000. Today, Reid serves as majority leader of the Senate, serving as an example of how a Las Vegas–area politician (he was born in the tiny town of Searchlight, southeast of Las Vegas) can survive the pitfalls of his home base and achieve the leadership positions that were mentioned briefly for Cannon but never seriously pursued.

For all his hard work and accomplishments, Cannon evoked few laudatory memorials. Those who appreciated his quiet behind-the-scenes method of getting things done were themselves low-key and ignored by all but insiders. Dorothy Robyn's chronicle of the trucking deregulation battle is one example, and the *Almanac of American Politics* is another. Just as *Congressional Quarterly*'s unsung reporters covered the day-in-and-day-out progress of legislation, and were unique in their appreciation of senators who abetted that progress, the *Almanac* captured Cannon's contributions better than any other publication in its 1982 edition. "Barely known outside his home state, Cannon made himself one of the chamber's pure power brokers. . . . He presided over enactment of an exceptional array of aviation, trucking, railroad, maritime, communications and consumer legislation. . . . Some of the most significant economic deregulation measures since the New Deal became law in large part because of Cannon's support."

When Cannon died on March 6, 2002, of congestive heart failure after suffering from Alzheimer's disease for several years, a few of his contemporaries showed they appreciated his contributions. Richard Bryan, who capped a political career as attorney general and governor by winning back Cannon's Senate seat from Hecht, eulogized Cannon as "the most underappreciated public figure in my time." Bryan, whose father, Oscar, was a contemporary of Cannon in the political skirmishes of Las Vegas in the 1950s, cast the first vote in his life in favor of Cannon's 1958 Senate bid. He accurately pegged Cannon as "essentially a modest and shy man." He added: "He was the antithesis of the flamboyant politician. His life was extraordinarily colorful, yet almost nobody knew anything about it."

Cannon's daughter, Nancy, helped make life comfortable for Howard and Dorothy after they returned to Las Vegas. She made sure a gentle palomino named Bandit was always stabled at his home, and remembers her dad gaining pleasure from simply petting the animal almost until his last day. Howard and Dorothy both suffered from Alzheimer's in their last years, but Cannon recognized his wife and drew comfort from her presence until the end. Dorothy, who would pass away on May 11, 2003, a little more than a year after her husband, would occasionally tell her daughter to help her pack for a return to Washington, flashing on memories of the innumerable trips the couple took together. But, as vivid as those memories were in Dorothy's fading mind, there were no more trips for her and Howard.

Notes

INTRODUCTION : AN HONORABLE MAN

1   "Defeat Reality": *U.S. News and World Report,* June 11, 2001 (cover story).

1 : BLOOD MATTERS

7   His great-grandfather: This and succeeding accounts of the Cannon family's role in St. George history are taken from a handwritten account by David Henry Cannon, Howard's grandfather, on March 13, 1917, and from a speech Howard Cannon delivered at the centennial celebration of St. George on August 27, 1961, which was placed in the *Congressional Record* on August 28, 1961, s16116. David Cannon rendered a slightly different account, this one typewritten, for a presentation on February 19, 1922.

10   moved in with: Author interview with Evelyn Jay, Cannon's sister.

11   sold the motel: Ibid. The deed for the sale is also in Cannon's private papers.

11   "stern but loving": Nancy Cannon Downey interview with her father, December 29, 1990.

12   rented a basement room: Jay interview.

12   "Put your shoulder": Downey interview.

12   Howard's intelligence: Rose manuscript.

13   "It was kind": Downey interview.

13   "Howard and Gene": Rose manuscript.

14   awarded a music scholarship: Downey interview.

14   "I was pretty good": Ibid.

15   An article: The clipping is in a personal scrapbook of Cannon's, but the source is not indicated.

15   "could have been": Downey interview.

16   Repeating the pattern: Several articles and letters in Cannon's scrapbook chronicle the progress of both groups.

16   played a weekly: Rose manuscript.

16   Howard's managerial skills: Letters from Cannon's scrapbook.

16   The boys had a major: Cannon's scrapbook holds the photo and caption, identified as from the *Seattle Post-Intelligencer,* but the date and page are not given.

16   landing a booking: Letters and other material from Cannon's scrapbook.

16   According to the ship's: Program in Cannon's scrapbook.

17   His excellent grades: Downey interview.

17   "chummed around together": Martinez.

17   Something else had: Rose manuscript.

18   "I had a date": Ibid.

18   Addressed to "Friend Dorothy": Letter to Dorothy, June 18, 1936.

19   Dorothy's fiancé: *Washington County News,* March 7, 1935, 1.

19   Howard's girlfriend: *Reminder,* April 16, 1940. The tragedy was reported in a local publication identified only as the *Reminder.*

19   "He was really": Jay interview.

2 : WAR CLOUDS

21   sitting county attorney: *Washington County News,* November 1, 1934, 19.

21   Cannon filed for: Ibid., August 2, 1938, 2.

21   He came close: Ibid., November 4, 1938, 1.

21   accepted a position: Ibid., January 5, 1939, 3.

22   "Howard Cannon's Work": Page and date unavailable.

22   Cannon also became: *Washington County News,* June 22, 1940, 1.

22   Cannon prevailed by: Ibid., November 6, 1940, 4.

22   Cannon also followed: Various articles in the *Washington County News* in 1941 detailed Cannon's service in this unit.

22   Cannon found himself: *Washington County News,* March 13, 1941, 1.

22   Cannon was assigned: Ibid., April 3, 1941, 1.

23   A newspaper story: *Los Angeles Times,* November 11, 1941, page unavailable.

23   "I was playing": Downey interview.

23   "I didn't hesitate": Martinez.

23   "I was amazed": Rose manuscript.

24   had a "shaky beginning": Remarks by Col. Krebs, U.S. Air Force Academy, October 10, 1986, dedicating a memorial plaque to the 440th Troop Carrier Group.

25   Although military leaders: Young, 53.

26   managed to train: Ibid., 54.

26   For their part: Cannon detailed these activities and the trip to England in a long letter to his sister, Evelyn, and brother-in-law, George Jay, on May 12, 1945, written at a base near Metz, France. The detail indicates he kept a diary during the war.

26   It began with the buildup: These and successive details were provided in a second letter Cannon wrote from France on May 16, 1945, this time addressed to his parents.

27   *Stoy Hora:* Information supplied to author by radio operator Bill Quick.

27	Commanding officer: Young, 149.
27	Cannon and Krebs relied: Krebs's words that follow are from his Air Force Academy remarks, Cannon's from his May 16, 1945, letter to his parents.
28	lying in ambush: Young, 149.
28	In vivid contrast: BBC correspondent Smith's written account was carried in a *News of the World* dispatch on June 6, 1944, that was picked up by numerous publications.
28	A chronic problem: Young, 233.
29	Orders for the: The most thorough account of Cannon and Krebs's crash landing and evasion of Nazi troops in Holland is in Young, 291–97.
29	*Miss Yank:* Information supplied by Bill Quick.
29	"Perfect flying weather": Sullivan, 2.
30	described the flight: Young, 291.
30	"We put him": Ibid. Hils emphasizes the importance of the pinpoint drop achieved by the Krebs-Cannon crew, along with an assessment of the Normandy mission as "a good drop." Hils vigorously disputes numerous disparaging accounts of the TCG's record as tainted by bad information and dubious sources, and, in fact, is petitioning for a rewrite of the official military history of the Normandy invasion.
30	Cannon recalled seeing: Young, 291.
30	Cannon thought initially: This is Hils's conclusion from studying all available information about the event.
30	Krebs's account is: Young, 291.
31	"As we drifted": Ibid., 292.
31	"We lay flat": This detail was supplied in an account of the ordeal that appeared under Cannon's byline in the March 26, 1961, edition of the nationally syndicated Sunday supplement *Family Weekly.*
31	A Dutch farmer: His identity was revealed to Cannon in correspondence between members of the Dutch Underground after the war. The successful concealment of Cannon, Krebs, and the others was a source of great pride for the Underground and was extensively related in news articles in Holland.
31	As Cannon recalled: "Escape to Freedom."
31	"I frightened him": Young, 292.
31	Wary, tired: "Escape to Freedom."
31	"We were quartered": Young, 293.
32	The group of: Ibid., 294.
33	two young Dutch: In correspondence with Frans and Charles many years later, Cannon expressed surprise that they were twenty and twenty-two years old, respectively, when assisting him. Cannon said he and Krebs thought they were fifteen or sixteen at the time.

33   "This was our": Ibid.

33   Finally, after what: Ibid., 296.

35   "despite the most": Unidentified newspaper account.

35   Krebs had broken: Information provided by Christine Goyer, Krebs's daughter, in a letter to the author.

36   "It was the greatest": Associated Press story in unidentified newspaper, January 13, 1946.

36   Dorothy's younger sister: Interview with author.

37   and that afternoon: A good account of the wedding was in the *R-J*, December 22, 1945, 4.

37   "still a small town": Greenspun, 68.

38   it was the ultimate: Moehring, 46.

38   "the thing that excited": *R-J*, November 10, 1958, 2.

3 : CITIZEN CANNON / SENATOR CANNON

41   "If you're asking": Interview with author.

41   "It wasn't uncommon": Interview with author.

41   He soon was able: Cannon, letter to Dorothy.

41   who had established: *Humboldt Star,* July 31, 1942, 1.

42   The crime blotter: *R-J*, December 21, 1946, 2.

42   Claiborne remembered: Interview with author.

42   achieved his first: *R-J*, March 15, 1950, 1.

42   In the inevitable: *Sun,* May 2, 1952, 2.

42   On June 5: *R-J*, June 5, 1952, 1.

43   Cannon received: Cannon private papers.

43   following scenario: *Nevada Report,* January 3, 1970, 7–8.

44   filing as a candidate: *R-J*, April 3, 1947, 2.

44   "a constant visitor": *R-J*, April 12, 1947, 2.

44   "hot and close": *R-J*, March 31, 1949, 2.

44   Cannon's victory margin: *R-J*, May 4, 1949, 1.

45   Cragin had been: Moehring, 56.

45   A public-power: Ibid., 27.

45   took a sudden: Ibid., 28.

45   "worst political crisis": Ibid., 31.

46   This amounted: Ibid., 219.

46   C. D. Baker: Ibid., 56.

47   had their main: Edwards, 28.

47   The airline had provided: Wright, 5.

48   His announcement: *Sun,* March 7, 1953, 1.

48   sniffed out the: *R-J*, March 7, 1953, 1.

49	numbered only around 50: Kaufman, 326.
49	Migration of: Ibid., 340.
49	segregated housing: Moehring, 37.
50	overt segregation: Kaufman, 341.
50	The standard reply: Ibid., 354.
50	introducing a bill: *Sun,* February 21, 1953, 5.
51	indefinitely postpone it: *Sun,* March 17, 1953, 1.
51	appearing before: *R-J,* August 6, 1953, 7.
51	Greenspun chimed in: *Sun,* August 6, 1953, 1.
51	In a memo: Cannon private papers.
52	At a special: *Sun,* January 8, 1954, 1.
52	in a letter: *R-J,* January 14, 1954, 1.
53	"[Cannon] came back": Wilson oral history, 88.
53	As Ralph Denton: Interview with author.
53	National polls suggested: See, for example, Gallup Poll in *Nevada State Journal,* October 1, 1958, 4.
53	He had surprised: *Sun,* December 2, 1955, 1.
54	Cannon and Baker: *R-J,* December 20, 1955, 1. This article contains Baker's official withdrawal, but there was no official announcement by Cannon.
54	Dickerson's son: Letter to Nancy Cannon Downey, March 13, 2002.
54	Cannon announced: *Sun* and *R-J,* May 3, 1956, 1.
54	"revealed Cannon's unreal": Interview with author.
55	"He knew where": Interview with author.
56	Sawyer moved first: *R-J,* July 10, 1958, 1.
56	"Sawyer Spikes": *Sun,* July 11, 1958, 1.
56	Cannon told the leader: Downey, 3.
56	"Howard and Dorothy": Interview with author.
57	"Cannon was programmed": Interview with author.
58	"Business Men": Downey, 8.
58	He founded: *Sun,* September 13, 1955, 1.
59	The brutal murders: *Sun,* December 4, 1958, 1.
59	According to these reports: Cannon's report to the secretary of the Senate.
59	"The bulk of": *Congressional Quarterly Almanac, 1965,* 1572.
60	Bramlet in the '50s: "First 100 Persons."
60	"Significant in the 1958": *R-J,* August 3, 1958, 5.
60	"[Conlon] handled": Rose manuscript.
61	his five horses: *R-J,* October 12, 1958, 30.
61	controversial Berkeley Bunker: Bunker was a central figure in many of the Democratic Party's setbacks in the '40s and '50s. He was a surprise choice of Governor E. P. "Ted" Carville in 1940 to fill in for U.S. senator Key

Pittman, who died shortly after winning reelection to what would have been his sixth term. Forced to stand for election on his own two years later, Bunker was defeated for the Senate seat by former governor James Scrugham. He later won election to Congress, but earned the enmity of numerous Democrats by seeking the Senate again in 1946. His opponent then was the same man who had appointed him to take Pittman's place, former governor Carville. Carville had resigned the governorship and had himself appointed to the Senate when Scrugham died in 1945. Bunker defeated Carville in the primary, but lost to Malone.

63   bizarre positions: These included his 1957 call to expunge the Senate record of its vote to censure Senator Joseph McCarthy (*Sun,* May 10, 1957, 3), a 1955 trip to Russia that included praise for the Soviet government's balanced budget (*Sun,* September 18, 1955, 1), and a March 2, 1958, appearance on Edward R. Murrow's popular TV show *See It Now,* in which he predicted the imminent onset of the "greatest depression in history" because of the perfidy of New York financial institutions.

63   "ran the campaign": Rose manuscript.

4 : EDUCATION OF A SENATOR

65   The *New York Times: Times,* November 6, 1958, 24; *Post,* November 6, 1958, A2; *Washington Star,* November 7, 1958, A4.

66   "The Democratic tide": Ibid., *Times.*

66   "He didn't mind": Interview with author.

66   "met the press": *Post,* December 6, 1958, page unavailable.

67   house on West Charleston: The house had been built by Buck Blaine, the Golden Nugget executive who attended Cannon's wedding. According to an article by Florence Lee (Cahlan) Jones in the *R-J* (July 22, 1979, page unavailable), it had several famous residents in addition to the Cannons. While Blaine was overseas in World War II, it was rented to Rex Bell, the western movie star, Nevada lieutenant governor, and husband of "It Girl" Clara Bow. When the Cannons moved to Washington, its most famous resident was Perle Mesta, the D.C. "hostess with the mostest." Among many parties she hosted there was one for her nephew William S. Tyson, a Reno dairyman who was running for Congress. He was unsuccessful, but the party was spectacular, according to Ms. Jones. The house has since been torn down to make way for a state building.

67   It was a "lovely home": *R-J,* date and page unavailable.

68   "a Mormon and": Interview with author.

68   "When Cannon asked": Interview with author.

68   His sister: Interview with author.

69   "He always joked": Interview with author.

71   "Insiders who watched": *R-J,* January 15, 1959, 5.

71   Cannon received a letter: Cannon papers, 86th Congress, Box 2, Folder 49.

71   Just as Cannon: Ibid., Box 1, Folder 2.

71   His ultimate dream: Archie, in fact, became the fifth African American to practice law in Nevada, but the first who was a product of the Las Vegas school system. He later was named head of Nevada's 450-person State Employment Security Department.

72   The new senator's: Ibid.

72   "My appreciation": Ibid.

72   McMillan added: Ibid.

73   The *Sun* carried: *Sun,* January 15, 1959, 1.

73   The *Sun* editorialized: *Sun,* January 17, 1959, 12.

74   "We are enjoying": Cannon papers, 86th Congress, Box 30, Folder 485.

74   He wrote letters: Ibid.

75   They cosponsored: Ibid., Box 34, Folder 530.

75   and, in an effort: Ibid., Box 34, Folder 535.

76   Bible introduced: Ibid., Box 32, Folder 502.

76   "This is probably": Ibid. The letter was from Dick Toothman of the Stockmen's Motor Hotel in Elko.

77   he was successful: *Nevada State Journal,* July 3, 1964, 3.

77   He had been warmly: One of several gracious letters from Stennis to Cannon, this one expressed how pleased Stennis was that Cannon was joining the subcommittee (Cannon papers, 86th Congress, Box 3, Folder 72).

78   Cannon's handwritten: Ibid.

78   Within a year: *R-J,* May 13, 1959, page unavailable.

78   The figure would: *Reno Evening Gazette,* April 27, 1961, page unavailable.

78   "placing a dollar": *San Antonio Express and News,* June 24, 1961, B1. Cannon was speaking before a meeting of the Reserve Officers Association in San Antonio.

78   The price tag: *Boulder City News,* January 25, 1962, page unavailable.

78   Kennedy's historic challenge: "Special Message," 10A.

79   *Sun* revealed: *Sun,* May 26, 1961, 1.

80   Senate floor speech: *Congressional Record,* August 20, 1962, 16051–59. Copy found in Cannon papers, 87th Congress, Box 6, Folder 72.

80   "No speech by": *Omaha World-Herald,* August 22, 1962, 1.

80   "We think this": *Washington Star,* August 22, 1962, page unavailable.

83   Cannon received praise: *Congressional Record,* September 15, 1961, 18478.

83   Mansfield added: Cannon papers, 87th Congress, Box 22, Folder 272.

84   on behalf of: Cannon papers, 87th Congress, Box 2, Folder 43.

84	and pleading various: Ibid., Box 3, Folder 45.
84	gave startling evidence: Ibid., 88th Congress, Box 31, Folder 390, contained the *Post*'s May 27 rendition of the Evans-Novak column, but there is no further discussion, memos, and so on.
86	The president hailed: *Mineral County Forum,* June 14, 1961, page unavailable.
87	the president addressed: *Sun,* September 29, 1963, 1.
87	most difficult vote: Cannon papers, 88th Congress, Box 9, Folder 110.
88	calling it a: *R-J,* November 23, 1963, 3.
89	but Cannon voted no: Titus, *Nevada Historical Society,* 15.
89	He voted "yea": Ibid., 17.
89	been on the telephone: *Nevada State Journal,* June 20, 1965, 1.
89	Senate historian revealed: The U.S. Senate historian's office sent the author a facsimile of the official tally, which recorded Cannon's vote as the seventieth in favor of cloture.
90	editorialized the *Sun: Sun,* June 20, 1964, 8.
90	a prepared statement: Cannon papers, 88th Congress, Box 4, Folder 53.

5 : CONFLICT AND CHALLENGE

91	closest Senate contest: Nevada's intrepid state archivist, Guy Louis Rocha, recently established this fact through an exchange of e-mails with the U.S. Senate historian.
92	While a student: *R-J,* November 24, 1958, 1.
93	"Conlon was relentless": Denton and Green, 237.
93	"Jack took the lead": Ibid., 247.
95	first major political: *R-J,* September 29, 1963, 2.
95	He replied: *Nevada State Journal,* October 30, 1963, page unavailable.
96	Organized by: Goffstein was general chairman of the dinner and its toastmaster. He was regarded as the leading Las Vegas businessman instrumental in the dinner's success.
96	drew a sold-out: *R-J,* April 21, 1963, 1.
97	"special agent": *Nevada Appeal,* June 25, 1964, 1.
98	a paper fortune: *Congressional Quarterly Almanac, 1964,* 948.
98	LBJ might not make it: Dallek, *Flawed Giant,* 38–41.
99	lead to an indictment: *Post,* January 30, 1967, 1.
99	"I do not intend": *Congressional Quarterly Almanac, 1964,* 955.
100	Mollenhoff had broken: Mollenhoff, *Investigative Reporting,* 293.
100	The vending-machine company: *Congressional Quarterly Almanac, 1964,* 952.
100	"marriage was hatched": Interview with author.

101	"high-style hideaway": Mollenhoff, *Investigative Reporting*, 283.
101	matched paisley top: *New York Herald-Tribune*, March 8, 1964, page unavailable.
102	chartered an airplane: *Nevada State Journal*, March 21, 1964, 1.
102	reportedly not attended: Opinions vary on this point, as some participants at Cannon's dinner said Baker was not in the crowd and some said they remember seeing him. Baker's name was not listed on a passenger manifest for the flight (Special Collections, University of Delaware Library, papers of Senator Williams), but some news accounts contend he attended along with his girlfriend, Carol Tyler, who was on the passenger list (*Washington Daily News*, March 5, 1964, 20).
102	would defeat Cannon: Claiborne letter to author, November 28, 2003.
103	over the edge: *Nevada State Journal*, July 4, 1964, 16. Laxalt said the reapportionment decision was not the "controlling issue" in his decision, "but was the straw that broke the camel's back."
103	Cannon agreed: See *Reno Evening Gazette*, September 6, 1964, 6; and *Nevada State Journal*, September 6, 1964, 6.
103	Laxalt settled for distorting: See *Nevada State Journal*, October 24, 1964, 4. This forceful editorial from a newspaper in Laxalt's Reno–Carson City stronghold silenced the Laxalt campaign on the reapportionment issue. It laid out the equivocations and half-truths necessary to support Laxalt's contention that Cannon had somehow sacrificed Nevada's interests in his voting on reapportionment.
103	Among the figures: *R-J*, August 12, 1964, 1.
104	Looking back: Claiborne letter to author, November 28, 2003.
104	"progressive moderation": *R-J*, September 2, 1964, 1.
104	ominous-sounding twist: *Nevada Appeal*, September 2, 1964, 1.
104	"two leading Republicans": *Nevada State Journal*, October 25, 1964, editorial page. This nonbylined column offered one of the few bombshell-level facts uncovered in the entire Bobby Baker episode. That Laxalt felt the issue was so important to his cause that he dispatched two "leading Republicans" to Washington to try to dig up dirt should have raised media eyebrows throughout the state. Perhaps because it came so late in the campaign, it did not catch on as an issue.
105	"been doing favors": R. Laxalt, 189.
105	"an endless squadron": Ibid., 190.
105	"But neither Abner": Ibid., 204.
105	"Very soon": Ibid., 208.
105	"influence peddlers": Ibid., 209.
105	"Ask yourselves": Ibid., 210.

106	Cannon had been lobbying: The original idea of a presidential visit, however, was Governor Sawyer's. John Gilbertson, a history teacher at Reno High School, uncovered this fact by researching Johnson's papers at the presidential library in Austin, Texas.
106	deliver the word: *R-J*, October 10, 1964, 1.
107	"the largest crowd": *Nevada State Journal,* October 13, 1964, 1.
107	"the biggest": Ibid., 3.
107	stood atop a bus-stop bench: Ibid., 2.
107	Another member: *Nevada Appeal,* October 26, 1964, 1.
107	remembers an encounter: Denton and Green, 273.
108	he had contacted: Cannon papers, 89th Congress, Box 32, Folder 324.
108	In a eulogy: *Valley Times,* June 13, 1984, page unavailable.
108	"relatively quiet": *Reno Evening Gazette,* October 29, 1964, 7.
108	the general consensus: *R-J*, November 5, 1964, 1.
109	The scene was: Sobsey interview with author. Snyder, who was a friend of Sobsey's and a strong Cannon supporter, may have let his personal feelings influence his odds on the Cannon-Laxalt race. On election eve he made Cannon a 7-to-2 favorite over Laxalt, saying Cannon had been gaining momentum since Johnson's visit while Laxalt was "reacting in desperation with an old worn-out accusation [regarding Baker] and TV commercials" (*Sun,* October 31, 1964, 1).
109	In his memoir: P. Laxalt, 99.
109	Reed had discovered: *R-J*, November 5, 1964, 1.
110	"We don't need": R. Laxalt, 224.
110	When the Clark County: *R-J*, November 14, 1964, 1.
110	he also demanded: *Nevada State Journal,* November 14, 1964, 1.
110	handwriting expert: *Reno Evening Gazette,* November 16, 1964, 1. Reporters followed the progress of this expert closely, but Laxalt never announced the results of his scrutiny. Given the fact that Laxalt overlooked no strategy in his attempt to overturn the election result, it can be assumed the expert found no actionable irregularities.
111	"Give me just one vote": Interview with author.
111	a team of lawyers: *Sun,* November 12, 1964, 1.
112	recalled the brief: Interview with author.
112	"long, slow, tedious": *Reno Evening Gazette,* November 30, 1964, page unavailable.
112	Cannon scored: *R-J*, November 30, 1964, 1.
112	the final result: *Nevada State Journal,* December 3, 1964, 1.
113	not enough to convince: *Reno Evening Gazette,* December 5, 1964, 1.

113   as the court dismissed: *Nevada State Journal,* December 11, 1964, 1. "Laxalt Concedes" was the headline.

113   Claiborne reminded: Cannon papers, 89th Congress, Box 32, Folder 324.

6 : MOVING ON

115   was having trouble: Cannon papers, 89th Congress, Box 31, Folder 315.

116   Veteran observer: *Sun,* December 9, 1965, page unavailable.

117   Cannon had issued: *R-J,* August 19, 1964, 23.

117   historic actions: *Congressional Quarterly Almanac, 1965,* 65.

118   resisting only: Ibid., 95.

118   "one man, one vote": Ibid., 87, 95.

118   reported Drew Pearson: See *Nevada State Journal,* October 31, 1964, 5.

119   dryly noted: *Congressional Quarterly Almanac, 1966,* 485.

119   "it will present": Cannon papers, 89th Congress, Box 6, Folder 56.

119   was approved: *Congressional Quarterly Almanac, 1966,* 485.

119   even agreeing to drop: *Congressional Quarterly Almanac, 1967,* 567.

120   to unanimous approval: Ibid., 568.

120   was named vice chairman: Various letters of congratulations are found in Cannon papers, 91st Congress, Box 9, Folder 110.

120   "Look for Sen.": *Aviation Daily,* March 31, 1969, 157.

122   was approved unanimously: *Congressional Quarterly Almanac, 1968,* 621–24.

122   most interesting amendment: *Congressional Quarterly Almanac, 1970,* 171.

122   photo of the event: One placement was in the *Elko Daily Free Press* on June 18, 1970, page unavailable.

123   his second star: *R-J,* January 18, 1966, 5.

123   Stennis rewarded: The news was carried throughout Nevada. See *Sun,* March 13, 1969, 3. Cannon immediately began exercising his new power, leading the subcommittee in an investigation of the "major weapons systems associated with tactical air power." He reported the subcommittee's findings in a Senate floor speech on July 10, 1969 (*Congressional Record,* s7865).

123   delivered in a Denver: *Journal,* August 24, 1966, 1. This was a comprehensive look at troubles facing the Nevada gambling industry, including Mob issues. Running on the front page of the prestigious *Wall Street Journal* and on several pages inside, it was a sign that the world was watching activities in Nevada very closely.

123   letter to *Sun* publisher: *Post,* October 28, 1966, A3.

124   ordered an investigation: *Times,* August 21, 1966, 68.

127   included among the seven: Cannon private papers.

124   The casino opened: A *Sun* photo and story on the structure's "topping out" party on April 25, 1971, 9, shows Cannon standing proudly among various dignitaries.

124   He came to: Taken from a biography prepared for a board meeting of the Union Plaza Hotel and Casino, plus additional details drawn from newspaper accounts.

125   Scott remained: *Sun,* October 2, 1969, 1.

125   Greenspun referred: *Sun,* June 4, 1971, 1.

126   Swackhamer's ingenious idea: *R-J*, May 1, 1968, 14. Columnist Gabriel Vogliotti attributed the idea to Swackhamer.

126   Cannon and Bible: Cannon papers, 88th Congress, Box 30, Folder 358.

127   He struck on: *Congressional Quarterly Almanac, 1971,* 430–54.

127   expanding the rebate: *Congressional Quarterly Almanac, 1978,* 238; *R-J*, November 13, 1978, B2.

128   To federal prosecutors: For a more benevolent view, see Sheehan, 48–67. This profile is by former *Sun* and *R-J* newsman A. D. Hopkins.

129   he turned to: Private papers.

130   could only hazard: Interview with author.

130   made another effort: Private papers.

130   "no special connection": Interview with author.

131   ended the practice: *Reno Evening Gazette,* October 4, 1967, 8.

131   severed his relationship: *R-J*, June 28, 1967, 1.

131   died of heart failure: *Sun,* October 7, 1968, 1.

132   "I really wanted it": Interview with author.

132   with smiling photos: *R-J*, February 6, 1969, 1.

133   "virtually opened": *Reno Evening Gazette,* March 23, 1968, 4. According to columnist Norman Cardoza, Sawyer "landed a post that will keep his hand in state and national politics while waiting for another election year, and knowledgeable observers say he has already decided he will tackle Cannon in '70."

133   Nixon made no: *Times,* March 3, 1970, op-ed page. This column by veteran political analyst Tom Wicker examined the problems facing Nixon in replacing Cannon.

134   "law and order" climate: One of the issues that surfaced between Cannon and Raggio was the notorious killing of protesting students on the campus of Kent State University. When asked about the proper role of the National Guard in such circumstances, Cannon said he did not think they should carry live ammunition. Raggio jumped on the statement as simplistic, insisting that Guardsmen should have the right to arm themselves in potentially violent situations.

134	proved to be a lackluster: One tip-off that Raggio was not another Laxalt came in his announcement speech as a senatorial candidate, delivered on May 2, 1970, to the Nevada State Republican convention in Reno. Instead of blasting Cannon and laying out his own convictions, Raggio spoke about Republican Party principles and detailed the tribulations he underwent trying to decide whether to oppose Cannon. He did not impress many by saying he decided to run after receiving a telephone call from Vice President Agnew, particularly since his audience knew well of Nixon's efforts to get Laxalt in the race. The unstated message was that the second-team candidate was recruited by the White House's second team.
134	never considered it: Sawyer, Elliott, and King, 120.
134	won rather easily: Del Papa, 293.
135	Cannon came back: *Congressional Quarterly Almanac, 1973*, 453.
135	a plea-bargaining: The deal was this: Agnew would resign and plead nolo contendere to avoiding federal taxes on unreported income that came from Maryland contractors.
136	not be a candidate: J. Cannon, 210–11.
136	The Twenty-fifth Amendment: *Congressional Quarterly, 1965*, 573–81.
137	less certainty in the Senate: *Congressional Quarterly, 1973*, 1060.
137	"the most thorough": Ibid., 1062.
138	impeach Nixon: *Congressional Quarterly, 1974*, 903.
140	a comprehensive attack: Ibid., 743.
140	thirteen contentious days: Ibid., 611–12.
141	"instrumental in working": *Post*, October 2, 1974, 1.
141	praised Cannon: *Nevada State Journal*, May 19, 1974, 4. The Common Cause endorsement was carried at the bottom of a glowing editorial headlined "Sen. Cannon Leader in Election Reform." Calling him a "key figure in a historic undertaking," the editorial nevertheless pointed out "election reform probably has less appeal to voters in free-wheeling Nevada than in most states." For whatever reason, Cannon never received the acclaim for his efforts in election reform that he did for those in defense and aviation.
141	To help a small: *Congressional Quarterly Almanac, 1976*, 671.
141	become a major force: *Congressional Quarterly Almanac, 1971*, 340, 359. See also *Miami Herald*, September 14, 1975, A32.
141	moved to strike: *Congressional Quarterly Almanac, 1976*, 671.
143	"For example": *Nevada Historical Society Quarterly* (Spring 2001): 6.
143	commenting in a 1961: Ibid.
144	"If this bill passes": Cannon papers, 91st Congress, Box 28, Folder 337.
144	They authored separate: Ibid., Folder 339.
144	worked his magic: *Congressional Quarterly Almanac, 1974*, 197.

144   "Even at 2%": *Nevada Historical Society Quarterly* (Spring 2001): 8.

145   *Sun* columnist: *Sun,* February 4, 1975, 9. In a similar vein a little later that
        year, the *Nevada State Journal* (May 9, 1975, 4) noted that the past year had
        been a "dramatic time" for Cannon. "And he has broadened his reputa-
        tion from that of an effective, conscientious Nevada Senator, to a national
        figure, familiar to thousands of Americans."

7 : THE BARRIERS FALL

147   "The dynamic of": Interview with author.

148   the CAB's rationale: Barnum, former acting secretary of transportation,
        International Bar Association, Vancouver, British Columbia, September
        15, 1998.

150   join him for dinner: Clymer, 227.

151   These were accounting: Barnum, op. cit.

151   the CAB proposed: Clymer, 228.

151   most concrete result: *Congressional Quarterly Almanac, 1974,* 709.

151   used the word: Clymer, 230.

151   much Washington lore: Ibid., 228–29.

152   "We wanted $30,000": Interview with author.

152   issued a position paper: *Congressional Quarterly Almanac, 1975,* 729.

152   Cannon conducted: Clymer, 242.

154   "Everybody thought": Interview with author.

154   be about half-full: Barnum, op. cit.

155   The initial stage: *Congressional Quarterly Almanac, 1978,* 498.

155   "only clear champion": *Congressional Quarterly Almanac, 1977,* 554.

157   "After the [first round of]": Interview with author.

158   swallowed Danforth's proposal: *Congressional Quarterly Almanac, 1977,*
        554.

158   adjourn for the August: Ibid., 555.

160   it was amended by Cannon: *Congressional Quarterly Almanac, 1977,* 559.

162   Senator Kennedy offered: *Congressional Quarterly Almanac, 1978,* 500.

163   "lacked almost all": Ibid., 501.

163   "By the time": Interview with author.

164   "strengthened in conference": *Congressional Quarterly Almanac, 1978,* 504.

164   "all he wanted": Ibid., 496.

164   resonated in Barclay's memory: Interview with author.

165   "Four days before": *Congressional Quarterly Almanac, 1978,* 497.

165   would actually improve: *R-J,* January 31, 1979, 1.

166   "for political reasons": *Nevada State Journal,* February 12, 1979, 4.

166   Cannon International: *Nevada State Journal,* July 13, 1979, 1.

166   a compromise name: *R-J*, November 13, 1981, 5.

166   a survey conducted: The AP's Carson City Bureau, headed then and now by Brendan Riley, released the story on May 12, 1980.

8 : MISTAKEN IMPRESSIONS

168   "I almost had": Interview with author.

169   "But to the": Robyn, 42.

169   had been tapping: Neff, 315.

169   something more interesting: Ibid., 320.

170   A flyer sent: Cannon private papers.

170   In late December: This detail, like many others to follow, was spelled out in a memorandum Cannon produced as part of his defense against DOJ allegations.

172   Dorfman was: Dorfman is a prime subject of Mob literature. Profiles of him can be found in Neff, Pileggi, and Brill.

172   "Allen speaks for me": Brill, 217.

172   Teamsters' man in Las Vegas: Not just to Cannon. In a 1971 letter to President Nixon he later repudiated, Laxalt urged Nixon to release Jimmy Hoffa from prison because he was "a political prisoner." In that letter, Laxalt referred to an extended discussion with Dorfman, "with whom I've worked closely the past few years" (Neff, 335). In his memoir, Laxalt says he "foolishly wrote President Nixon a letter," but he does not elaborate, nor does he mention his endorsement of Dorfman (176). His brush with the underworld evidently stayed with him, as Cannon's lawyer John Dowd recalled seeing Laxalt several times while in the Russell Senate Office Building visiting Cannon. "[Laxalt] would laugh and say, 'They're after the wrong guy,'" Dowd said (interview with author).

173   particularly bold move: A Cannon staff member received a briefing on the action from a Commerce Committee staffer later that month, which Cannon reviewed. The briefing called the ICC's decision "undoubtedly the most controversial move the ICC has made to date." Attached to the memo was a clipping from the *New York Times* (November 30, 1978, page unavailable) detailing the negative effect the ICC ruling had on trucking stocks.

173   He was to contact: This information, unreported in all the media accounts of the investigation, was contained in a chronology prepared by Dowd's office. It establishes the legitimate purpose of the fateful January 10 meeting.

173   Alverson eventually: Alverson, a beautiful, extremely capable woman who was a fixture of Cannon's Las Vegas office, detailed all her contacts with Dorfman in a memo prepared in the course of the investigation. This information, also unreported by the media, is important because it establishes

that Dorfman was seeking a meeting with Cannon instead of the other way around. Alverson succumbed to cancer in 1996.

174   "My best recollection": Cannon memo. This encounter is the crucial moment in the potential case against Cannon. To DOJ prosecutors it was vital that they show a corrupt bargain was reached sometime on January 10 in Cannon's office. They got no solace from the private meeting among Cannon, Williams, Wheeler, and Dorfman, as the participants unanimously stated that nothing other than ICC regulatory actions was discussed. Therefore, the meeting in Cannon's reception area became critical. Sitting outside was a Dorfman confederate named William Webbe and Cannon's son-in-law, Bob Bjornsen. Neff gives full credence to the Justice Department's claim that in this meeting Cannon and Williams engaged in an incriminating conversation. "You take care of our end and we'll take care of your end," Williams allegedly said to Cannon, according to Neff (313–14). To which Cannon supposedly replied, "Don't worry about it, I'll have that committee. You tell me what you want . . . and we can work this thing out together." Notwithstanding the suspension of disbelief it would take to imagine Cannon engaging in such a blatantly unethical conversation in full voice in the Las Vegas Federal Building with visitors and staff close enough to overhear instead of in the privacy of his own office, Webbe recanted the alleged conversation during the trial of Williams et al. (*Reno Evening Gazette,* November 18, 1982, A3).

174   A fuller examination: This is obviously a subjective judgment, but it was shared unanimously by Cannon's staff, the author included. Although everyone close to Cannon was appalled by his bad judgment in mentioning the land deal to Dorfman, no one gave any credence to the government's contention that a deal was reached that day. For a full year before news of the investigation was leaked, Cannon and his Commerce Committee staff had worked diligently on paving the way for enactment of a strong trucking deregulation bill. There was simply no evidence, either on paper, through wiretaps, or from our personal observation of Cannon's action, that he gave any thought to the land deal in connection with the trucking bill.

174   "He just didn't realize": Interview with author.

175   classic Mob shakedowns: A good account is in Pileggi, 216ff.

176   "Why would you": Interview with author.

176   "I got whistled in": Cannon's copy of wiretapped conversations.

177   One group was led: Cannon's private papers include a memo describing this group.

177   a suspicious loan: Glick's story is also well chronicled by both Pileggi and Brill.

177	Glick withdrew: Neff, 316–17.
178	All but painting: Taken from Bjornsen's handwritten notes of his questioning by a Chicago grand jury.
178	Dorfman himself: Chronology prepared by Dowd's office.
179	much publicized press conference: Robyn, 34.
179	Cannon made it clear: Ibid., 35.
180	"We're mad as hell": Ibid., 40.
180	"completely unacceptable": Ibid., 42.
181	Roller was concerned: Neff, 321.
181	"The FBI suspects": ABC News provided a transcript of the report for Cannon's files.
181	"that has been languishing": *Post,* February 6, 1980, 1.
181	"died in his committee": *R-J,* February 6, 1980, 1.
182	"From that point": Interview with author.
183	held an oversight: From a chronology of Commerce Committee action on trucking issues prepared in connection with the Teamsters investigation.
183	Ris sent Cannon: The memo is in Cannon's private papers.
185	cautiously indicated: *Reno Evening Gazette,* February 6, 1980, 1.
185	almost a comic monologue: The AP released a story carried in Nevada under the headline "Cannon the Comic" (*Reno Evening Gazette,* February 22, 1980, 8).
186	"These are my heroes": White House press secretary, July 1, 1980.
186	"the *Times* learned": *Valley Times,* March 7, 1980, 1.
188	"close call": The *Times* first quoted an unnamed "federal investigator who is familiar with the case" as saying the Cannon matter was a "close call" on November 30, 1980. In that story, it reported that the Justice Department would reach a decision on whether to indict by the end of the year. When the decision not to indict was announced on December 18, the paper quoted "sources close to the inquiry" describing the decision as a "close call" (*Times,* December 19, 1980, 22).
188	"When all is said": Interview with author.
189	make one point: Interview with author.
189	"The senator was tough": Interview with author.

9: THE HEARTBREAKING FALL

192	compiled consistently large: Del Papa, 325–26.
192	was born and raised: Barone and Ujifusa, 730.
192	"typical Washington windbag": *Valley Times,* January 12, 1979, 4.
192	"only hyperactive adult": *Nevada State Journal,* May 9, 1981, 2.
192	In seeking reelection: *Sun,* June 29, 1976, 11.

193   Southern Nevada Water Project: That Santini would claim a role in this project, which piped Lake Mead water to Las Vegas, at such a late date seemed remarkable to Cannon. Cannon and Bible had championed the project since the early '60s, and Bible claimed even earlier provenance because of his work as a private attorney in arguing Nevada's claim to a 300,000-acre-foot annual allotment of water from the Colorado River to fuel the growth of southern Nevada. Cannon and Bible had introduced the original bill to fund the $80 million–plus project, had labored through innumerable committee hearings to obtain appropriations, had endured slowdowns from Presidents Johnson and Nixon, and had exhausted every persuasive bone in their bodies to keep funding alive for the project, with key milestones coming in 1971 (launch of Phase I) and 1977 (launch of Phase II). Although Santini would be able to cast some votes for appropriations measures in the project's later years, the major battles had been fought long before he came to Congress.

193   "He'll take an easy": *Nevada State Journal,* August 27, 1978, 1.

193   "After [Cannon] had his problems": Interview with author.

194   "very serious consideration": *Valley Times,* February 3, 1981, A5.

194   "I think I could": *Reno Evening Gazette,* February 5, 1981, 1.

194   "Some sources": *Valley Times,* February 8, 1981, 2.

194   respondents overwhelmingly favored: This poll was covered extensively throughout Nevada. See *Sun* and *R-J,* May 7, 1981, 1; and *Nevada State Journal* and *Reno Evening Gazette,* May 6, 1981, 1.

194   Sara Denton: Interview with author.

195   "matching Mr. Santini": *Valley Times,* January 3, 1982, 10.

196   issued an indictment: The *Wall Street Journal* (May 26, 1981, 6) provided a comprehensive account of the indictment.

196   send all evidence: *Reno Evening Gazette,* May 28, 181, 1.

197   "It's a tough case": Portions of the CBS News broadcast were detailed in a letter from Cannon to Senator Howell Heflin (D-AL), vice chairman of the Senate Ethics Committee (author's files).

197   touching off a new wave: *R-J,* July 2, 1981, 1.

197   more comprehensive poll: *Sun,* July 23, 1981, page unavailable.

197   handwritten notation: This was on a Digilio column in the *Valley Times* following the May poll (author's files).

198   headlines proclaiming: *Nevada State Journal,* December 1, 1981, 1.

198   shook Cannon's staff: *Nevada State Journal,* February 3, 1982, 1. The headline said it all: "Cannon Campaign Fund Lagging Behind Santini's." Cannon and Sobsey were "really impressed," according to the author's notes.

198   "have been digging": *R-J,* November 27, 1981, B23.

199   "It is time": *R-J,* February 17, 1982, B1. Santini greatly exaggerated alleged flaws in the financial disclosure rules recently imposed on members of Congress. They were actually quite revealing of the kinds of things he said he was interested in, such as assets, business deals, and approximate net worth. As a salve to the concerns of members, however, the disclosure forms allowed them to value their assets in various ranges—such as "$250,000 or above." Although this provision prevented media and opponents from placing an exact dollar amount on a member's wealth, it did show in detail what were the sources of his or her income. Cannon's response to Santini was to point out that he had filed his financial disclosure form with the secretary of the Senate on May 15, 1981, and would do so again on May 15, 1982. He refused to release his income tax forms.

199   "trying to 'hide something'": *Nevada State Journal,* April 14, 1982, 4. This was a column written by Everett Landers, managing editor of the *Journal*'s sister paper, the *Reno Evening Gazette.* Landers wrote an allegorical tale about strange goings-on during the political season. He imagined a scholar commenting on some of Santini's claims about financial disclosure: "Notice the strategy of this Santini," he intoned. "This man has read his Henry Mencken. He knows about the great Boobus Americanus. . . . Those stupid dolts who believe there's something to this income tax crap."

200   richer than the average Joe: Ibid., Landers continued: "Santini has the boobs despising Cannon because beyond what he's hiding on his tax forms they will also show he's rich. And you know how the boobs hate the rich."

200   recommended to its: *Nevada Appeal,* February 14, 1982, A7.

200   a "traitor": *Nevada State Journal,* May 3, 1982, 1.

200   "Don't look now": *Nevada State Journal,* March 7, 1982, H1.

201   Cannon had used: *R-J,* July 9, 1982, A5.

201   Cannon was full: *Sun,* July 20, 1982, 12; *Nevada State Journal,* July 20, 1982, C3.

202   raising some $1.2 million: *Post,* November 12, 1980, A10.

202   Nevada media was hostile: Some sample headlines included: "NCPAC a Failure Against Cannon" (*R-J,* August 27, 1982, B10); "NCPAC: Dangerous to Nevada Voters" (*Sun,* September 2, 1982, 18); "Facts Disprove NCPAC Charge Against Cannon" (*Valley Times,* May 24, 1982, A10); and "Cheap-Shot Artists Not Welcome Here" (*R-J,* November 16, 1980, B2).

203   approved by both sides: *R-J,* August 4, 1982, 1.

203   headlined a Reno paper: *Nevada State Journal,* August 29, 1982, B1.

204   It was then: *R-J,* September 1, 1981, B7.

204   too close to call: *Nevada State Journal,* September 7, 1982, 1.

205   Cannon said: *Sun,* September 15, 1982, 5.

205   by five percentage points: *R-J,* September 17, 1982, A17.

205   political journalists: A good example of this analysis was Martin Griffith's in *Nevada State Journal,* September 17, 1982, D1.

205   "The old man": Telephone call to author.

205   congratulatory calls: *R-J,* September 17, 1982, A17.

206   "I'm more likely": Interview with author.

206   most telling finding: "Report on Findings: A Survey of the Political Climate of Nevada," Study no. 1769, vol. 2, September 1982, Frank M. Goldsmith.

207   Instead of dismissing: Cannon's natural political instincts told him how to challenge Hecht, as a speech he gave to the Nevada State AFL-CIO Convention in Las Vegas shortly after the primary indicated. Cannon "charged head first down the campaign warpath Friday, labeling his Republican opponent a 'rubber stamp' for Reaganomics," the *Sun* reported (September 18, 1982, 7). "I intend to make this administration's record an issue in the US Senate campaign because my Republican opponent has made no secret of his allegiance to its cause," the story continued. As simple and effective as it would have been against Hecht—similar to the "empty chair" campaign against Malone—the rubber stamp never became a consistent campaign theme.

207   Hecht recalled: Interview with author.

207   "If Reagan people": *Valley Times,* August 26, 1982, A12.

207   as if he were a head of state: "Nofziger Stumps for Hecht" was the *R-J*'s headline on August 25, 1982, B3.

208   devised a formula: This strategy was no secret and was noted by numerous Nevada news outlets. Even an outsider such as William Twombley, a reporter for the *Los Angeles Times* who dropped in on the Hecht-Cannon campaign in October, picked up the essentials. "Chic Hecht, on the other hand, hardly campaigns at all," Twombley wrote (October 21, 1982, 16). "He has made few public appearances and even fewer speeches, perhaps because his shy personality, lisp and high-pitched voice combine to make him an ineffective speaker."

208   flight of negative ads: *Nevada State Journal,* October 31, 1982, 1.

208   "I refused that": Interview with author.

209   front-page headline: "Cannon Legal Fund Unveiled," *R-J,* May 16, 1982, 1.

209   "very much on trial": *Los Angeles Times,* October 29, 1982, page unavailable.

209   wire-service accounts: For instance, "Prosecutor: Union President Offered Cannon Vegas Land Deal," *Nevada State Journal,* October 22, 1982, 1.

210	he added with a chuckle: Interview with author.
210	with just $153,065: This is the amount listed in Cannon's official filing with the FEC, although, in interviews, Cannon referred to having less than $100,000 on hand (*R-J*, September 17, 1982, A17).
210	raised a respectable amount: Both Cannon's and Hecht's figures are taken from official FEC reports.
210	"pure, unadulterated": Author's notes.
211	*R-J* managing editor: In a letter to Cannon dated November 4, 1982.
211	spent two-thirds: *Nevada State Journal,* November 5, 1982, 1.
212	"go on with our strategy": Interview with author.
212	Homecoming Day crowd: *Reno Evening Gazette,* October 8, 1982, 1.
212	"It's very hard": *R-J*, October 24, 1982, 1.
213	an endorsement from: *Nevada State Journal,* October 27, 1982, 5.
213	Cannon offered: Author's notes.
213	"it is frightening": *Nevada State Journal,* October 27, 1982, 5.
213	Hecht's 5,657-vote win: Del Papa, 301.
214	win a "fluke": Interview with author.
214	"Laxalt, Laxalt, Laxalt!": Interview with author.
214	"He was dedicated": Interview with author.
215	"He was a cold fish": Interview with author.
215	most telling personality: Interview with author.
215	sort out problems: Cannon's private papers.
216	Sitting in the well: *Congressional Quarterly Weekly Report,* October 11, 1986, 2569.
216	As he answered "No": *Post,* November 30, 1982, A6.
216	Dorfman was shot: Neff, 404–5.
218	"Barely known outside": Barone and Ujifusa, 724.
218	"most underappreciated": *R-J*, March 7, 2002, 1.
219	would occasionally tell: Interview with author.

Bibliography

The official papers of Senator Cannon's twenty-four-year Senate career are housed in the Special Collections Department of the Lied Library at the University of Nevada–Las Vegas, under the direction of Su Kim Chung, manuscript librarian. The papers for Cannon's first two terms are organized clearly, with a published index. They were extremely useful for researching Cannon's first two terms.

Unfortunately, the papers for the last two terms were transferred to microfilm and are much less useful. The main problem is lack of indexing, which renders the material in a disorganized and unhelpful manner. Several attempts by Ms. Chung to unravel this material and discover its key were unsuccessful. Future scholars and historians may have better luck than I did in dealing with the microfilmed material, and I wish them well. From a purely personal point of view, the best solution would be to use the system for the first two terms throughout the collection. Whether the original Cannon material still exists, or whether UNLV has the desire or manpower to accomplish this task, is unknown.

Additional material came from the Robert Laxalt Collection at the University of Nevada–Reno, which is under the capable direction of Jacquelyn Sundstrand.

In addition to his Senate papers, extensive personal files are under the control of Cannon's daughter, Nancy Cannon Downey. These papers, consisting of letters, memos, and documents, cover sensitive issues, including investigations by the Senate Ethics Committee and the U.S. Department of Justice, Cannon's involvement in the Howard Hughes marriage to Jean Peters, Cannon's efforts to obtain clemency for Benny Binion, and family matters.

Mrs. Downey also possesses letters from Cannon to his wife, Dorothy, both before and shortly after their marriage. There are a few letters from Cannon to other family members from his World War II service.

The author was a member of Cannon's staff throughout his final term, 1977–1982. He kept extensive notes on the 1981–1982 reelection campaign, along with files on the Teamsters investigation, the 1980 *New York Times* article impugning Cannon's character, and campaign activities. References are to the author's notes or author's files.

Perhaps the most valuable resources on Cannon's life, also in Mrs. Downey's keeping, are scrapbooks meticulously maintained since Cannon's days as Las Vegas city attorney from 1949 to 1958 and continuing to the end of his Senate career in 1982. Virtually every mention of Cannon in newspapers from Nevada and other locales was clipped and pasted into these huge scrapbooks. They provide an excellent overview of his life, and the author recommends all public figures to consider the usefulness of this tool. The only blemish on the scrapbook material is that sometimes dates or page numbers of articles were omitted. This accounts for occasional indications of "page unavailable" in the chapter notes.

GOVERNMENT DOCUMENTS

Cannon, Howard W. "Proposed Civil Rights Ordinance." Interoffice memo, Las Vegas, November 30, 1953.

———. "Report to the Secretary of the Senate, Dec. 1, 1958." National Archives and Records Administration, Washington, D.C.

Carter, Jimmy. "Remarks of the President at the Signing Ceremony for S2245, the Trucking Deregulation Bill." Washington, D.C., July 1, 1980.

Congressional Record. Various issues.

Federal Election Commission. Candidate Reports of Receipts and Expenditures. Howard W. Cannon, 1975–1976, 1981–1982. Chic Hecht, 1981–1982. Washington, D.C.

Federal Express Corporation. Application for Exemption, Civil Aeronautics Board, Washington, D.C., September 26, 1975.

Kennedy, John F. "Special Message on Urgent National Needs." May 25, 1961, 10A.

NEWSPAPERS

Newspapers played a more important role in researching the life of Howard Cannon than they would for other political figures. This is because of several factors: very little written record—either in books, monographs, or scholarly articles—of Nevada politics in general, and Cannon in particular, exists; Cannon did not keep diaries or write memos or even letters save for the time spent overseas in World War II; Cannon did not seek acclaim for his Senate accomplishments and, so, received very little; and, finally, Cannon's exploits as Las Vegas city attorney from 1949 to 1958 occurred at a time when Las Vegas was out of the national spotlight. It was a small town in a small state, dealing with mundane issues such as adequate utility, communications, and transportation services.

Fortunately, the *Las Vegas Sun* appeared on the scene just about the same time (1950) that Cannon was achieving prominence in the city. It was not that the existing newspaper, the *Las Vegas Review-Journal,* was doing a poor job of covering city hall but that the existence of the *Sun* made that coverage better. *Sun* publisher Hank Greenspun, although an internationalist at heart, concentrated his paper's meager resources on local issues at its outset, and the *Sun* went after those issues with a vengeance. The combination of assiduous coverage by beat reporters and Greenspun's commentary in his "Where I Stand" column provided an excellent record of the daily life of Las Vegas.

The *R-J* made its impact felt in a big way through publication of the excellent series "The First 100 Persons Who Shaped Southern Nevada," appearing in 1999. Frequent references to it are made throughout the biography.

Another factor moving newspaper articles to the forefront in this biography was Cannon's use of scrapbooks. He instructed his staff, from his earliest days as city attorney through his Senate career, to clip and save any mention of him in newspapers in Nevada or wherever his name might appear. Thus, references to somewhat obscure Nevada weeklies or community newspapers will occur, thanks to the scrapbooks. Listed below are the many newspaper sources cited in the book.

Arizona Range News
Arizona Republic
Aviation Daily
Boulder City News
Elko Daily Free Press
Elko Independent
Ely Daily Times
Eureka Sentinel
Gardnerville Record-Courier
Henderson Home News
Humboldt Star (Winnemucca)
Las Vegas Life
Las Vegas Review-Journal (*R-J*)
Las Vegas Sun (*Sun*)
Los Angeles Examiner
Los Angeles Times
Miami Herald
Mineral County Forum
Nevada Appeal (*Appeal*)
Nevada Report
Nevada State Journal
New York Herald-Tribune
New York Times (*Times*)
New York Tribune
North Las Vegas Valley Times (*Valley Times*)
Omaha World-Herald
Reminder
Reno/Carson City
Reno Evening Gazette
San Antonio Express and News
San Francisco Chronicle

Tonopah Times-Bonanza
Wall Street Journal (Journal)
Washington County (Utah) News
Washington Daily News
Washington Post (Post)
Washington Star

INTERVIEWS

Barclay, Charles M. October 15, 2003.

Bissell, Laurene (Lari). November 15, 2002.

Breyer, Stephen. January 29, 2004.

Carlino, Phil. June 11, 2002.

Carson, Eileen. December 18, 2002.

Claiborne, Harry E. June 18, 2002.

Dahlke (Marcus), Barbara. December 18, 2003.

Denton, Ralph. October 24, December 18, 2002; February 5, 2003.

Denton, Sara. February 24, 2004.

Dowd, John. October 8, 2003.

Downey, Nancy Cannon. February 25, 2004.

Drendel, John Squire. November 15, 2002.

Ferris, Charles. October 23, 2003.

Foley, George. October 28, 2003.

Foley, Joseph. May 22, 2002.

Gastanaga, Gene. January 27, 2003.

Goffstein, Dottie. August 8, 2002.

Goyer, Christine. February 10, 2003.

Griffin, Patrick. October 17, 2003.

Hall, Edwin King. October 18, 2003.

Hall-Patton, Mark P. July 12, 2003.

Hawkins, Prince. November 6, 2002.

Hecht, Chic. February 26, 2004.

Hedger, Sydney. April 14, 2003.

Houssels, J. Kell, Jr. February 16, 2003.

Jay, Evelyn. June 16, 2002.

Jones, Herb. June 3, 2002.

Laxalt, Paul. October 7, 2003.

Morris (Hafen), Vella Ruth. October 29, 2002.

Murphy, Florence. August 3, 2002.

Nathan, Irwin. October 12, 2003

Notti, Robert. November 24, December 18, 2002.

O'Callaghan, Mike. July 22, 2003.

Revert, Bob. July 1, 2002.

Rietz, Ken. April 12, 2004.

Riley, Brendan. March 24, 2004.

Ris, Will. October 16, 2003.

Rocha, Guy Louis. November 5, 2002.

Rogich, Sig. February 27, 2004.

Sarvis, Aubrey. October 10, 2003.

Smith, Chester. June 27, October 30, 2002; January 10, June 20, 2003.

Smith, Fred. January 15, 2004.

Sobsey, Chester. June 10, December 18, 2002; August 26, 2003.

Stewart. Jeanne (Houssels). March 25, 2003.

Thornton, William. November 20, 2002; August 18, 2003.

Walker, Lee. June 10, 2003.

Young, Clifford. November 26, 2002.

OTHER SOURCES

Anderson, Fred. "Participation in Party Politics, 1952–1964." Oral history, University of Nevada–Las Vegas, 1971.

Baker, Robert Gene. *Wheeling and Dealing: Confessions of a Capitol Hill Operator.* New York: W. W. Norton, 1978.

Barnum, John W. "What Prompted Airline Deregulation 20 Years Ago." International Bar Association Annual Meeting, Vancouver, B.C., September 15, 1998.

Barone, Michael, and Grant Ujifusa. *The Almanac of American Politics.* 1975. Reprint, Washington, D.C.: Barone, 1982.

Biltz, Norm. "Memoirs of the Duke of Nevada." Oral history, University of Nevada–Las Vegas, 1967.

Brill, Steven. *The Teamsters.* New York: Pocket Books, 1978.

Cahlan, John F. "Reminiscences of a Reno and Las Vegas, Nevada, Newspaperman, University Regent and Public Spirited Citizen." Oral history, University of Nevada–Las Vegas, 1968.

Cannon, David H. "A History of the Cannon Family." Presented at a meeting of the Daughters of the Pioneers, St. George, Utah, February 19, 1922.

Cannon, Howard W. "Are We Being Too Peaceful in Space?" *Saturday Evening Post,* June 15, 1963, 10.

———. "Escape to Freedom." *Family Weekly,* March 26, 1961.

Cannon, James. *Time and Change: Gerald Ford's Appointment With History.* New York: HarperCollins, 1994.

Caro, Robert A. *The Years of Lyndon Johnson: Master of the Senate.* New York: Alfred A. Knopf, 2002.

Clymer, Adam. *Edward M. Kennedy.* New York: William Morrow, 1975.

Congressional Quarterly Almanac, 1959–1982. Washington, D.C.: Congressional Quarterly.

Dallek, Robert. *Flawed Giant: Lyndon Johnson and His Times, 1961–1973.* New York: Oxford University Press, 1998.

———. *An Unfinished Life: John F. Kennedy, 1917–1963.* New York: Little, Brown, 2003.

Davies, Richard O. "Only in Nevada: America's Unique Experiment With Legalized Sports Gambling, 1931–2000." *Nevada Historical Society Quarterly* (Spring 2001): 3.

———, ed. *The Maverick Spirit: Building the New Nevada.* Reno: University of Nevada Press, 1999.

Del Papa, Frankie Sue. *Political History of Nevada.* 9th ed. Carson City: State Printing Office, 1990.

Denton, Ralph, and Michael Green. *A Liberal Conscience.* Reno: University of Nevada Oral History Program, 2001.

Denton, Sally, and Roger Morris. *The Money and the Power: The Making of Las Vegas and Its Hold on America, 1947–2000.* New York: Alfred A. Knopf, 2001.

Downey, William T. "Howard W. Cannon: Political Beginnings in Nevada." Research paper, University of Nevada–Las Vegas, April 23, 1997.

Driggs, Don. "The 1958 Election in Nevada." *Western Political Quarterly* 12 (1959): 317.

Edwards, Jerome E. *Pat McCarran: Political Boss of Nevada.* Reno: University of Nevada Press, 1982.

Elliott, Gary E. *Senator Alan Bible and the Politics of the New West.* Reno: University of Nevada Press, 1994.

Gearhart, Dona. "The 1960s Revolution: UNLV Style." *Nevada Historical Society Quarterly* (Summer 1997): 183.

Gilbertson, John. "Plane Politics: Lyndon Johnson, Howard Cannon and Nevada's 1964 Senatorial Election." *Nevada Historical Society Quarterly* (Winter 2003): 257.

Greenspun, Hank. *Where I Stand: The Record of a Reckless Man.* New York: David McKay, 1966.

Gup, Ted. "Eye of the Storm." *Columbia Journalism Review* (May–June 2001).

Highton, Jake. *Nevada Newspaper Days: A History of Journalism in the Silver State.* Stockton, Calif.: Heritage West Books, 1990.

Hulse, James W. *Forty Years in the Wilderness.* Reno: University of Nevada Press, 1986.

———. *The Nevada Adventure: A History.* Reno: University of Nevada Press, 1966.

Hutcheson, Austin, and Don Driggs. "The 1956 Election in Nevada." *Western Political Quarterly* 10 (1957): 133.

Johnson, Lubertha. "Civil Rights Efforts in Las Vegas, 1940s–1960s." Oral history, University of Nevada–Las Vegas, 1988.

Jones, Florence Lee, and John F. Cahlan. *Water: A History of Las Vegas.* Vol. 1. Las Vegas: Las Vegas Valley Water District, 1975.

Kaufman, Perry Bruce. "The Best City of Them All: A History of Las Vegas, 1930–1960." Ph.D. diss., University of California–Santa Barbara, 1974.

Koskimaki, George E. *D-Day With the Screaming Eagles.* Sweetwater, Tenn.: 101st Airborne Division Association, 1989.

Land, Barbara, and Myrick Land. *A Short History of Las Vegas.* Reno: University of Nevada Press, 1999.

Laxalt, Paul. *Nevada's Paul Laxalt: A Memoir.* Reno: Jack Bacon, 2000.

Laxalt, Robert. *The Governor's Mansion.* Reno: University of Nevada Press, 1994.

Martinez, Marty. "Capitol Hill's 'Mr. Aviation.'" *Air Line Pilot*, December 1971.

McCarthy, Fran. "Our Man in Washington." *Reno,* September 1979.

McMillan, Dr. James B. "Fighting Back: A Life in the Struggle for Civil Rights." Oral history, University of Nevada–Las Vegas, 1997.

Moehring, Eugene P. *Resort City in the Sunbelt.* 2d ed. Reno: University of Nevada Press, 2000.

Mollenhoff, Clark R. *Despoilers of Democracy.* Garden City, N.Y.: Doubleday, 1965.

———. *Investigative Reporting, From Courthouse to White House.* New York: Macmillan, 1981.

Moody, Eric N. *Southern Gentleman of Nevada Politics: Vail M. Pittman.* Reno: University of Nevada Press, 1974.

Neff, James. *Mobbed Up.* New York: Dell Publishing, 1989.

Oberdorfer, Don. *Senator Mansfield.* Washington, D.C.: Smithsonian Books, 2003.

Paher, Stanley W. *Las Vegas: As It Began—As It Grew.* Las Vegas: Nevada Publications, 1971.

Pileggi, Nicholas. *Casino: Love and Honor in Las Vegas.* New York: Pocket Books, 1995.

Reid, Ed, and Ovid Demaris. *The Green Felt Jungle.* New York: Pocket Books, 1964.

Robyn, Dorothy. *Braking the Special Interests: Trucking Deregulation and the Politics of Policy Reform.* Chicago: University of Chicago Press, 1987.

Roemer, William F., Jr. *War of the Godfathers.* New York: Ivy Books, 1990.

Rose, Carolyn. Ms. Rose began a biography on Senator Cannon in 1998, but did not finish it.

Rothman, Hal. *Neon Metropolis: How Las Vegas Started the Twenty-first Century.* New York: Routledge, 2002.

Rothman, Hal, and Mike Davis. *The Grit Beneath the Glitter: Tales From the Real Las Vegas.* Berkeley and Los Angeles: University of California Press, 2002.

Sawyer, Grant, Gary E. Elliott, and R. T. King. *Hang Tough!* Reno: University of Nevada Oral History Program, 1993.

Sheehan, Jack, ed. *The Players: The Men Who Made Las Vegas.* Reno: University of Nevada Press, 1997.

Sullivan, Ward. "A Refinement of War." 1980.

Titus, A. Costandina. *Bombs in the Backyard: Atomic Testing and American Politics.* Reno: University of Nevada Press, 1986.

———. "Howard Cannon: The Senate and Civil Rights Legislation, 1959–1968." *Nevada Historical Society Quarterly* (Winter 1990): 13.

Viehe, Fred W. "The Recall of Mayor Frank Shaw: A Revision." *California History* 59, no. 4 (1980): 290.

Wilkerson, W. R., III. *The Man Who Invented Las Vegas.* N.p.: Ciro's Books, 2000.

Wilson, Woodrow. "Race, Community and Politics in Las Vegas, 1940s–1980s." Oral history, University of Nevada–Las Vegas, 1990.

Wright, Frank. *A Short History of Clark County Aviation, 1920–1948.* Clark County Heritage Museum Occasional Paper no. 1. Las Vegas: Clark County Heritage Museum, 1993.

Young, Charles H. *Into the Valley: The Untold Story of USAAF Troop Carrier in World War II.* Dallas: PrintComm, 1995.

Index

Cannon, Walter: health concerns, 36; Howard's law studies and, 15–16; life of, 10–11; relationship with Howard, 12

Cannon, Wilhelmina, 9, 10

Cannon museum. *See* Howard W. Cannon Aviation Museum

Cannon-Danforth compromise, 158–59

Cannon International Airport, 166

cargo planes. *See* air-cargo industry

Carousel Motel, 101

Carson, Eileen, 55, 60

Carswell, G. Harold, 133

Carter, Jimmy: airline deregulation and, 153, 164; Jim Santini and, 192; trucking industry regulation and, 183, 186

Carville, Edward P., 69, 92

casino industry: Cannon and, 124, 125, 126; FBI investigations, 123–24; reputation of, 5–6; Frank Scott and the Union Plaza, 124–26; slot machine tax rebate, 126–27

casino taxes, 126–27

CBS Evening News, 197

C-47s, 26

charter airlines, 151

Christensen, M. J., 58

city attorney: of Las Vegas, 44–48, 49–53

Civil Aeronautics Authority, 149

Civil Aeronautics Board (CAB), 83; abolished, 163; airline deregulation and, 148–52 *passim,* 154, 155, 159, 162; air service affecting Nevada and, 84; FedEx and, 142; Alfred Kahn named head of, 162–63

civil aviation policy. *See* airline deregulation; aviation policy

civil rights: Cannon and, 51–53, 67, 71, 88–90; Las Vegas and, 49–53; school desegregation and, 67

Civil Rights Act of 1957, 88

Civil Rights Act of 1964, 88–90

Civil Rights Commission, 88

Claiborne, Harry: 1964 senatorial recount in Nevada and, 111–12, 113; as an attorney in Las Vegas, 41; the Binion pardon case and, 127, 128; campaign for the Senate, 97–98, 102, 104; on Cannon as an attorney, 41; impeachment, 215–16; relationship with Cannon, 130–31

Clark, Ed, 45

Clark, Joseph, 119, 120

Clark, Ramsey, 129, 130

Clark County: 1964 Senate race and, 109–10

Clark County Democratic Central Committee, 49

Clark County Planning Commission, 170

Clymer, Adam, 151

combat engineers, 22–23

Commerce Committee: airline deregulation and, 152, 153, 154–55, 158–60; Cannon becomes chairman of, 161; significance of, 161

Committee for the Re-election of the President (CRP), 140

Common Cause (lobby), 141

Congressional Quarterly, 155

Congressional Staff Directory, 132

Conlon, Alberta "Bunny," 131, 215

Conlon, Jack: background of, 92; Bobby Baker and, 100; Cannon's 1958 Senate race and, 56–57, 60, 63; Cannon's 1964 Senate race and, 109; on Cannon's Washington staff, 68–69; death of, 131; early association with Cannon, 48–49; labor unions and, 60; Lido Bar and, 63; Nevada politics and, 92–93; personality of, 68–69; relationship with Cannon, 68, 69, 131

Conlon, Laurene. *See* Bissell, Laurene

Conlon, Lee, 69

Connally, John, 136

Corrupt Practices Act, 59, 82, 139

Cragin, E. W. "Ernie," 45, 46, 58

labor unions, 59–61. *See also* Teamsters Union

"Lady Integrity" (political ad), 204

Lamb, Ralph, 132

Lardner, George, Jr., 181, 185

Larson, Corwin, 17

Last Frontier (resort), 38

Las Vegas (Nev.): 1964 Senate race and, 110–11, 112–13; Amtrak service, 166; Cannon as city attorney, 44–48, 49–53; Cannon settles in, 37; Cannon's law career in, 41–44; growth of, 5; President Johnson's visit to, 106; President Kennedy's visit to, 87; racial discrimination and civil rights in, 49–53; reputation of, 6

Las Vegas Chamber of Commerce, 74

Las Vegas Country Club, 170

Las Vegas Hotel Association, 58

Las Vegas Land and Water Company, 46

Las Vegas Review-Journal: 1982 Senate election and, 212; coverage of Cannon, 47, 101, 181, 209; endorsement of Santini, 204; President Johnson's influence over, 108; resignation of Robert Brown, 107; Chet Sobsey and, 70

Las Vegas Sun, 2, 47–48

Las Vegas Valley Water District, 46

law career: early years in, 20–22; in Las Vegas, 38, 41–44; as Las Vegas city attorney, 44–48, 49–53; passes bar exams, 20; student years, 15–16, 17

Lawlor Special Events Center (UNR), 127

Lawson, Samuel, 45, 46

Laxalt, Dominique and Theresa, 94

Laxalt, Paul, 193; 1964 U.S. Senate race, 95–96, 102–13 *passim,* 116; 1970 U.S. Senate race and, 133; election to the Senate, 145; Chic Hecht and, 206, 214; overview of, 93–94; qualities as a politician, 94, 95; retirement, 218; slot-tax rebate and, 127

Laxalt, Peter, 112

Laxalt, Robert, 94, 104–6, 110

Legion, Ralph, 58, 61

Levinson, Ed, 100, 124

Levitas, Elliott, 163

Lewis, J. R., 41

Lido Bar (Las Vegas), 63

List, Robert, 191

Lombardo, Joey (the Clown), 188

"Long, Long Time" (political advertisement), 204

Long, Russell, 77, 118, 122, 126, 127, 144

Lumberjack Collegians, 15

MacArthur, Horace, 19

Magnuson, Warren "Maggie," 153, 154, 155–56, 157, 161; concern for Boeing Aerospace, 152

Malone, George "Molly," 47, 55, 61–64

Manatos, Mike, 129

Mansfield, Mike, 83, 89, 118

Marijnissen, Frans and Charles, 33

Marshall, George E., 44

McCarran, Pat, 44, 47, 54, 84, 92

McClellan, John, 161

McMillan, James B., 71, 72, 102

McNamara, Robert, 131

Mechling, Thomas, 54

Melcher, John, 158, 159, 160

Mendez, L. G., 30

Mesta, Perle, 101

military career: with the 440th Troop Carrier Group, 24–28; Air Force Reserve, 38, 84; Army Air Force training, 23–24; Battle of the Bulge, 35; behind German lines, 30–34; fighter-jet program, 123; flights into Germany, 35; impact on Cannon, 39; medals and honors, 35–36; Normandy invasion, 26–28; Operation Market Garden, 29–30; postwar service, 37; in the Utah National Guard, 22–23

military construction projects, 78

133, 134; Jack Conlon and, 92–93; gambling corruption in Nevada and, 124; Nevada politics and, 93

scandals: Bobby Baker, 98–102; Lyndon Johnson and, 98–99. *See also* Teamsters Union bribery scandal

school desegregation, 67

School of Hotel Management (UNLV), 58

Schwartz, Hugh, 212

Scott, Frank: Cannon's 1958 Senate race and, 56, 57–58; Cannon's bribery scandal and, 187; Cannon's land deal in Las Vegas and, 177; Cannon's relationship with, 194; Union Plaza hotel-casino and, 124–25

Scott Corporation, 124, 125, 126, 200

Scrugham, James, 92

Serv-U Corporation, 100

slot machine tax rebate, 126–27

Smith, Chet, 215

Smith, Fred, 142

Smith, Hyrum, 8

Smith, Joseph, 8

Smith, Ward, 27, 28

Snow, Glenn E., 21–22

Snow, Patsy, 67

Snyder, Jimmy "the Greek," 109

Sobsey, Chet: becomes Cannon's aide, 131–33; on Cannon and Benny Binion, 130; on Cannon and Harry Claiborne, 130; on Cannon's 1958 election, 63–64; on Cannon's 1964 election, 109; on Cannon's personality, 54–55, 214; on Cannon's politics, 66; on Cannon's Washington staff, 69–70; on Jack Conlon, 68; relationship with Cannon, 215

Sol Estes, Billy, 99

Sourwine, Julien "Jay," 54

Southern Motors Carriers Rate Conference, 173

Southern Nevada Central Labor Council, 58, 60–61

Southern Nevada Power and Telephone, 45

Southwest Airlines, 148

space-based defense, 80–82

Space Committee. *See* Aeronautical and Space Sciences Committee

space program, 78–79. *See also* space-based defense

sports gambling taxes, 143–44

Sports Illustrated, 143

Sputnik, 73

Staggers, Harley O., 192

Stardust Hotel, 175, 176, 177

"Star Wars," 80

Stennis, John, 77, 122–23

Stevens, Ted, 158

St. George (Utah), 9

Stoy Hora (plane), 27

Subcommittee on Administrative Practice and Procedure, 150, 151, 152

Sullivan, Edward J., 27

Sullivan, Leah, 10

Sullivan, Ward, 29

"sunset legislation," 163

"supply-side economics," 79

Swackhamer, William, 126

Sweet Promised Land (Robert Laxalt), 94

Symington, Stuart, 73

Tactical Air Power Subcommittee, 123

tactical fighter jets, 123

Taft-Hartley Act, 118

Taylor, John, 7–8

Taylor, R. G. "Zack," 177, 194–95

Teamsters Union: Cannon's alleged bribery and, 169, 171, 172, 173–79 *passim;* trucking industry deregulation and, 169, 173, 180, 184. *See also* Teamsters Union bribery scandal

Teamsters Union bribery scandal: background to, 170–73; Cannon's defense fund and, 209; Cannon's efforts in trucking industry deregulation during, 179–80, 182–86; Cannon's meet-

as, 136–38; Nelson Rockefeller is
confirmed as, 138–39
Victor H. Palmieri and Company, 171–72
Vostok III and IV, 80

wagering tax, 143–44
Walker, Lee, 68, 215
Wanniski, Jude, 79, 97, 108
Warden, Lubertha, 51
War on Poverty, 117
Washington Post, 141, 181, 185
Washoe County: 1964 Senate race, 110,
115–16
Washoe County Airport Authority, 166
Webbe, William, 178
Webster, William, 185
Weinzettel, Roy, 34
Western Air Lines, 47, 148
West Point, 14
Westside, Las Vegas: 1964 Senate race and,
110–11, 112–13
Wheeler, Edward K., 173, 174
Willard, Bill, 63
Williams, Edward Bennett, 99
Williams, Franklin H., 52

Williams, Harrison "Pete," 64
Williams, James, 16
Williams, John J., 98, 99
Williams, Roy: indictment of, 196;
Teamsters Union bribery scandal
and, 173, 174, 176, 180, 190; trial of,
209, 216
Wilson, Woodrow, 51, 52–53
Withagen, Piet, 31
Wolverton, Robert, 27, 28
Woodburn, Bill, 68
World Series of Poker, 128
World War II: Battle of the Bulge, 35;
Cannon and (*see* military career);
Normandy invasion, 26–28;
Operation Market Garden, 29–30;
troop carrying, 24, 25, 26–28
Wyman, Lois, 145

Young, Brigham, 9
Young, Charlie, 24
Young, Clifton, 54

Zimmerman, Ralph, 24